TREASON

TREASON

NIXON AND THE 1968 ELECTION

DON FULSOM

PELICAN PUBLISHING COMPANY
Gretna 2015

Copyright © 2015
By Don Fulsom
All rights reserved

*The word "Pelican" and the depiction of a pelican are
trademarks of Pelican Publishing Company, Inc., and are
registered in the U.S. Patent and Trademark Office.*

Library of Congress Cataloging-in-Publication Data

Fulsom, Don.
    Treason : Nixon and the 1968 election / by Don Fulsom.
        pages cm
    Includes bibliographical references and index.
    ISBN 978-1-4556-1949-8 (hardcover : alk. paper) -- ISBN 978-1-
4556-1950-4 (e-book) 1. Presidents--United States--Election--1968.
2. Nixon, Richard M. (Richard Milhous), 1913-1994. 3. Vietnam
War, 1961-1975--Political aspects--United States. 4. Vietnam
War, 1961-1975--Diplomatic history. 5. United States--Politics
and government--1963-1969. I. Title. II. Title: Nixon and the 1968
election.
    E851.F85 2015
    324.973'0924--dc23

                                        2015006598

Printed in the United States of America

Published by Pelican Publishing Company, Inc.
1000 Burmaster Street, Gretna, Louisiana 70053

For Avi McClelland-Cohen, whose help was absolutely indispensable

Contents

Acknowledgments

From idea to proposal and from chapter outlines to complete chapters, Avi McClelland-Cohen has been a chief partner in this endeavor. Avi is a brilliant former student of mine at American University. Among her contributions: indexing the X Envelope, compiling research, composing several sections, contacting experts, selecting photos and documents, and editing initial drafts.

Another former student, James Tsouvalas, deserves high praise for his fine writing and editing—and for bolstering the book in its final stages. Jimmy wrote one full chapter and beefed up many others. He edited the entire manuscript and made key agent and publisher contacts.

The best literary agent in the business, Jane Dystel, quickly found an enthusiastic publisher in Pelican and its savvy editor-in-chief, Nina Kooij. And, in Erin Classen, Nina brought a very sharp editor into the publishing process. This is their book too. Thanks!

My gratitude also goes out to Margaret Harman and Holly Reed of the National Archives and Records Administration, Director Mark Updegrove and Deputy Director Tina Houston of the LBJ Library, and Dick O'Neill and Steve Greene of the Nixon Project at the National Archives in College Park, Maryland.

I also want to thank family members who offered continuous support and encouragement, led by my daughter, Beth Willett, and my sister, Deanna Nowicki, and their spouses—my son-in-law, James Willett, and brother-in-law, Frank Nowicki.

Others who offered advice and support include: Jay Bell and Mary Mariani; Ted and Cornelia McDonald; Pat O'Connor; Maya O'Connor; Fred Tracy; William Klein; Bob and Nancy Sloan; Melissa and Jay Crews; Tina and Igor Rafalovich; Rick Boardman; David and Patti Victorson; Mitch Kominsky and Sarah Lerman; Carol and Max Hershey; Kim Mealy; Kelly Lux; Liz Specter; Steve and David

Toth; Penny Pagano; Marc Borbely; Bill Stoffel; Kenneth Williams; Joe Gomez; Al Schumm; Tom Foty; Tom DeLach; Gene Kuleta; Mary Chamberlayne; Sid Davis; Muriel Dobbin; Al Spivak; Bill McCloskey; Pat Sloyan; David Taylor; Dan Moldea; Stanley Kutler; Glenn Fuchs; Devra Marcus; Rob Enelow; Dan Deutsch; Tom Gauger; Jim McManus; Bob Moore; Bill and Marsha Greenwood; Ford Rowan; Eric, Mihun, and Cosworth Esplund; Rob and Romani Thaler; Jane Berger and Roger Gittines; Gordon MacDougall and Linda Geurkink; Linda Cashdan; Dave Rosso; Jenny Tsouvalas; Linda Anderson; Bill Wilson; Frank Sciortino; Bill Scott; Nicole Hollander; Rowena Gear; and Margaret Southern.

Cast of Characters

Richard Milhous Nixon (1913-1994)

Richard Nixon stands as one of America's most fascinating historical figures. As the leader of a criminal presidency, his actions would irreparably alter that office.

Born in Yorba Linda, California, in 1913, Nixon attended Whittier College and Duke University School of Law (where he committed one of his earliest break-ins, to view his grades before they were released) before returning to his home state to practice law. After serving in the Navy during World War II, Nixon won election to the House in 1946, then to the Senate in 1950.

A staunch anti-communist who once accused an electoral opponent of being "pink down to her underwear," Nixon gained national renown for his voracious pursuit of Alger Hiss in the House. In 1952, Dwight "Ike" Eisenhower chose Senator Nixon as his running mate, and Nixon served as vice president for two terms. He and Ike, however, were not close—a fact Eisenhower made known publicly, inspiring Nixon's resentment. Nixon lost a presidential race to Sen. John F. Kennedy in 1960 and suffered another defeat almost immediately in the 1962 gubernatorial race in California.

After disappearing briefly from politics, Nixon returned to the scene for another White House bid in 1968. Paranoid that a last-minute peace deal would turn the electoral tides to Democratic candidate Hubert Humphrey, Nixon conspired with the South Vietnamese to torpedo Pres. Lyndon Johnson's peace talks and thus win the election. Though his actions were discovered by the Johnson White House, they were not made public, and Nixon won the race, taking office in January 1969.

Rather than providing a better peace deal—as he had promised—Nixon escalated the war in Vietnam. Millions of Vietnamese, as well as twenty-one thousand American soldiers, lost their lives under Nixon's reign before he finally declared the war over in 1973 and announced the withdrawal of all troops. The war did not end, however, until 1975, when communist forces overran Saigon.

Nixon is often known for opening the door to renewed U.S. relations with China and encouraging détente with the Soviet Union. But his name has truly become synonymous with Watergate, referring to the criminal conspiracy that ended his presidency. An investigation that followed a June 1972 break-in at the Watergate offices of the Democratic National Committee revealed that Nixon had at least orchestrated the subsequent cover-up. Among Nixon's multitude of other illegal activities were the collection of a huge campaign slush fund and the targeting of political opponents by the Internal Revenue Service.

Facing certain impeachment, Nixon resigned in 1974, the only president to ever do so. A month later, he was pardoned by Pres. Gerald Ford, Nixon's carefully chosen vice president and presidential successor. Highly unpopular, the pardon made Nixon ineligible for prosecution for any crimes he had committed during his presidency. It also doomed Ford's chances of becoming an elected president when he ran for that office in 1976.

As an ex-president, Nixon did manage to somewhat salvage his legacy by making numerous trips overseas in the role of an elder statesman and by publishing nine books. He died in 1994 after suffering a massive stroke.

Lyndon Baines Johnson (1908-1973)

Lyndon B. Johnson, thirty-sixth president of the United States, was undoubtedly one of the shrewdest politicians of the twentieth century. Known for the "Johnson Treatment" — coarse, gruff political dealing with a bit of physical roughhousing thrown in — Johnson is one of only four people to hold all four elected federal offices (representative, senator, vice president, and president). For better or worse, his policies as president would shape the country's destiny for decades.

After spending several years as a teacher, LBJ followed the footsteps of his father, a Texas legislator, into the political arena. He became a congressional aide, personally befriending the likes of

Rep. Sam Rayburn and numerous aides to Pres. Franklin Roosevelt, before running for Congress himself in 1936. He won and served in the House of Representatives until 1949, when he was elected to the Senate. He spent the next dozen years there, half of them in leadership positions.

In 1960, after his own failed bid for the White House, Johnson became Democratic presidential nominee John F. Kennedy's running mate. On the dark day of Kennedy's assassination in November 1963, Johnson fulfilled his constitutional duties and was sworn in as president. The next year, he won the presidency in his own right, defeating Barry Goldwater in the 1964 election.

Johnson is best known domestically for crafting the "Great Society" legislation responsible for civil rights advances, Medicare and Medicaid, environmental protection, urban and rural development, economic aid that lifted millions of people out of poverty, arts funding, and improved education. Though Kennedy's presidency paved the way, it was Johnson who signed the Civil Rights Act and Voting Rights Act to outlaw racial discrimination.

Overseas, however, Johnson escalated the war in Vietnam. The Gulf of Tonkin Resolution in 1964 essentially gave Johnson carte blanche to run the war however he saw fit, without any legal declaration of war. American personnel on the ground in Vietnam increased from sixteen thousand advisors to over half a million troops between 1963 and 1968. Massive bombing raids devastated the north, and the deadly chemical weapon Agent Orange soaked the land in both parts of Vietnam. Soldiers and civilians were dying in numbers almost too great to count, and victory—if there was ever a possibility for one—remained worse than elusive.

Early in 1968, Johnson announced he would reduce the bombing of North Vietnam in order to kindle hope for peace negotiations. He also announced, after an early primary defeat and massive criticism of his war policies, that he would not be seeking another presidential term. Vice Pres. Hubert Humphrey became the eventual Democratic candidate, though Johnson and Humphrey had, at best, a lukewarm relationship.

With much political maneuvering, it seemed by the end of 1968 that a peace deal was in sight, with parties agreeing to meet in Paris to discuss future action. At the last minute, though, South

Vietnamese president Nguyen van Thieu pulled out of the talks. Shortly after, Johnson found out that the Republican presidential nominee, Richard Nixon, was working behind the scenes to sabotage the negotiations.

Johnson never went public with the information about Nixon, and after the transfer of power he and Nixon maintained a close professional relationship, visiting each other in the White House and at Johnson's Texas ranch. That relationship, however, grew increasingly toxic as Nixon failed to end the war, tried to blackmail the ex-president, and made clear his intention to dismantle the Great Society. Two days after Nixon's second inauguration, on January 22, 1973, Lyndon Johnson died of a heart attack. That night, Nixon announced the war would finally draw to a close. Yet it did not end until a communist victory in 1975.

Anna Chennault (b. 1925)

A friend and political ally of Richard Nixon, Asian-American socialite Anna Chennault played a key role in the sabotage of the 1968 peace negotiations. Her exertion of political influence and role as an informal covert operative would shape the course of geopolitical history at the height of the Vietnam War.

Anna married American general Claire L. Chennault in her native China in 1947. He was the founder of the Flying Tigers, the first American Volunteer Group of the Chinese Air Force, which defended Chinese airspace by shooting down thousands of Japanese aircraft during World War II. In 1958, after the general lost his last battle to cancer, Anna and their two daughters moved to Washington, DC, and the young widow began developing her status as a thoroughly red-white-and-blue yet simultaneously fascinatingly exotic hostess. She became known for her sharp mind and keen eye for both parties and politics and attracted two nicknames: she was called "Little Flower" by some, "the Dragon Lady" by others.

Having broken barriers as the first female reporter for China's Central News Agency, Chennault's hard-nosed journalistic skills served her well in making friends and influencing people. She drew eyes in her flamboyant, brightly colored, authentic Chinese silk dresses, and her intellect won the ears of many a politician.

She rose in the ranks of the Republican Party as a campaigner and fundraiser, and by 1968 she was co-chairperson of Women for Nixon-Agnew.[1]

During the campaign, Chennault served as a go-between in secret message relays from Nixon to the South Vietnamese and back. She met often with John Mitchell, and sometimes with Nixon himself. She was placed under FBI surveillance by President Johnson, which failed to hinder her actions but established a historical record of her direct involvement in collapsing the Paris negotiations. It was Chennault herself who gave the message that South Vietnam should refrain from negotiating with Johnson because Nixon would surely provide a better deal when elected.

Her shrewd political mind did not prevent Chennault from being double-crossed, and indeed Nixon deeply betrayed her by failing to end the Vietnam War as he had promised. Nevertheless, her political career continued. She served as a personal liaison for a total of eight presidents and in 1980 was part of President Reagan's special envoy to Taiwan and mainland China; her reputation grew as a goodwill ambassador between China and the U.S.—a reputation that might have been far different had the 1968 sabotage become public.

Now a vivacious octogenarian, Chennault founded and chairs the Council for International Cooperation (CIC), a non-profit, non-political organization that aims to foster global cooperation. Focused primarily on building relationships between the U.S., China, and Taiwan, CIC promotes educational exchange programs and provides annual scholarships worldwide.[2]

John Mitchell (1913-1988)

Sometimes referred to as the ultimate Nixon loyalist, John Mitchell started his career as a municipal bond lawyer in New York City. He practiced there from 1938 to 1968, with the exception of three years spent as a naval officer during World War II. Mitchell met Richard Nixon when their firms merged in 1967. As Nixon's 1968 campaign manager, Mitchell was a key communication point between the GOP candidate and Anna Chennault, Nixon's clandestine go-between with the South Vietnamese government.

After Nixon took office, Mitchell was appointed attorney general.

But the nominee escaped the standard background check for someone of such high office — thanks to the new president's unusual appeal to FBI director J. Edgar Hoover. Once in office, Mitchell favored "law and order" policies over civil liberties protections. He advocated the use of non-court-ordered wiretaps in national security cases, as well as preventative detention of criminal suspects. The attorney general compared Vietnam War protesters to Nazi Brownshirts and brought criminal conspiracy charges against war critics.

In 1972, Mitchell resigned as attorney general to run Nixon's re-election campaign. Later it was discovered that he controlled an illegal campaign slush fund used to spy on Democratic opponents and was one of the key conspirators in both planning the Watergate break-in and covering up White House involvement.

Tapes from the Nixon White House are stained with incriminating evidence against Mitchell, and at trial he was found guilty of conspiracy, obstruction of justice, and perjury. Sentenced to two-and-a-half to eight years in prison, Mitchell had time reduced for health reasons. He spent only nineteen months behind bars under minimum-security conditions. Mitchell holds the dishonor of being the only United States attorney general to serve prison time.

Many years later, it emerged that Mitchell had lied about key parts of his military service. He had not, as he'd claimed, commanded a heroic World War II junior officer named John F. Kennedy. Nor was Mitchell awarded two Purple Hearts and the Navy's Silver Star, as the eulogy delivered by his lifelong friend Richard Moore at Arlington Cemetery asserted.[3]

After his early release from prison, Mitchell lived quietly in the Georgetown area of Washington, where he served as a consultant to business schemes of dubious propriety. He granted no interviews and published no accounts of the Watergate affair, which he called the "White House horrors." Like Nixon, Mitchell never spoke or wrote about the sabotage of 1968 Vietnam peace efforts. The former attorney general died of a heart attack in 1988 and was buried with full military honors at Arlington National Cemetery.[4]

Hubert Horatio Humphrey (1911-1978)

Before ever harboring political aspirations, Hubert Humphrey was a licensed pharmacist, assisting at his father's drug stores in the 1930s. In 1940, he became a political-science instructor at Louisiana State University, where he had just graduated with a master's degree. During World War II, he returned to Minnesota (where he had attended college) to supervise the Works Progress Administration and helped found the Minnesota Democratic-Farmer-Labor Party (DFL). He was elected mayor of Minneapolis on the DFL ticket in 1945 (having lost as a Democrat in 1943) and co-founded Americans for Democratic Action, a liberal anti-communist group, in 1947.

In 1948, the Democratic Party added to its platform a plank to end racial segregation, and Humphrey made a notable speech at the convention in which he urged Democrats to "walk into the sunshine of human rights." He was elected to the Senate that year and served three terms, until being chosen as Lyndon Johnson's vice presidential nominee in 1964. (He also made two failed presidential primary bids during that time, in 1952 and 1960.) While in the Senate, Humphrey introduced the first resolution to create the Peace Corps, chaired the Select Committee on Disarmament, and was the lead author of the Civil Rights Act of 1964.

As vice president, Humphrey remained loyal to Johnson's Vietnam War policies—which disappointed many liberal anti-war Democrats when Humphrey made his third White House bid in 1968. Challenged by anti-war senators Eugene McCarthy and Robert F. Kennedy, Humphrey used a shrewd delegate strategy (focused on winning over the delegates from non-primary states) and secured the nomination. But the Democratic National Convention in Chicago that summer became a bloody hotbed of protest and police brutality—what might, in hindsight, be viewed as a death knell for Humphrey's presidential dreams.

Humphrey might have stood a chance in the November 1968 general election against Richard Nixon had the Paris peace negotiations been successful. But Nixon ensured they were not, and the war raged on. Humphrey lost the election, yet he never went public about Nixon's sabotage. His campaign manager, Larry O'Brien, went on to chair the Democratic National Committee, whose offices were broken into in the Watergate scandal of 1972.

In 1971, after a political hiatus during which he returned to teaching in Minnesota, Humphrey returned to the Senate. He served there until his death in 1978.

Nguyen Van Thieu (1923-2001)

Nguyen Van Thieu was born in a deeply impoverished village in the lowlands of Vietnam (then French Indochina) in 1923. Educated at Catholic schools, Thieu worked in his father's rice fields during the Japanese occupation of World War II. His nationalistic sentiments drove him to join the Viet Minh, the anti-French nationalist liberation army, in 1945. But Thieu quickly became disillusioned, realizing he had joined a communist organization. He turned to the Vietnamese National Military Academy, which the French had established to train anti-Viet Minh fighters, and received his commission in 1949. He quickly became known as a brave and capable leader, and in 1954 he led a battalion to oust the communists from his home village.

Thieu was introduced to politics in the early 1960s, when he assisted in a successful and deadly coup against President Ngo Dinh Diem, a corrupt, American-backed, South Vietnamese leader known for imprisoning political opponents by the thousands. The Military Revolutionary Council took control, and Thieu began to accrue influence.

In 1965, Thieu set up his own military government in South Vietnam. He was the tenth national leader in nineteen months and received an endorsement by the United States as "the best available candidate."[5] He reigned strong against the communists, imposing martial law, growing the military through conscription, and arresting hundreds of political opponents.

In 1968, Thieu's ambassador to the U.S., Bui Diem, communicated with Anna Chennault and the Nixon campaign about holding off on the peace talks. Thieu was unhappy with prospects under Johnson—one reason being that Thieu wanted South Vietnam, not the U.S., to lead the anti-communist side at the table. So Thieu, communicating with Nixon through Chennault, agreed to refrain from negotiating until the GOP candidate became president and a better deal was available. Thieu refused to send a delegation to Paris, and the peace talks crumbled.

In the end, Nixon did not offer Thieu a better deal; Thieu felt betrayed. When Nixon announced plans to withdraw U.S. troops from Vietnam, Thieu became even harder for Nixon to deal with. Nixon made a thinly veiled threat on Thieu's life to get him to support final U.S. peace efforts. When the last American forces withdrew from Vietnam in March of 1973, Thieu controlled most of the South. But the ceasefire broke down less than a year later.

In 1975, Saigon fell to communist forces, and Thieu fled — reportedly taking along suitcases rattling with millions of dollars in gold bullion.[6] It was later determined that Thieu's corrupt regime was also riddled with communist spies, and there was, in reality, little chance he could ever have had a fighting chance at victory on his own. In his final speech before being safely flown out of the country in an American aircraft, Thieu blamed the military defeat of his government on "American betrayal."

Thieu relocated to Britain and later to America, where he lived out his days quietly in Massachusetts. He rarely made public statements. The last president of South Vietnam, he died in 2001.[7]

Bui Diem (b. 1923)

Bui Diem was South Vietnam's ambassador to the United States under President Nguyen van Thieu. Deeply involved in his country's politics, Diem was part of the delegation to the Geneva Conference in 1954, and in 1965 he was Prime Minister Phan Huy Quat's chief of staff. His status allowed him to work closely with American diplomats, including Robert McNamara and Henry Kissinger.

In 1968, Diem met personally with Anna Chennault, at the behest of Richard Nixon, and transmitted messages to President Thieu. These communications, and Nixon's promise to Thieu that a better peace deal would be available if Nixon were elected president, led to Thieu's withdrawal from the Paris negotiations and the collapse of the peace talks.

The war continued for several years. Near the end, as American support evaporated, Diem lobbied Congress for $700 million in emergency aid that never came. In 1975, Saigon fell, and the communists took over the country.

When South Vietnam collapsed, Diem and his family moved stateside to Rockville, Maryland, bringing only two suitcases and a few thousand dollars. Initially he worked at a local deli to support his wife and young son; he later took a faculty position at George Mason University and became a scholar at both the Woodrow Wilson International Center for Scholars and the American Enterprise Institute. With the goal of fostering public understanding of the war, he published *In the Jaws of History* (co-authored with David Chanoff), a book about the Vietnam War from the perspective of those it affected most — the Vietnamese.[8]

Henry Alfred Kissinger (b. 1923)

Born Heinz Alfred Kissinger to Jewish parents in post-World War I Germany, Henry's family fled their home country for New York in 1938. Five years later, Kissinger became a naturalized citizen and was drafted into the Army to deploy in the Second World War. He returned to Germany, this time in uniform and ready to fight the Nazis who had chased his family from their home.

Upon returning stateside, Kissinger attended Harvard University, ultimately attaining a Ph.D. from the department of government in 1954. His studies there influenced his views on foreign policy, which generally cherished order, no matter how flawed, over political tumult. He joined the department's faculty upon graduation, securing tenure in 1959.

Even during his time as a professor, Kissinger involved himself in policymaking, serving as a special advisor to both JFK and LBJ during their presidencies. In 1968, Kissinger served as Richard Nixon's mole in Johnson's peace negotiations, providing Nixon with information he needed to sabotage the talks; he was rewarded with an appointment to national security advisor when Nixon took office in 1969 and left his position at Harvard.

Kissinger and Nixon claimed to seek "peace with honor" in the Vietnam War. Kissinger used both diplomatic maneuverings and massive military firepower (including covert operations in Cambodia that led to the Khmer Rouge's rise to power and ensuing genocide) in attempts to simultaneously lure North Vietnam to the negotiating table and maintain credibility on the world stage. In 1973, a semblance of peace was achieved, though with questionable honor, when Kissinger and his North Vietnamese counterpart, Le Duc Tho, finally reached an agreement to end U.S. involvement in

Southeast Asia. Kissinger and Tho shared the Nobel Peace Prize for their efforts, though millions had died under Kissinger's foreign-policy guidance.

Kissinger also paved the way for the Nixon administration to open relations with China and played a key role in détente with the Soviet Union, negotiating the Strategic Arms Limitation Treaty (SALT I) in 1972. He orchestrated the coup that overthrew the Allende government in Chile, ushering the violently dictatorial but U.S.-backed Pinochet regime. Kissinger was appointed secretary of state by Nixon in 1973 and remained in office following Nixon's resignation, stepping down when President Ford left office in 1977.

Kissinger would go on to advise Presidents Ronald Reagan and George H. W. Bush, continuing his prolific career as one of the United States' most prominent, if Machiavellian, statesmen.

Lawrence "Larry" O'Brien Jr. (1917-1990)

Larry O'Brien had his first taste of politics at age eleven when his father, a local Democratic Party official, recruited him to volunteer on Al Smith's 1928 presidential campaign. The experience hooked him on politics, and at age twenty-two, with a newly minted bachelor's degree in law, he was elected leader of his chapter of the Hotel and Restaurant Employees Union. It was the only elected office he would hold, but he would go on to help some of the most prominent political figures of the twentieth century attain theirs.

Larry O'Brien Sr., an Irish immigrant and staunch Democrat, passed on his political connections to his son, but the young man would quickly prove himself in his own right. After serving as a local director for three House of Representatives election campaign cycles in Massachusetts, O'Brien was chosen to lead John F. Kennedy's Senate campaigns in 1952 and 1958. In 1960, he helped Kennedy to victory in the presidential race against Richard Nixon. He became a member of the "Irish Mafia," Kennedy's inner circle of friends and confidantes. O'Brien was charged with staffing the new Kennedy White House, and later with overseeing its congressional relations.

The presidential campaign strategy O'Brien had developed for the Democrats in 1960—which focused on strong communication with convention delegates and alternative delegates, voter registration, telephone canvassing, and recruiting volunteers (particularly women, who would hold tea with friends to promote the candidate) — became a national standard. O'Brien's status as a brilliant political player solidified. In 1964, he led Johnson's campaign to victory, and in 1965 Johnson appointed him postmaster general, a position he occupied for three years while continuing as a congressional liaison.

In 1968, O'Brien served as Humphrey's campaign lead and was privy to Nixon's underhanded intervention in the Vietnam peace talks immediately before the election. Though Humphrey lost, O'Brien was elected by the Democratic National Committee (DNC) as its chairman. He still held that position in 1972 when his office became the prime target of the infamous Watergate burglars — who may have been searching for documents incriminating Nixon in the 1968 sabotage.

After Watergate, O'Brien gravitated away from politics, though he left an indelible mark on campaign strategy. From 1975-1984, he served as commissioner for the National Basketball Association (NBA), stabilizing the organization. He died of cancer in 1990.[9]

Timeline of Events

"Had this information been made public at the time, it would surely have destroyed Nixon's presidential hopes — then and forever."
— Nixon biographer Anthony Summers

1954

When the French withdraw from Vietnam after a major military defeat, Vice Pres. Richard Nixon becomes the first elected U.S. official to urge the dispatch of American troops to Indochina.

President Dwight Eisenhower rejects such advice, proclaiming: "The sun's still shining . . . Dien Bien Phu (where the French were defeated) isn't the end of the world . . . it's not that important."[1]

1960-1961

American advisors are sent to Vietnam in the Eisenhower era in small numbers. Under Pres. John F. Kennedy, that number increases to about sixteen thousand.

1961

Vice Pres. Lyndon Johnson visits Pres. Ngo Dinh Diem in Saigon. LBJ assures Diem that he is crucial to American aims in Vietnam and calls him "the Churchill of Asia."

April 1964

Former Vice President Nixon says North Vietnam must be attacked if South Vietnam is to win its anti-Communist war.[2]

August 1964

Congress passes the Gulf of Tonkin Resolution. It authorizes

President Johnson to "take all necessary measures to repel any armed attack against forces of the United States and to prevent further aggression."

1965
Using his new powers, President Johnson begins bombing targets in North Vietnam and escalating America's military buildup in the South.

1965-1968
From 1965 to 1968, about 643,000 tons of bombs are dropped on the North. U.S. troop strength grows rapidly and reaches its peak in 1968 with five hundred thousand troops on the ground.

1968
Republican presidential hopeful Richard Nixon claims to have a plan to "end the war and win the peace" in Vietnam. But he keeps the plan to himself, Nixon asserts, so as not to upset ongoing peace efforts.

March 31, 1968
LBJ surprises the nation and announces he will not run for re-election in order to devote the remainder of his presidency to the search for peace.

July 1968
Nixon holds a secret meeting at his Manhattan apartment with his campaign manager, John Mitchell; Anna Chennault, an avid Nixon fund-raiser with solid ties to South Vietnam; and South Vietnam's ambassador to Washington, Bui Diem.

As a result of this meeting, private citizen Nixon begins illegally engaging in clandestine negotiations with the South Vietnamese. Nixon promises Saigon a "better deal" if he is elected. His secret emissary is Chennault, a.k.a. "the Dragon Lady." The operation is code-named "Little Flower."[3]

Nixon goes on to obtain inside intelligence on the peace talks from his secret "mole" in the United States delegation in Paris–Henry Kissinger.

August 1968
Accepting the GOP presidential nomination, Nixon pledges that, if elected, his first objective "will be to bring an honorable end to the war in Vietnam."

September 30, 1968
Seeking to separate himself from LBJ on Vietnam, Vice Pres. Hubert Humphrey, the Democratic presidential nominee, promises to end the bombing of North Vietnam and calls for a ceasefire.

October 20, 1968
Nixon asks LBJ if he can restrain Humphrey on Vietnam:

> **RN:** Can you keep . . . your vice president and others, keep them firm on this? The hell with the god damned election! We must stand firm on this!
>
> **LBJ:** Very frankly, I don't know. That's the honest answer. I just plain don't know . . .
>
> **LBJ:** You [Nixon] can have every reason to be proud of what your platform is.
>
> **RN:** I won't take any advantage of you.
>
> **LBJ:** I know that [or] I wouldn't be calling you. I'm going to keep you informed . . .[4]

October 29, 1968
Through CIA, NSA, and FBI surveillance, President Johnson gets solid proof of Nixon's "treason."

October 31, 1968
To convince Hanoi to come to the bargaining table, Johnson orders a halt in the bombing. This gives Humphrey an immediate boost in public-opinion polls. A onetime eighteen-point Nixon lead is soon sliced to two percentage points.

November 1, 1968
Operation "Little Flower" succeeds, as Thieu reneges on a

promise to Johnson and announces his country will not participate
in the Paris peace talks.

Many years later, LBJ biographer Charles Peters notes that
Thieu's announcement "appeared in the American press the weekend before the election, dashing any hope for peace. Humphrey's
momentum came to a dead stop and went into reverse."[5]

November 2, 1968

The President asks Senate Minority Leader Everett Dirksen for
help in stopping Nixon's sabotage. Johnson hints he might leak the
full story of Nixon's duplicity to the press:

> **LBJ:** I don't want to get this in the campaign . . . They oughtn't to
> be doing this. This is treason.
> **ED:** I know.[6]

Dirksen, the top elected Republican official, promises to get in
touch with Nixon.

When LBJ later informs Sen. Richard Russell of Nixon's treachery,
Russell says: "I never did have any respect for [Nixon], but damn, I
never thought he'd stoop to anything like that."[7]

After Humphrey learns of Nixon's moves to undercut peace, the
enraged Democratic candidate asks an aide, "What kind of guy
could engage in something like this?"[8]

November 3, 1968

Nixon denies to LBJ that he has been trying to scuttle the peace
process. He pledges to cooperate with the president's peace plans
and even to go to Paris or Saigon if needed.

November 4, 1968

Defense secretary Clark Clifford tells the president: "Some
elements of the story are so shocking in their nature that I'm
wondering whether it would be good for the country to disclose the
story and then possibly have a certain individual [Nixon] elected. It

could cast his whole administration under such doubt that I think it would be inimical to our country's interests."[9]

In the interests of national security, neither Johnson nor Humphrey blows the whistle on Nixon.

November 6, 1968
Nixon edges out Humphrey in the presidential election.

In Saigon, South Vietnamese leaders toast Nixon's victory with vintage French champagne. One celebrant reportedly declares: "We did it. We helped elect an American president."[10]

November 17, 1968
Syndicated columnists Drew Pearson and Jack Anderson report on a U.S.-South Vietnamese "backstage fight" over the peace talks. They say Saigon's leaders backed out of the negotiations because they felt LBJ rushed through a bombing-halt agreement "just before the election in order to win votes for Hubert Humphrey."

Early January 1969
Tom Ottenad of the *St. Louis Post-Dispatch* writes an article saying a top Nixon official "secretly got in touch with representatives of South Vietnam shortly before the presidential election. It was in connection with an apparent effort to encourage them to delay joining the Paris peace talks in hopes of getting a better deal if the Republicans won the White House."[11] The Ottenad piece gets no public traction, no press follow-ups, and is soon forgotten.

January 20, 1969
Declaring he has a "sacred commitment" to peace, Richard Nixon assumes the presidency from Lyndon Johnson.

LBJ gets early word to the new president "that Johnson would never reveal how Nixon had used Anna Chennault to torpedo the peace talks until Humphrey was defeated," as LBJ biographer Charles Peters disclosed in 2010.[12]

March 1969

President Nixon illegally orders the secret bombing of Cambodia. Neither Congress nor the American people are told.

The bombing continues for more than four years, until Congress discovers and stops it.[13]

July 1969

The president holds a quick, *pro forma* meeting with Thieu in Saigon and then choppers to a nearby U.S. Army base. Nixon tells aide Bob Haldeman that he was overwhelmed by the character of the troops, adding: "Never let those hippie college boys in to see me again . . ."[14]

March 1970

CIA director Richard Helms refuses Nixon's request for the CIA's detailed files on possible connections among LBJ's bombing halt, the Paris talks, and the U.S. presidential campaign. (Nixon eventually fired Helms for his refusal to turn over these files—as well as for his refusal to involve the agency in the Watergate cover-up.)

April 1970

American and South Vietnamese troops begin a two-month invasion of Cambodia. This, along with the secret bombings, helps destabilize the country.

1970

Shortly after the invasion ends, Gen. Lon Nol instigates a coup and displaces Prince Norodom Sihanouk of Cambodia. (Racked by turmoil, in 1975 the country witnesses the rise to power of Pol Pot and the Khmer Rouge—a communist political and military organization.)

June 30, 1971

President Nixon approves a firebombing and break-in at the left-leaning Brookings Institution in Washington in order to steal its Vietnam files, which he believes include documentation of his 1968 moves to block peace.

The break-in is ultimately called off, but only after proceeding to near-implementation. (John Dean managed to convince other top aides that it was too dangerous. Nixon's approval of this crime was only recently confirmed on new Nixon White House tapes.)

June 17, 1972

DC cops catch Nixon's ham-handed Watergate burglars as they replaced a broken bug they had previously placed on the telephone of Democratic Party chairman Larry O'Brien. They also had rolls and rolls of film on which to photograph opposition political documents.

The burglars were on a fishing expedition to locate dirt they could use against the Democrats, or that O'Brien might use against them, as an election-year "October Surprise." Could Nixon have thought O'Brien might have had copies of the Vietnam files that disclosed Nixon's Vietnam treachery?

1973

Early in his Watergate-truncated second term, the president tries to find out whether Johnson ordered the rumored FBI bugging of Nixon's 1968 campaign jet. When Johnson finds out, he explodes and makes what Nixon aide Bob Haldeman described as "a direct threat from Johnson" to expose Nixon's Vietnam treachery.[15]

Lyndon B. Johnson dies on January 22.

August 1974

Nixon is forced to resign from office over the Watergate scandal.

September 1974

President Ford grants Nixon a pardon for all crimes Nixon committed as president. (Nixon's "treason," of course, took place *before* he became president. But Nixon's sabotage of the Paris negotiations was not confirmed until after Nixon's 1994 death.)

April 30, 1975

The United States loses its first war, as North Vietnamese troops overrun Saigon.

1994

Richard Nixon, the man accused by Lyndon Johnson of being a traitor, dies in Yorba Linda, California, after suffering a stroke. He was eighty-one.

1995

LBJ aide Walt Rostow's "X Envelope" is finally opened, leading to a declassification of many of the "Top Secret" and "Secret" documents it contains on Nixon's 1968 "treason."

1999

Key FBI documents from the X Envelope are released to Nixon biographer Anthony Summers. They verify that Nixon himself called the shots in the sabotage of the U.S. peace plan for Vietnam. The author concludes: "The fact that Nixon covertly intervened . . . deliberately flouting the efforts of the American authorities, was indefensible. The way in which he involved himself remains to this day undefended."[16]

2002

A bitter Anna Chennault admits her role in the 1968 sabotage, telling the *Shanghai Star:* "To end the war was my only demand. But after [Nixon] became president, he decided to continue the war. Politicians are never honest."[17]

2008

The LBJ Library releases riveting audiotapes concerning Nixon's 1968 attempts to torpedo U.S. peace efforts. Included is the president's description of Nixon's actions as "treason." Johnson opined that the GOP candidate had "blood on his hands."

2010

Declassified documents from the Nixon White House reveal just how eager Nixon was to obtain the CIA's intelligence data on his 1968 anti-peace machinations.

2014

In a declassified oral history, 1968 Nixon aide Tom Charles Huston confirms the sabotage plot and says it's *inconceivable* Nixon didn't manage it.

TREASON

Chapter 1

Setting the Scene

Few figures in U.S. history have proven as brilliant at high-stakes power-wielding and brokering as Lyndon B. Johnson. The same could be said of Richard Nixon, his political rival, but according to former White House correspondent for the *Baltimore Sun* Muriel Dobbin, "Nixon was different, and I think you have to be careful to draw the difference. Johnson was ruthless and probably terrifying. But . . . there was nothing [Nixon] would not do."[1] As the 1968 election approached, these two giants clashed in a high-stakes political battle royale, one of the nation's most dramatic and important little-known events.

As we are only now grasping, the Johnson-Nixon showdown involved a potential national security crime of the highest magnitude—an unpatriotic act so extreme that it challenged the legitimacy of the election. Johnson caught Nixon embroiled in a clandestine attempt to torpedo United States-sponsored peace negotiations in Paris by manipulating the Vietnam War for his own political ends and by portraying himself as a dove in hawk's clothing. Nixon's moves were designed to bolster his own chances of defeating Democratic nominee Hubert Humphrey, Johnson's vice president.

Most of the information President Johnson uncovered came from unimpeachable intelligence sources. It was considered so shocking by the president and his advisors that Johnson took it with him when he left the White House in 1969. This evidence was turned over to the LBJ Library, where it was placed in what came to be known as the "X Envelope." The envelope was sealed and was not supposed to be opened for fifty years. This book will fully examine and analyze this evidence, which Johnson's national security advisor Walt Rostow eventually came to believe should be made public much earlier than its originally prescribed release date.

Indeed, much of the X Envelope's material was made available

33

to researchers in the late 1990s. It has been augmented by tape recordings from the LBJ White House in 2008, as well as by declassified records and phone calls from the Nixon White House in 2010. (Johnson taped selectively, while Nixon recorded almost all of his phone conversations—and Oval Office meetings—on an automated system.)

The Ballot Develops

The Paris peace talks began in May of 1968, about one month after President Johnson stopped bombing parts of North Vietnam. But they went nowhere until mid-September, when Hanoi's delegates finally agreed to expand the talks to include South Vietnam immediately after a complete halt to the bombing. Ironing out details of this promising development, however, would take additional time—and the U.S. election clock was ticking.

GOP front-runner Nixon had formally entered the 1968 campaign on February 1, confidently asserting, "I believe that I will be the strongest [Republican] candidate, and I believe that I can beat Lyndon Johnson." Nixon scored a resounding win in the first important primary in snowy New Hampshire on March 12—winning 79 percent of the vote against Michigan governor George Romney. The former vice president went on to easily capture the Republican nomination that summer.

It was obvious by February that the fall campaign would center on Johnson's highly unpopular war policies. So, from the start, on the hustings and in TV commercials, Nixon—at heart a war hawk—promoted himself as the peace candidate. He repeatedly pledged to implement an unspecified plan that would "end the war and win the peace." That probably sounded pretty good to many dovish voters who thought Humphrey was too tightly tied to LBJ's military misadventures.

As president, Johnson's mastery of domestic affairs—especially on civil rights, anti-poverty measures, and health care—was overshadowed by his failed Vietnam War policies. The situation on the faraway battlefront had steadily deteriorated on his watch and took a big turn toward disaster just before Nixon entered the race.

On January 30, 1968, Johnson and his top military advisors—along with hundreds of thousands of United States and allied forces in Vietnam—were totally surprised by the intensity and range of a major enemy attack that had been anticipated for months. Known as the Tet Offensive, enemy troops advanced on five of South Vietnam's six largest cities—and on most of its provincial capitals. Before Tet was repulsed, Viet Cong forces even attacked the U.S. Embassy compound and the presidential palace in Saigon.

LBJ biographer Mark Updegrove says "the sheer ferocity of Tet meant, in essence, that [enemy forces] were winning the war." Johnson, according to his biographer, "monitored the developments of Tet at all hours, getting little sleep and wearing himself down further. During the crisis, Richard Russell visited with him privately at the White House, where he watched his former mentee weep over the situation."[2] (Senator Russell had been Johnson's mentor in the Senate.)

On the home front, the war was becoming even more divisive. Public confidence in Johnson fell sharply after legendary TV news anchor Walter Cronkite returned from a fact-finding trip to the battlefront. CBS's avuncular journalist, "whose wisdom Americans seemed to take as an article of faith," as Updegrove notes, broadcast a one-hour special on February 27. Cronkite reported: "It seems now more certain than ever that the bloody experience of Vietnam is to end in a stalemate." After the program aired, Johnson told an aide, "If I've lost Cronkite, I've lost the country."[3]

Exasperated by the war, and believing he might not even be renominated, Johnson surprised the nation and quit the presidential race on March 31, 1968. In doing so, in a nationally televised address, he dramatically pledged to devote all of his remaining term to the search for peace:

> With America's sons in the fields far away, with America's future under challenge right here at home, with our hopes and the world's hopes for peace in the balance every day, I do not believe that I should devote an hour or a day of my time to any personal partisan causes or to any duties other than the awesome duties of this office—the presidency of your county.[4]

After the TV cameras went off in the Oval Office, as Johnson got up from his desk, his wife and daughters rushed to his side. Lady Bird Johnson gave her husband a kiss and a hug and whispered into his ear, "Nobly done, darling."[5] A little later, while eating a bowl of tapioca and wearing a powder blue turtleneck, a relaxed president bantered with a small group of reporters in the family residence. Opening with a joke—"I fooled y'all, didn't I?"— Johnson soon turned serious, according to *Washington Post* reporter Carl Bernstein:

> [T]hen we asked some questions about the war and what led to his decision [not to seek a second term], and he talked in very emotional terms about what the war was doing to the fabric of the country and his presence if he continued as President as this terribly divisive issue was [affecting] the county. And he became emotional at that point. I think we were all emotional in the sense of knowing this was an incredible moment in history.[6]

The news was astonishing—a healthy sitting president deciding not to run for a second term. It was so unexpected, one White House radio reporter lost his job for wrapping up a live broadcast of the event without any mention of the bombshell. He had been relying on the White House handout of the president's prepared remarks and had not paid suitable attention to LBJ's brief but critical insert. The reporter must have left his particular audience double-dazed. In his conclusion, the reporter began his comments by saying: "And so, President Lyndon Johnson has ordered a total halt to the bombing of North Vietnam in order to bolster peace prospects."[7]

LBJ's withdrawal announcement was followed by another 1968 political shocker: Sen. Robert Kennedy, who was running as an anti-war Democrat, was murdered—and Hubert Humphrey wound up as the party's standard-bearer. Richard Nixon then figured that if he could just keep the president from attaining peace before the November election, he, rather than Humphrey, would win.

The "Peace Candidate"

In the campaign, Nixon was mostly silent or vague on the details of his secret plan for peace. He said that to discuss such matters might wreck the Paris talks. This led Humphrey to run a TV spot that, in the words of Nixon biographer Rick Perlstein, "deflated Nixon's very masculinity." The ad opens with twelve seconds of silent film of Nixon speaking and gesticulating. Then comes a voiceover that says, "Mr. Nixon's silence on Vietnam has become an issue itself." It ends with a quote from Republican senator Mark Hatfield: "The Paris peace talks should not become the skirt for timid men to hide behind."[8]

Reporters were not able to regularly and frequently quiz Nixon about his supposed peace plan — because he refused to hold news conferences and only appeared on live TV before friendly pre-screened studio audiences. His standard stump speech was so well-memorized by campaign reporters that they could say it along with him. He also refused to debate Humphrey. At the time, some Nixon PR specialists dubbed this strategy (focusing on prime-time TV commercials) "The Living Room Campaign."

This allowed the tightly wound Nixon to avoid confrontations or crowds that might cause him to come unglued. And it was an ideal strategy for trying to be all things to all people. So the GOP candidate regularly donned his brash disguise as *the* peace candidate. In one of his most dovish TV spots, Nixon's own soothing baritone is heard over the sounds of battle, as a visual collage of the bloody Vietnam fighting fills the screen:

> Never has so much military, economic and diplomatic power been used so ineffectively as in Vietnam. If, after all this time and all this sacrifice and all of this support there is still no end in sight, then I say that it is time for the American people to turn to new leadership not tied to the political mistakes of the past. I pledge to you that we will have an honorable end to the War in Vietnam.[9]

On October 9, Nixon fired yet another Vietnam volley at both Johnson and Humphrey, declaring: "Those who have had a chance for four years and could not produce peace should not be given another chance."[10]

In the race's final days, in a near panic, Nixon actually accused Humphrey of endangering the "delicate" Paris peace talks with the "fastest, loosest tongue ever in American politics." He charged his

Democratic rival with speaking from both sides of his mouth on the "great issue" of a bombing halt. Nixon added: "He's been for it unconditionally, and then he has said we should have conditions. He has been unable to mind his tongue when negotiations are going on."[11]

Nixon's blast might have been connected to signs of significant progress in Paris, just the kind of "October Surprise" the paranoid GOP candidate was dreading. Nixon first got word of a possible Paris breakthrough from his prized mole in the U.S. delegation, Henry Kissinger. Nixon's future national security advisor, the urbane Harvard professor regularly delivered confidential information from the talks to Nixon, mostly through Nixon's campaign manager John Mitchell. Mitchell, of course, went on to become President Nixon's attorney general, and then the chairman of Nixon's 1972 reelection campaign. An eventual Watergate felon, Mitchell wound up as Prisoner Number 23171-157 in the Alabama correctional system.[12]

By the end of October 1968, President Johnson was huddling with his top advisors on the advisability of a total bombing halt. The U.S. field commander in Vietnam, Gen. Creighton Abrams, was secretly flown to Washington and sneaked into the White House in a disguise. LBJ grilled the general on the potential battlefield ramifications of a bombing cessation. General Abrams told the commander in chief: "Mr. President, you will be plunged into a cesspool of controversy. This will be interpreted as a political act, but if I were you I would do it."[13]

Johnson also received assurances from the joint chiefs of staff that such a move "would be a perfectly acceptable military risk." At the end of his meeting with the joint chiefs, the president declared: "I know I will be charged with doing this to influence the election. The doves will criticize us for not doing this earlier. The hawks will say I shouldn't have done this at all."[14]

On October 31, the hawkish Johnson announced a total halt in the bombing of North Vietnam to entice the enemy into serious bargaining. By election eve, Nixon's early 18 percent lead over Humphrey had evaporated to a mere two percentage points. (Segregationist Alabama governor George Wallace's third-party bid was siphoning votes from both major party candidates, but mostly from Humphrey.)

The closer peace seemed to be at hand, the harder Nixon covertly tried to block it. Just days before voters went to the polls, Nixon convinced Nguyen Van Thieu to renege on a firm pledge to Johnson to participate in the Paris negotiations.[15] Saigon's boycott paid off big time for Nixon, who defeated Humphrey by less than one percentage point of the popular vote. In Electoral College voting, Nixon won with 301 to Humphrey's 191 and Wallace's 46.

The indomitable Johnson had waged a skillful and relentless fight — not only *against* Nixon, but also *for* peace in Indochina (where twenty thousand more Americans and millions of Indochinese would die during Nixon's presidency). But every time Johnson personally, or through intermediaries, called Nixon on the carpet on the sabotage issue, the Republican standard-bearer would play hide-and-go-seek with the truth.

Fearful LBJ might go public with the indisputable evidence he held, Nixon had nervously phoned Johnson just before the election. The soon-to-be president falsely assured LBJ that the "rumblings around about somebody trying to sabotage the Saigon government's attitude . . . certainly have no — absolutely no — credibility as far as I'm concerned."[16]

Johnson's proof of the Republican nominee's treachery had given him a huge advantage in his direct and indirect confrontations with Nixon in the fall of 1968. At his presidential fingertips was a cornucopia of top-secret intelligence data from FBI wiretaps, CIA surveillance, and NSA intercepts. Through those means, Johnson was, as he told Senate Republican Leader Everett Dirksen, "looking at [Nixon's] hole card." Using the lexicon of poker, the president was confiding to his longtime Republican friend that he had identified the exact scope of Nixon's anti-peace meddling.

Later in the same conversation, Johnson asked Dirksen to deliver a message to Nixon and his confederates: "You better tell 'em they better quit playing with [negotiations]. You just tell 'em that their people are messing around in this thing, and if they don't want it on the front pages, they better quit it."[17]

Johnson's ability to read Nixon's full poker hand had revealed to the president and his top advisors a scandal of truly immense proportions. As LBJ peace negotiator Richard Holbrooke later observed, Nixon's people had "massively, directly and covertly interfered in a major diplomatic negotiation—probably one of the most important negotiations in American diplomatic history."[18]

How did Richard Nixon's Vietnam sabotage system work? It was a rather Byzantine scheme. The candidate used a go-between to tell Saigon to resist LBJ's peace initiatives until after the election. During a Nixon presidency, the candidate told Thieu, he would get a better deal.

Nixon's secret channel to Thieu was acquainted with both men. She was Madame Anna Chennault, a glamorous forty-three-year-old Chinese-born intrigue- and gossip-loving Washington socialite, and an effective lobbyist for right-wing causes. Nixon's messages went from John Mitchell to Chennault, who forwarded them to South Vietnam's ambassador to Washington, Bui Diem, who in turn sent them on to President Thieu, the final link in the conspiracy chain. All the participants in this plot—with the exception of Thieu—had secretly conferred at Nixon's Manhattan apartment in July to set it in motion. Chennault later explained: "Nixon told Ambassador Bui Diem that any message to President Thieu will go to Anna Chennault, or any message President Thieu of Vietnam wanted to give to me [Nixon], you may give it to Anna."[19]

Chennault was somewhat of an odd pick. First, Nixon had great disdain for the female mentality. Second, he knew she had loose lips—not a terrific trait for a secret emissary engaged in a highly sensitive mission.

The future presidential candidate saw this flaw in Chennault up close and personal on a trip to Taipei in 1967. Not a "people person" to begin with, Nixon ran into Chennault during his visit, much to his displeasure. When she was out of sight, Nixon ordered aide Pat Hillings: "Get her away from me, Hillings. She's a chatterbox." LBJ aide William Bundy later described Chennault's key drawback as a trustworthy back-channel messenger a little more politely, saying that Chennault was "a bit too conspicuous and not always discreet in speech and action." But she was well-positioned to serve as a covert go-between with South Vietnam's government.

Through Chennault—a.k.a. "the Dragon Lady"—Nixon repeatedly urged Thieu to block Johnson's peace plans. But, by the fall, FBI wiretaps on Chennault's phones—installed at the direction of a suspicious Johnson—picked up this key November 2 message from

Nixon via Chennault to South Vietnam: "Hold on. We are gonna win."[20]

As we have seen, "Operation Little Flower," as Team Nixon dubbed it, worked splendidly. Despite Johnson's hard proof of Nixon's treachery, the president remained silent, and Nixon edged out Humphrey on November 6, 1968.

President Johnson wrestled with the question of whether to blow the whistle on Nixon's 1968 perfidy. After failed backstage efforts to cajole, coerce, and threaten Nixon into stopping his sabotage, LBJ felt he could do no more. He could not reveal Nixon's skullduggery without endangering the peace talks or divulging highly sensitive diplomatic, military, and intelligence secrets. Disclosure might also have created a crisis of confidence in America's government, at home and overseas. As Johnson himself explained to Sen. George Smathers, a friend of Nixon: "Obviously, it's so sensitive I can't say anything about it, except just say 'quit it.'"[21]

A newly released tape gives us a much clearer idea of the moral and ethical depths to which Nixon had sunk in committing what LBJ describes as "treason." On the other end of Johnson's phone line, Senator Dirksen, putting country above party, responds: "I know."[22]

Were the president and the senior Senate Republican right in their conclusion? Apparently. The U.S. Constitution says treason includes giving "aid and comfort" to the enemy. The subversion of negotiations with a foreign power in opposition to official American foreign policy certainly seems like something that could benefit an enemy. The top penalty for treason is death. But a traitor could get off with as few as five years in prison, a fine of $10,000, "and shall be incapable of holding any office under the United States."[23]

American University professor Chris Edelson—a constitutional law expert—thinks Nixon's action might well have qualified as treasonous: "South Vietnam was not the enemy, of course, but it seems Nixon was undermining his own government's efforts to make peace. It could also be improper dissemination of classified information—the same thing that got [President] Nixon so incensed at [Pentagon Papers leaker Daniel] Ellsberg."[24] At the least, Nixon deliberately violated the Logan Act, which prevents unauthorized private citizens from conducting United States foreign policy. A violator of this 1799 law could be imprisoned for up to three years.[25]

To his credit, President Johnson had given Humphrey a pre-election look at his intelligence goodies and an opportunity to go public with them. Learning about the full extent of the Nixon-Thieu contacts while on a campaign plane, Humphrey exploded to aides: "By God, when we land, I'm going to denounce Thieu. I'll denounce Nixon. I'll tell about the whole thing."[26]

Before the jetliner landed, however, Humphrey had a change of heart. He kept his mouth shut—reportedly concluding that outing Nixon's treachery might backfire. Some voters, he thought, might view such Humphrey charges as sour grapes—or even a dirty trick against Nixon. LBJ was reportedly "furious" with the vice president's decision not to implicate Nixon, calling it "the dumbest thing in the world not to do it."[27]

Humphrey campaign manager Larry O'Brien later explained that Humphrey held his fire because he didn't want to "be accused of playing cheap politics at the end of a desperation effort to win an election." Yet O'Brien said the even-keeled, often ebullient Democratic candidate, nicknamed the "Happy Warrior," was "shocked" when apprised of Nixon's actions, asking: "What kind of a guy could engage in something like this?"[28]

LBJ aide Tom Johnson describes Nixon's behavior as "reprehensible," adding: "I remain amazed that LBJ and Humphrey did not publicize the actions taken by the Nixon side in this ultra-sensitive matter. It is my belief that Nixon would not have been elected if the public had learned [of the sabotage]. This was kept as a very closely guarded secret."[29]

"Johnson was a master of leaking to the press," says Ford Rowan, a former NBC-TV reporter who covered the Nixon White House. "It's not clear why he was talked out of it in the hours before the election, even though a few reporters had picked up the scent of the Nixonian sabotage."[30]

Senior LBJ advisor Clark Clifford, one of those in the loop on this tightly held national security matter, later opined: "The activities of the Nixon team went far beyond the bounds of justifiable political combat. It constituted direct interference in the activities of the executive branch and the responsibilities of the Chief Executive, the only people [that is, members of the Executive Branch] with authority to negotiate on behalf of the nation." Clifford concluded that the sabotage "constituted a gross, even potentially illegal, interference in the security affairs of the nation by private individuals."[31]

"The Most Wicked Action in American History"

Despite the mild scent of duplicity, reporters covering the Nixon campaign were largely unaware of Nixon's anti-peace conspiring, but they were aware that the GOP candidate and his advisers were deeply worried that LBJ's bombing halt and Humphrey's separation from Johnson's hardline on Vietnam could produce a huge comeback victory for Humphrey, who trailed Nixon by more than twenty points in some early polling.

Indeed, campaign aides privately admitted that Nixon could well be robbed again of his fondest political dream. But Nixon and his American anti-peace co-conspirators, John Mitchell and Anna Chennault, kept their interference in the Paris negotiations completely to themselves.

Humphrey press aide Al Spivak now recalls, "I didn't have first hand-knowledge [*sic*] of [the sabotage], but I remember those of us in the HHH campaign apparatus knew in October of 1968 that here was *important* info on Nixon that might turn the tide of the November election. It just sort of vanished; we weren't told why. One theory is that HHH vetoed any use of the info as being harmful to the USA. I think a better suspicion is that LBJ vetoed it."[32]

As the election approached, LBJ's bombing halt and Humphrey's move away from Johnson's war policies were alone enough to convince many political junkies that Humphrey could pull off a political miracle.

(My United Press International colleague Bill Greenwood, a gent with a wry sense of humor who was covering Humphrey, was so confident of a coming HHH victory that he proposed we make a huge, multi-faceted bet on the outcome. I knew this proposed wager would likely be a put-on, one he knew I'd decline. Indeed, Greenwood set the stakes so much in his favor [including a codicil that I would give up the White House beat to him if Humphrey won] that I had to decline the bet—even though I was fairly certain Nixon would prevail.)

Nothing of importance in government or politics usually stays secret for long (the JFK assassination being a notable exception), so the non-spillage of Nixon's 1968 sabotage secret—at least during his own lifetime—was a rare exception to the ways of Washington. For Nixon, this was likely his most successful cover-up.

After the election, President Johnson—acting on the advice of Clark Clifford and a few other trusted aides—decided that national interests were best served if he did not expose a conspiracy so tawdry it could have crippled Nixon's ability to govern. Johnson also knew that news of Nixon's anti-peace maneuverings would almost certainly compromise U.S. intelligence-gathering "sources and methods."

Nonetheless, what Nixon had managed to pull off was a capstone of unscrupulousness and duplicity. As Christopher Hitchens has stated: "Nixon's illegal and surreptitious conduct not only prolonged an awful war but also corrupted and subverted a crucial presidential election: the combination must make it the most wicked action in American history."[33]

This sordid saga also stands out as underreported history; and history—the evil as well as the laudable—often holds valuable lessons. This particular tale even has a hero or two: Lyndon Johnson's public silence about a national security breach by a political rival was a rare display of nobility in modern American presidential leadership. Hubert Humphrey's silence deserves an equally honorable mention.

One can only hope that future history textbooks contain at least a few lines about the scandalous 1968 presidential campaign of Richard M. Nixon. "Ironic" is too weak a word to use in noting that, in 1974, this same corrupt politician was forced from the Oval Office by a 1972 campaign scandal called Watergate. One man; two tainted elections.

The two scandals might even be related. By 1972, one of the few Democrats who knew of Nixon's 1968 un-American activities was Larry O'Brien, who headed the Democratic National Committee. Did President Nixon's burglars break into O'Brien's Watergate offices and bug his phone to find out whether the Democrats might blow the whistle on Nixon's 1968 "treason"? Let's not rule out that possibility, which will be fully explored in Chapter Twelve.

Chapter 2

Nixon and Humphrey

The election of 1968 not only presented two highly distinct visions for the country moving forward but also a choice between two polar-opposite candidates who seemed nothing short of Shakespearian foils. Hubert Humphrey, the ever-affable and optimistic champion of liberal causes nicknamed "The Happy Warrior" by his colleagues in the Senate, had virtually nothing in common with the awkward and morose Nixon, who in college earned a nickname of his own: "Gloomy Gus." Never before in American history had so vastly different men battled each other for the nation's highest office.

A careful examination of the fires that forged these monumental political figures of the twentieth century, from their earliest years to the origins of their political careers, paints a compelling contrast of virtues that proved fateful for not only the outcome of the 1968 election but also the eventual demise of Nixon's presidency. Their backgrounds provide an essential context for understanding the actions taken by each that shaped the political climate for decades to come. As Nixon historian Kenneth Franklin Kurz put it, "The old adage, 'character is destiny,' decidedly applies to Richard Nixon. He created a presidency, staffed his White House, and conducted his relations with Congress all in such a way that made Watergate inevitable. Nixon got into the Watergate mess because he was Nixon."[1]

Yet just as Nixon's lack of moral conviction forced him out of the White House in 1974, Humphrey's deep ethical commitment prevented him from storming it in 1968. Armed with evidence that his opponent had committed a crime of the highest sort against his own country, Humphrey refused his aide's plan to reveal Nixon's sabotage of the Vietnam peace talks largely out of a fear that doing so would shatter any semblance of political efficacy during one of the most trying times in American history. Perhaps no one has more succinctly summed up these two antithetical men than Humphrey's own former press secretary Norman Sherman, reasoning, "Campaigns generally do reflect their principals. Humphrey was open, cheerful, and a bit chaotic. I think that defined our campaign and staff. Nixon was devious, secretive, duplicitous and his staff and his campaign reflected his 'values.'"[2]

The central task thus becomes determining how these two men, born less than two years apart to such seemingly similar middle-class families, who shared the same historical context in their formative years during the Great Depression and the Second World War, could be so at odds. A thorough inspection reveals an incredible contrast involving their childhoods, fathers, personalities, and personal motivations that explains their eventual clash on the national stage in 1968.

Hubert Horatio Humphrey – Early Years

Hubert Horatio Humphrey Jr. entered the world on the 27 of May, 1911, in a tightly-packed second-story room above the drugstore his father, Hubert Sr., owned in the small town of Wallace, South Dakota. Within a few years his family moved across the state to the somewhat larger Doland (though it had only six hundred residents) where Hubert would spend his entire childhood. By all accounts Hubert, or "Pinky" as everyone in Doland called him, had what can only be described as a wonderful early childhood. The second of four children, he engaged in all of the activities one might expect of a young midwestern boy, later writing of "hard work, but also fun in the outdoors, riding the hay wagon, driving the cattle from pasture to the barn . . . freedom to run through the fields."[3] Humphrey would often run clear across the entire sixteen-block town after school to the railroad tracks, gazing down them while dreaming of the big world outside of South Dakota.[4]

That being said, life in the Midwest did not lack incredible hardships for the many struggling families in the years leading up to the Great Depression. In fact, the trials of growing up in South Dakota during that time played a key role in shaping the nature and views of future-Vice President Humphrey. Tornadoes, droughts, and unrelenting storms intermittently brought disaster in the form of deep poverty that left Humphrey unable to forget his past and the plights of the common man, even years later as a member of the United States Senate. "I learned then something that is never far out of mind as I work on agricultural legislation, " he wrote after returning to the Senate years after the 1968 election, "that farmers are always puppets of the weather . . . Life was not only hard, it was capricious."[5] Humphrey's motivations for entering politics stemmed from a genuine desire to alleviate the suffering that was at times omnipresent in the rural Midwest.

Humphrey always possessed that cheerful disposition that would define him throughout his political career. Particularly during the darkness of the Depression, "to live, not just survive, required good spirits and hope, " and Humphrey possessed both.[6] Once as a young boy after misbehaving, he ran away from his mother and hid in the crawlspace under the front porch of his family's large wooden home. When Humphrey's father arrived, he was dispatched by his wife to find and discipline the eight year old. As Hubert Sr. began crawling under the porch, the son shouted to his father, "Come on in! Is mother after you, too?"[7] His sense of humor and optimism combined with his athleticism made Humphrey popular among his peers in Doland, where they often played in the fields long into the night.

Early in life, Humphrey learned the value and virtue of an honest day's work. Just as a young Richard Nixon worked in his family's grocery and gas station, in grade school Humphrey began helping out at his father's drugstore. His list of duties around the store was endless, involving helping with everything from picking up the "big, wooden, ice-filled tubs shipped from a factory in Watertown, with the five-gallon containers of vanilla [ice cream] packed like capsules inside" to washing dishes in the back of the store. As a young boy he also took up extra work selling newspapers to earn money of his own. As Humphrey himself later put it, "I was brought up to believe in work. I started writing checks when I was ten years old. I kept a ledger . . . I was independent . . . I'd make up to $3 to $5 a week. I'd keep my money in one of those little ice cream cartons. Bought all my own clothes from the time I was twelve."[8]

Before he was even a teenager, Humphrey bought all the

magazines his father intended on selling in the store for $50 in hopes of selling them faster and for a higher price. The young boy ambitiously bit off far more than he could chew, later explaining, "I proceeded to lose $100 on the magazines in three months because I was just too busy with too many activities—*Argosy, Bluebook, Redbook*—I didn't tear off the covers soon enough to get credit for those I didn't sell."[9] He learned an important and humbling lesson, gaining a deeper respect for the father who had an important role in shaping the young man's character.

As Humphrey later wrote in his memoirs, "The kind of public man I am has been overwhelmingly shaped by two influences: the land of South Dakota and an extraordinary relationship with an extraordinary man, my father."[10] He saw the deep suffering of his humble, rural homeland alleviated by a decisive governmental response in the leadership and programs of President Franklin Delano Roosevelt, infusing in him a brimming optimism in the potential for government to play a virtuous role in the lives of everyday Americans. The combination of this optimism with the confidence, compassion, and love of country inspired by his father propelled him into the field of public service.

Hubert Humphrey, Sr. was a large man who had a deep love for his family, especially his second son, Hubert, who was tasked with carrying on his namesake. By all accounts he was the wellspring of laughter and kindness that formed the famous amiable nature of his son. Prior to Hubert Jr.'s birth, Hubert Sr. had stepped away from the drugstore business for a period of time to sell candy across South Dakota. Humphrey would later describe his father as having "an unshakable faith in his own strength, in other people, and in this country." Humphrey Sr. instilled in his children a willingness to sympathize with their fellow countrymen, often sitting them down for a quick lesson. "Just think of it, boys," he once spoke to them, "here we are in the middle of this great big continent, here in South Dakota, with the land stretching out for hundreds of miles, with people who can vote and govern their own lives, with riches enough for all if we will take care to do justice." One can think of no more likely candidate for the father of the future "Happy Warrior."[11]

These words were not a hollow creed for the father of four, as he set a tangible example that his son followed during a long career of public service. Once, during the height of the Great Depression, Humphrey Sr. waived off a staggering thirteen thousand dollars' worth of debts owed to the drugstore by local members and businesses of Doland. Just as important, the father made clear to his son that forgiving the debts and thereby foregoing the money that they desperately needed to pay their own bills was not an act of charity but one of "elemental justice and fairness."[12] All were working hard, and all were suffering, so all needed to live and work together to get the country back on track.

The father's lessons did not fall on deaf ears, as Hubert and his brothers embraced his philosophies of kindness and generosity from their earliest years. One school day, young Hubert witnessed his friend Jonathan muddle through a brutal winter without shoes. When it got so bad that Jonathan's feet began turning blue, Hubert immediately brought the shivering child straight to his father's drugstore. "My father took one look, pushed the 'NO SALE' on the cash register, took out some money, and walked Jonathan down the street to buy him woolen socks and a pair of sturdy boots," Humphrey remembered.[13]

Yet it was not a blind tendency towards compassion alone that the father passed along to his son. The work ethic that complemented the cheerful disposition of the future politician Hubert Humphrey — the "Warrior" portion of his nickname — assuredly stemmed from his father as well. Hubert Sr. worked incredible hours at his drugstore, often stocking inventory late into the evenings and never taking a day off. "Dad set high standards for me," Humphrey reminisced. "The one fear I've had all my life was that I would disappoint him." From an early age his father would constantly remind him, "Son, you're not half as smart as you think you are. You're going to have to work twice as hard as you planned if you're going to succeed." This work ethic would prove Humphrey well.[14]

Humphrey's Political Motivation

There were, as with most who choose to run for political office on the highest stage, a multitude of forces that steered a budding

Hubert into a career in politics. One was undoubtedly the political nature of his father, inspired by his own desire to help his fellow man. Humphrey Sr. was known throughout the town just as much for his political gabbing as he was for his highly frequented drugstore and uncommon compassion. Around Doland the good-natured jest was that Hubert's father "never sells you a pill without selling you an idea." As young Humphrey worked behind the ice-cream counter, he took in lively philosophical discussions and political debates as the most respected figures in town considered the fundamental political questions of the day. Years later, the senator would recall, "I've attended several good universities, listened to some of the great parliamentary debates of our time, but have seldom heard better discussions of basic issues than I did as a boy standing on a wooden platform behind a soda fountain."[15]

Hubert Humphrey Sr.'s progressive views stood out in rural South Dakota at the time and laid the foundation for his son's own philosophies on government and politics. "In Doland, Dad was a Democrat," Hubert once said, "among friends and neighbors who took their Republicanism—along with their religion—very seriously." Humphrey Sr. had no qualms setting aside his kind and gentle demeanor "in political debate [to give] everything he had, and that could be considerable." He was a voracious reader of newspapers and would often wake his boys up in the middle of the night to point out a recent development from Washington, DC, more than one thousand miles away, saying, "You should know this, Hubert. It might affect your life someday."[16]

While his liberal leanings certainly were unpopular in the Re-publican town of Doland, home to no more than a few dozen Democrats, the affable pharmacist was nonetheless elected mayor. That being said, young Hubert certainly felt politically ostracized throughout his childhood, later commenting, "The equation was simple: Republicanism was synonymous with respectability and Protestantism. As a boy, I felt that to be a Democrat was to be, if not pagan, at least less than holy." Hubert's Republican mother cer-tainly instilled a strong religious sense within her son and forced her somewhat-unconvinced husband into the pews on most Sun-days. It was not long before Humphrey Sr. leveraged his charis-matic and convincing nature into election onto the church board and a position teaching Sunday school to both adults and children in the town. Central to his classes were the "social imperatives of religion" and the teachings of acceptance, togetherness, and unconditional generosity that seem more often absent from the current religious factions of the conservative party. Humphrey took these social lessons from religion to heart, convinced that "a heavenly city . . . could be created on earth through good works."[17]

As the Great Depression approached and banks began closing across the country, the pristine course of young Humphrey's early years was obstructed and took a much more somber turn. In 1927, the Humphreys were forced by the bank to sell their two-story house at the end of town; at sixteen years old Hubert Humphrey saw his father cry for the first time. "But our tears dried," Humphrey said later, and his father picked up the pieces and rented a much smaller house across town. He never lost his admirable outlook on life, nor his generous spirit. Humphrey was motivated by the conviction of his father, detailing, "Some people who enjoy the sunshine of living are unprepared for the storms. When they are shocked or hurt, they withdraw and cover up. Not my father. . . . He plunged on." Despite having to take on more work to get by, he stayed active in local politics and beamed with pride in 1928 when he was selected as a delegate to the Democratic National Convention in Houston, Texas.[18]

In 1929 Humphrey left his small-town lifestyle to attend college 310 miles away at the University of Minnesota. His father made the drive there with his son, dropping him off at a rooming house just off the campus. Before he left, he told his son, "From here on, it's on you."[19] The independence would be short lived, as a tense, decade-long saga began unraveling back home in South Dakota. Just after completing his freshman year, Hubert's father told him he would have to come back to work at the pharmacy. Hubert's brother Ralph had put off college to give Hubert the chance to pursue his own dreams, but he could no longer wait and demanded to make his own trip to the University of Minnesota. Humphrey Sr. pleaded with his son, "I can't have you and Ralph gone at the same time." Dejected, Hubert, returned to Doland, suspending his own lofty dreams of improving the country.[20]

Not long after, Hubert received a letter from his Uncle Harry, a kind-hearted plant scientist in Washington, DC, who stressed the importance of higher education and recognized the political potential of his nephew. Out of the letter fell a fifty-dollar check and a note: "Something to start you back in school." Humphrey's father permitted his son's return to university for the winter quarter provided he worked several jobs around the campus.[21]

Eventually, Humphrey's father had no choice but to give up on the economically depressed Doland, informing his son he was moving the family fifty miles south across the state to Huron. With the new store opening, Hubert was once again forced to return to South Dakota to work at his family's business. Hubert felt trapped in the small-town life and longed for the opportunity to better himself with education and to do something grand. He was thrust into a tense relationship with the father he so deeply admired, unable to bring himself to leave home in order to pursue his own dreams.

Seven years later, Hubert got the chance to further his education, though certainly not in the capacity he longed for. In 1936, President Roosevelt came to Huron, touring the desolation left in the wake of the four years of dust storms that covered the Midwest. Humphrey Sr. was invited onto the president's train, bringing his son to meet the commander in chief. It only served to deepen Hubert's discontent with his quiet lifestyle and spurred the political ambitions of both father and son. Humphrey Sr. began developing his own plans to run for Congress and quickly began considering who would man the pharmacy if he decided to pursue this dream. His father turned again to Hubert, "and summoning all his loyalty to his Dad, he agreed to go back to school, to the Capitol College of Pharmacy in Denver."[22]

The breaking point for the ambitious Hubert Humphrey finally came in 1935 when he took a trip to Washington, DC, with the Boy Scout troop of which he was the scoutmaster. Wide-eyed Hubert was blown away by the bustling seat of government. He stayed with his Uncle Harry, who so deeply understood his desires and took him immediately to the Jefferson Memorial, which Hubert had always longed to see. In that overwhelming trip, Hubert sat in the Senate gallery, listening to his idol, Huey Long, deliver one of his great oral spectacles. Hubert wrote to his sweetheart, Muriel Buck, whom he would go on to marry: "This trip has impressed one thing on my mind, Muriel,–the need of an education, an alert mind, clean living, and a bit of culture."[23]

Not long after returning to South Dakota, Hubert confronted his father. The elder Humphrey remained silent, eventually turning to him. "If that's the case, we'll have to make other plans," Hubert Sr. conceded. Hubert Humphrey Jr. returned to the University of Minnesota in 1937, earned a master's degree from Louisiana State University in 1940, and eventually began a successful academic career teaching political science.[24]

Humphrey was not content simply instructing; in 1943 he ran unsuccessfully for mayor of Minneapolis, only to return with a successful campaign in 1945 on the Minnesota Democratic-Farmer-Labor Party ticket he helped form the year before. He was committed to implementing the compassionate policies he heard the men in Doland debate at the ice-cream counter, and he was well on his way to succeeding. In 1948, Humphrey achieved the lifelong dream of his father — a seat in the United States Senate, representing Minnesota — and was thrust into the national spotlight for his proposal of expanding the platform of the Democratic Party to include eliminating racial segregation. The convention erupted in applause during his speech urging the party to "walk into the sunshine of human rights." Humphrey was well ahead of the nation in 1948 but was ready to lead them by the kindness and generosity his father had instilled in him.

Richard Milhous Nixon – Early Years

Hubert Humphrey's brightly shining early years lie in stark contrast to the dark episodes in Nixon's childhood and adolescence that molded him into the deeply troubled man who would go on to swindle his way into the White House. The strife of Nixon's formative years undoubtedly inspired him to consistently lie about and misrepresent his childhood after achieving political fame. Key aide John Ehrlichman commented on Nixon's exhaustive, two-part autobiography in 1978, saying, "Read that description of his family, they're all perfect, right? But what man can say his family's perfect? Those people are human . . . he makes them into waxwork dummies . . . if he doesn't come clean about them, how can he come clean about anything else?"[25]

Richard Milhous Nixon was born on January 9, 1913, in a humble house built by his father, Frank Nixon, in beautiful Yorba Linda, California. Nixon, the son of two devout Quakers, was raised in a solitary lifestyle with his parents and four brothers, and early on his family endured hardships that he spent his life trying to escape from.

Four of the five Nixon brothers were named after famous kings of England, some real, some fictional.[26] Richard was named after Richard I of England, also known as Richard the Lionheart. It is a great twist of irony that a child named after a British king would rise to be president of the United States and take office with the attitude of a royal's absolute right to rule. Interestingly, Nixon would eventually go on record as the only American president to flatly assert that the president of the United States was above the law. In a 1977 interview with British television personality David Frost, Nixon famously rebutted, "When the President does it, that means it is not illegal."

One of the earliest stories of a young Richard Nixon involves an accident that left the future president deeply scarred — physically and, perhaps, mentally. His mother, Hannah Nixon, had taken her three-year-old son Richard with her to the train station in neighboring Placentia to pick up her aunt, who was arriving for a family visit. As Hannah drove the horse and buggy back from Placentia, she asked a young girl from town who accompanied them on the trip to hold Richard while she managed the two horses. "As we were rounding the curve at the Anaheim Irrigation Ditch," Hannah later recounted, "something startled the horses and they bolted. The buggy swayed wildly from side to side and the little girl lost her hold on Richard. He fell out onto the road and a wheel cut into the side of his head. His scalp was badly lacerated, and blood spurted from a long, jagged gash that separated his scalp from the bone." In a stroke of luck, neighbors of the Nixons, the only family who owned a car in all of Yorba Linda, were able to drive Richard the twenty-five miles to the nearest hospital in time. As one of the emergency room doctors would later recount, "Had he reached the hospital emergency room just a few minutes later, Richard would have been dead on arrival."[27]

Nixon himself held a vivid memory of the incident, sharing the story years later in a rare candid recollection of his past with close aide Frank Gannon. "Well, curiously enough, my first memory is of running. . . . The buggy turned a corner and the horse took off and the neighbor girl dropped me. I fell out of the buggy. I got a crease in my scalp, and I jumped up afterwards, and I was running, running, trying to catch up, because I was afraid to be left behind."[28] Nixon seemed to lack faith in the love of a mother he would later go on to describe as a "saint" of a woman. His deep abandonment issues profoundly impacted the incredibly paranoid nature that would come to dominate the Nixon White House.

At the end of the ordeal, Nixon was left with a massive scar, "beginning just above the forehead and extending down to the neck."[29] For the rest of his life, he carefully parted his hair on the right side, so as to hide the scar from view. Beyond this literal mark, it is possible that Nixon suffered a concussion or other brain trauma from the accident, a potential explanation for the alcoholism, addiction, and psychological instability he struggled with in his adult life.

President Nixon would later confirm that he had his own fears about the deep impact this physical trauma had on his mental state, and it became one of the ghosts of his past that he tried desperately to hide. Responding to a question from Frank Gannon in regard to whether he amended his biography in his first congressional election to omit the carriage accident, Nixon responded, "Oh, yes. . . . You can't tell them that you got hit in the head by a carriage or wheel, because they'll think that that's why there's something wrong with your head. And so I haven't told that story too often lately." Nixon's own reply highlights his decision to concede that there was, in fact, "something wrong with [his] head" and that the incident would be used not merely to make the case that he was mentally unstable but to explain why.[30]

Young Richard had what can only be described as a seriously strained relationship with his parents, especially his abusive father, Frank, who Nixon described as "a scrappy, belligerent fighter, with a quick, wide-ranging raw intellect . . . a strict and stern disciplinarian."[31] Frank Nixon had also been the victim of a physically abusive father; as a parent himself, he likewise beat his children regularly. Family friends described him as "beastly . . . like an animal," and one especially rough beating of his son Harold drew horrifying screams that terrified neighbors. In another

incident, Frank Nixon threw Richard and one of his brothers into
a canal after catching them swimming in it, shouting, "You like
water? Have some more of it!" The situation escalated to the point
where one of Richard's cousins later recalled her Aunt Elizabeth
yelling, "You'll kill them, Frank! You'll kill them." Playmates of
the Nixon children feared going over to their household, afraid
of the "awful rough guy" that they knew was capable of savage
beatings.[32]

If young Richard turned to his mother for affection to compensate
for his father's abuse, he would have been deeply disappointed.
Hannah Nixon refused to show affection, even to her children,
leading Nixon to recall later in life, "I never heard her say to me
or anyone else, 'I love you.'" Nixon's personal psychiatrist, Dr.
Arnold Hutschnecker, told Nixon historian Anthony Summers that
Hannah was "not really close to Richard. . . . No woman ever gave
Nixon the support he really needed."[33]

According to Nixon, his family would spend the whole of their
Sundays in church, often going four times a day: "Sunday school
and a worship service in the morning, a young people's meeting
called Christian Endeavor, and another worship service in the
evening."[34] This strict religious upbringing had a profound impact
on young Nixon. In a particular boyhood anecdote Nixon aide John
Sears heard from the former president, Nixon stole a cookie from a
freshly baked plate his mother had made. When Hannah asked her
son whether he had eaten a cookie, "he didn't know any better than
to say yes, and she beat the daylights out of him. . . . But Richard
Nixon learned one thing from that. . . . That was a lifelong lesson to
him,"[35] namely the benefit of saying whatever would suit him best,
regardless of the truth.

From that day, Nixon inclined toward deception of his parents
and those closest to him, despite the strong religious and moral
environment he was exposed to. He once fixed a carnival game so
his grandmother would win, recalling:

> "At Slippery Gulch they had gambling. It wasn't legal, I guess,
> but some way — and Arizona was sort of a wide-open place. . . .
> I was a barker for a wheel of fortune where we gave away hams
> and bacon and other prizes. . . . I remember my grandmother; she

was in her eighties at that time, coming over on one occasion. And she, of course, didn't believe in gambling. And so I said, 'Look, Grandmother, you've got to do it just one time.' And believe it or not, she won a ham, and boy did we enjoy that ham, even though it was perhaps gotten in ways that she wouldn't appreciate."[36]

In a similar act of trickery, Nixon once spiked the Christmas pie his family made every year to celebrate the holiday. His parents "made excellent mincemeat, but they wouldn't put any brandy into it," Nixon explained. "One time Don and I . . . we sneaked in a bottle and put some in, and they thought it was the best mincemeat pie they'd ever made — but they didn't know why."[37]

The first of two formidable tragedies came in 1925 with the death Richard's younger brother Arthur at just seven years old. Richard, twelve years old at the time, seemed to be strongly affected by the sudden loss, most likely attributed to tuberculosis; his mother, Hannah, described him "staring into space, silent and dry-eyed in the undemonstrative way in which, because of his choked, deep feelings, he was always to face tragedy." The Nixons did not have long to recover, as before Arthur passed, Richard's older brother Henry had begun his own long and eventually fatal bout with tuberculosis. The twin tragedies went a long way in shaping Richard's gloomy demeanor and dour nature.[38]

Nixon's Political Tendencies

Despite winning a few class elections in his primary-school years, Nixon was never the most popular of students and lacked the friendships he witnessed among his peers. One of his classmates at Whittier College described him as "not universally popular. He was not what you would call a real friendly guy." His lack of popularity can be reconciled with his victory in class elections the same way his electoral successes could be: through an unmatchable willingness to say what was popular, regardless of what he really believed. For example, in a tightly contested campaign for the presidency of his freshman class at Whittier College, he ran on doing away with the recent prohibition on student dances, despite the fact that his Quaker parents strongly believed the ban was necessary—a personal belief that Nixon most assuredly shared himself at one point. Nixon went on to win the race, and his opponent would later remark, "He's a real smart politician, he knew what issues to use to get support." This ability to mislead without remorse would prove useful as Nixon, a longtime supporter of military intervention to combat Communism, specifically in Vietnam, would run as the peace candidate in 1968.[39]

Given his history, Richard Nixon most probably honed these morally objectionable political tactics throughout his first few congressional elections, eventually harnessing their full potential in the 1968 presidential election. In fact, his ethical and legal lapses nearly ended his political career in 1956, when incumbent president Dwight Eisenhower seriously considered dropping Nixon, his vice-presidential candidate, from the re-election ticket. The decision revolved not only around Eisenhower's personal distrust and disappointment in Nixon as a man and politician but also evidence that as a senator Nixon had broken the law. In 1952, Nixon had accepted a staggering $100,000 bribe from a wealthy Romanian industrialist by the name of Nicolae Malaxa. At the time, Malaxa had close ties with the communist regime in Romania and allegedly forwarded the money to Nixon in an attempt to purchase American citizenship through Congress. Although stories of the bribe were often considered rumors at the time, it became clear in 1996 that the CIA had uncovered damning evidence of the illegal act in the form of a photocopy of the check Malaxa deposited in Nixon's personal checking account at the Bank of California. Investigative journalist Seymour Hersh speculates that the Malaxa bribe—as well as the slush fund Nixon accepted from California businessmen—may have played a role in President Eisenhower's initial inclination to drop Nixon from the ticket. "The men in the upper echelon of the CIA knew that the vice presidential candidate was lying when he denied taking any bribes while in the Senate. Richard Nixon was not, in the CIA's phrase, 'an honorable man.'"[40]

More evidence of just how seriously unstable candidate Nixon was throughout his political career can be found in the 1956 election. During one campaign stop, Nixon exploded and physically flung himself upon aide Ted Rogers for setting up what had turned into a rough question-and-answer session with a group of Cornell students: "You son of a bitch, you put me on with those shitty-ass liberal sons of bitches. You tried to destroy me in front of 30 million people." It took a valiant effort from *Baltimore Sun* correspondent Phil Potter to pull the enraged Nixon off his own staff member. One can hardly imagine a more shocking display from a current United States vice president on the campaign trail.[41] Clearly a troubled politician, Nixon recognized how the demons of his past influenced his political behavior. He revealed to his director of communications, Ken Clawson, "What starts the process really are laughs and slights and snubs when you are a kid. . . . But if you are reasonably intelligent and if your anger is deep enough and strong enough, you learn that you can change those attitudes by excellence, personal gut performance, while those who have everything are sitting on their fat butts . . ."[42]

The upbringings and personal developments of Hubert Horatio Humphrey and Richard Milhous Nixon left little to chance in the 1968 election and created the two political figures vying for the United States presidency. Humphrey, out of a deep ethical commitment, refused to place politics above country and get down in the mud with Nixon, leaving him far too much of a Boy Scout to ever earn the top position in the nation. Nixon, on the other hand, would capitalize on his win-at-all-costs attitude only to have that same reckless ambition doom his political career less than a decade later.

Chapter 3

Vietnam and the 1968 Election

The year 1968 began in tumult and, fed by tragedy and discontent, progressed to a full-blown political typhoon. Though it had been slowly mounting since the early 1950s, the war in Vietnam was suddenly escalating exponentially. Resulting political dissent was met with police violence more suited to the battlefield than to city streets, progressive icons met deadly fates, and the Democratic Party found itself shattered.

At the height of the Vietnam War in the late 1960s, young anti-war protesters in Lafayette Park, a green expanse across the street from the White House, were demonstrating in full force day after day, night after night—jumping up and down and shouting "Hey, hey, LBJ! How many kids have you killed today?" or chanting "Hell no! We won't go!"

Luci Johnson and her sister, Lynda, had bedrooms on the north side of the thin-walled White House, and these were often the last words they heard at night as well as their morning wake-up calls. The president heard the shouts, too. In Johnson's own words, "I knew there was a long gulf between them and me, which neither one of us could do much about." He added: "I was doing what was right, right for them, and right for their future and their children. But they couldn't see that." Lynda remembered how much her father "could understand their sympathies. It didn't make him happy; he was angry and hurt and sometimes he exclaimed, 'I have tried to do so much for those people. Why don't they appreciate me? Why don't they understand?'"[1]

The shouts, which followed the president almost everywhere he went in public, "were so painful for him to hear . . . I so wish those protestors had known just how badly LBJ wanted peace, too," declared young LBJ press aide Tom Johnson—who noted that both of the president's sons-in-law, Marine Capt. Charles Robb and

Airman Patrick Nugent were serving in Vietnam.[2]

Though Vietnam—known as French Indochina until the mid-1950s—was the source of few valuable resources (it lacked oil, coal, and precious metals and was regionally important mostly due to its rich farming country for rice crops), it was viewed as strategically important in American policy due to the so-called "domino effect." This notion held that if one country became communist, the countries surrounding it would soon be taken over, leading to a global fall to this new political ideology. Although it was later proved a fallacy, this domino concern played a major role in U.S. policy formulation during the early Cold War.

Though not scrutinized by mass consciousness at the time, the United States was involved early on in Southeast Asia. During World War II, the Japanese took control of most of Indochina, which had previously been colonized by the French. France still desired control of the region, and America agreed to assist its ally in reasserting colonial influence.

Ho Chi Minh, the revolutionary leader of the Viet Minh independence movement, provided a communist foe against which the United States could ally with France without appearing overtly pro-colonist. Backed by Russia and China (he had personally met both Joseph Stalin and Mao Zedong), Ho Chi Minh's dream of a nationally unified Vietnam stood contrary to French interests, and the United States began heavily funding French efforts against him. In 1954, however, President Eisenhower rebuffed a French request for American planes and weapons, leading to a French surrender after a crushing defeat at the Battle of Dien Bien Phu.

Following this defeat, meetings were held in Geneva to discuss a ceasefire. The United States, however, refused to sign the peace accords. U.S. officials feared that a stipulation included for national elections to unify North and South Vietnam would lead to the election of Ho Chi Minh as national leader. Thus two states were formed: Ho Chi Minh's communist Democratic Republic of Vietnam in the North, and the State of Vietnam led by French loyalist Emperor Bao Dai in the South. The two states were separated by the seventeenth parallel.

In 1955, French-backed Ngo Dinh Diem overthrew the Southern regime and took the title of president, though he ruled as an autocrat. A Catholic while most Vietnamese practiced Buddhism, Diem befriended John F. Kennedy, then a Massachusetts senator of the same faith. Many Buddhists in Vietnam became increasingly opposed to Diem's dictatorial regime and accompanying raids on Buddhist temples. Monks self-immolated in high-profile protests to draw attention to the struggle. Ultimately, a Buddhist uprising during Kennedy's presidency led to Diem's assassination.

Kennedy took office as president of the United States in January 1961 and early in his term met with Charles DeGaulle, president of France, to discuss Vietnam. DeGaulle warned Kennedy that involvement in Southeast Asia would become a quagmire, yet Kennedy increased monetary assistance to the South Vietnamese regime and sent additional military advisors to aid with governing by a strategy of incremental escalation.

LBJ's Vietnam

On November 22, 1963, the day President Kennedy was murdered in Dallas, Lyndon B. Johnson assumed the presidency as the nation reeled from the violent public assassination. Images were bored into the national consciousness of Jackie Kennedy attempting to piece together her dead husband's skull following the kill shot in Dallas, and further trauma ensued when the accused assassin, Lee Harvey Oswald, was in turn murdered on live television by a shadowy Dallas figure, Jack Ruby.

Upon assuming office, Johnson focused on domestic policy and did little to rethink the Vietnam strategy — though his commendable ego certainly made him loath to surrender any battle. Early in Johnson's administration, communist freedom fighters known as the Viet Cong began to appear in South Vietnam. This became a domestic bargaining chip for Johnson, the great negotiator: in a grand bargain to garner Southern support for his civil-rights agenda, Johnson agreed to escalate American involvement in Vietnam with the goal of defeating the communists.

In late August 1964, Johnson deployed an additional five thousand military advisers to South Vietnam, but before massive escalation could occur (as any political strategist worth his or her salt knew) there would have to be a unifying event to rally public support. That event came quickly. On August 2, the destroyer USS *Maddox* came under attack by three North Vietnamese torpedo boats in the Gulf of Tonkin. United States forces returned fire using both the destroyer's artillery and nearby fighter jets, damaging all three torpedo boats and killing four North Vietnamese sailors. Only one U.S. aircraft was damaged, and there were no American casualties.

Following the initial incident, the *Maddox* and the USS *Turner Joy* were ordered to make their presence known fewer than eleven miles off the coast of North Vietnam. The weather that night, August 4, was rough, and the seas choppy. Radar and sonar signals indicated to the destroyers that they were again under attack, and the ships returned fire for two hours.

Despite claims that the ships managed to sink two torpedo boats, no wreckage, casualties, or any other evidence of the encounter were ever found. Word reached Washington that there might never have been any attack at all: there were signs that the destroyers may have simply spent the two hours firing on marine life that was distorted by the weather to appear as enemy fire. Cables sent from the destroyers to Washington throughout the next day indicated confusion and requested further investigation. But President Johnson, who did not immediately see these messages, had already decided what to do next. On August 5, LBJ ordered full retaliation, and within hours American planes were dropping bombs on North Vietnam.

Lyndon Johnson had the rallying event he needed. It wasn't until 1969 and the catastrophic (to Johnson) release of the Pentagon Papers (to be discussed later) that the American public learned the truth about the Gulf of Tonkin. In 1964, for all intents and purposes, it was a clarion call to war.

Johnson went before Congress requesting increased power to deploy force in Southeast Asia, and on August 7 the Gulf of Tonkin Resolution, officially known as the Southeast Asia Resolution, passed almost unanimously. (The vote in the House of Representatives was, in fact, unanimous, and only two senators — Wayne Morse of Oregon and Ernest Gruening of Alaska, both Democrats — voted in opposition.)

The Gulf of Tonkin Resolution greatly increased presidential war powers, giving LBJ broad authority to conduct military intervention without a declaration of war. Indeed, none of America's wars since World War II have been constitutionally codified with a legal declaration by Congress; it was Vietnam that set such a precedent and the Gulf of Tonkin Resolution that paved the way for much of the expansion the U.S. national security apparatus and presidential powers have since undergone.

For the rest of 1964, Johnson and his national security team — including Secretary of Defense Robert McNamara and Secretary of State Dean Rusk — developed a Vietnam strategy. In November, Johnson won the presidential election and retained his inherited seat in the Oval Office.

Early in 1965, the United States began Operation Rolling Thunder, a campaign of sustained bombing against North Vietnam. America now had boots on the ground and bombs dropping from the air. The full-scale intervention became a turning point for some, including Students for a Democratic Society (SDS), a group that had supported Johnson's civil-rights efforts but now turned on him in the face of a full-blown war.

Peace groups, including the Committee for a SANE Nuclear Policy (now Peace Action), led by celebrity spokesperson Dr. Benjamin Spock, began mobilizing against the war — demanding, instead, an international diplomatic agreement. In June, eighteen thousand protesters joined the Emergency Rally on Vietnam in Madison Square Garden; and, in November, thirty-five thousand "peacenicks" marched on Washington. Johnson, however, was not to be deterred. The American fight against Communism would persevere.

The Vietnam War was riddled with issues. First, access to resources and the ability to use force were completely disproportional: the United States, a global superpower, was waging an all-out war against a country that was essentially pre-industrial.

The low-tech North Vietnamese army was composed mostly of peasant guerillas. To American pilots looking down from thousands of feet in the air, these militant communists could hardly be differentiated from civilians — even women and children. The death toll of innocents rose at an incredible rate, fomenting Vietnamese sentiment strongly against the United States. With the rapid rise in anti-American sentiment, recruiting new fighters to the North Vietnamese army and its communist counterpart in the South — the

Viet Cong — was easy, and the death count inconsequential to their growing ranks. For each communist killed, another was radicalized to take his place; every civilian body yielded militants thirsty for justice, or revenge.

For South Vietnamese forces, in contrast, recruitment was difficult and the desertion rate was high. While the North Vietnamese were galvanized and personally dedicated to the struggle, their Southern neighbors took up arms out of necessity or force.

As for American soldiers, the war took an increasingly high toll, and the death count rose. From 1956 through 1962, annual American casualties remained at most in the single and double digits; in 1963 and 1964 combined, just under four hundred Americans died. But in 1965, when the war truly escalated, nearly two thousand young men lost their lives in Southeast Asia; in 1966, more than six thousand; in 1967, almost twice that — more than eleven thousand.[3] (There were few female casualties, though they did exist, because women service members were not generally allowed in combat.) The year 1968 was already shaping up to be the bloodiest yet, and the angry voices of young people chanting "Hey, hey, LBJ! How many kids did you kill today?" daily rang outside the White House and in streets around the nation.

In January 1968, many soldiers were led to believe by their generals and commanders that an end to the war was near, victory just around the corner. Thus, the shock of the Tet Offensive, which began on January 31, was tremendous. Massive numbers of communist troops infiltrated South Vietnam — taking initial control of the country to as far south as Saigon, where the U.S. Embassy came under attack. American forces were caught by surprise, and though they managed to push the communists back, the bad news quickly traveled to the States, where new questions began circulating. In coordinated attacks throughout South Vietnam, the Viet Cong assaulted major urban areas and military bases. Heavy battles went on for three weeks. As a result of the massive surprise attack, and gruesome TV and still pictures from the battlefronts, the U.S. press and public began to challenge LBJ's repeated assurances of eventual success in Vietnam.

At the same time as the Tet Offensive, the siege of Khe Sanh by North Vietnamese forces — directed by the legendary Gen. Vo

Nguyen Giap—"underscored the image of the war as an endless, costly, and pointless struggle," according to later analyses by military experts.[4]

Khe Sanh was a heavily fortified base in the northwest corner of South Vietnam. It was designed for use as a future staging point for American and South Vietnamese attacks on the Ho Chi Minh Trail—the main supply route from North Vietnam to the Viet Cong and NVA troops in South Vietnam. Some forty thousand NVA forces surrounded about six thousand marines and South Vietnamese soldiers at the remote hilltop outpost. Only through the use of massive U.S. artillery and air power—including nearly three thousand B-52 bomber runs—was the long siege ended.

Many in the Johnson White House, including the president, "saw Khe Sanh as a potentially catastrophic military defeat—much like the French had suffered in 1954 at Dien Bien Phu," according to presidential aide Tom Johnson, who quoted LBJ as telling his top military advisers: "I do not want any damn Dien Bien Phu!"[5] (In his post-White House days, Tom Johnson—known universally as a genial genius—headed CNN after serving as a top news executive at the *Los Angeles Times* and *Times-Mirror*.)

To Tom Johnson, Khe Sanh was a distressful eye-opener: "For me, the battle of Khe Sanh showed the incredible resolve of Hanoi to win the war at all costs. The best estimates are that the North Vietnamese lost up to 15,000 women and men in that siege. America lost 205 killed and hundreds of wounded. The siege lasted until April 1968. The base was abandoned three months later [in July 1968]."

Equally upsetting to Tom Johnson was the fact that Gen. William Westmoreland—the commander of U.S. forces in Vietnam—wanted to consider the use of tactical nuclear weapons at Khe Sanh. The general sent a message to the Pentagon saying, "If Washington officials are so intent on 'sending a message to Hanoi,' surely small tactical nuclear weapons would be a way to tell Hanoi something." Tom Johnson further reports that "the Pentagon ordered General Westmoreland to kill the idea. Reluctantly, he did."[6]

When General Giap died at age 102 in 2013, the *New York Times* wrote that "his willingness to sustain staggering losses against superior American firepower was a large reason the war dragged on for as long as it did, costing more than 2.5 million lives—58,000 of them American—sapping the United States Treasury and Washington's political will to fight, and bitterly dividing the country in an argument about America's role in the world that still echoes today."[7]

During a trip to Hanoi in 1997, Tom Johnson met General Giap— who told him America and North Vietnam never should have gone to war, that after Hanoi had driven out the Japanese and the French, in Johnson's words, "they asked America not to support the return of the French to Vietnam after the defeat of the Japanese." Instead, Johnson notes, "we supported the return of the French. General Giap told me that he and Ho Chi Minh saw the reuniting of South and North Vietnam no differently than our President Lincoln had seen in the reuniting of the South and the North in our own War Between the States, or Civil War."

Defense secretary Robert McNamara eventually came to the same conclusion as General Giap—that the Vietnam War was a mistake. After LBJ dismissed McNamara, partly because of their growing differences over the conduct of the war, McNamara "left government a broken man," according to Tom Johnson. President Johnson worried that the depressed McNamara "might kill himself as former Secretary of Defense James Forrestal had in 1949."[8]

Until his dying days, General Westmoreland claimed General Giap's Tet Offensive was a U.S. victory because the enemy was driven back with great losses of their fighting men. But most historians consider it a psychological victory for the communists, because it greatly increased domestic opposition to the Vietnam War and forced President Johnson to quit the race for reelection and hint that he might well go to the bargaining table with the communists to end the war.

While President Johnson had tried to sell the American people the idea that they could have both guns in Indochina *and* butter at home, General Giap's Tet Offensive seemed to decimate that argument. The Johnson administration "was forced to consider domestic consequences of its [war] decisions every day," observed Vassar College professor Robert Brigham. "Eventually," he writes, "there simply were not enough volunteers to continue to fight a protracted war and the government instituted a draft. As the deaths mounted and Americans continued to leave for Southeast Asia, the

Johnson administration was met with the full weight of American anti-war sentiments. Protests erupted on college campuses and in major cities at first, but by 1968 every corner of the country seemed to have felt the war's impact."[9]

On February 27, 1968, less than a month after the Tet Offensive, Walter Cronkite, the eminent anchor of the *CBS Evening News*, traveled to Vietnam to report directly. His sober voice and straightforward reporting had guided Americans through President Kennedy's assassination a few years before, and he was a trusted rock in the journalistic community as well as in the public eye. The closing words in his report were damning:

> To say that we are closer to victory today is to believe, in the face of the evidence, the optimists who have been wrong in the past. . . . To suggest we are on the edge of defeat is to yield to unreasonable pessimism. To say that we are mired in stalemate seems the only realistic, yet unsatisfactory, conclusion. On the off chance that military and political analysts are right, in the next few months we must test the enemy's intentions, in case this is indeed his last big gasp before negotiations. But it is increasingly clear to this reporter that the only rational way out then will be to negotiate, not as victors, but as an honorable people who lived up to their pledge to defend democracy, and did the best they could.[10]

Cronkite's words filtered into countless living rooms, kitchens, and conversations. The tide was, inevitably and irreversibly, turning American opinion against the war.

It was not known until many years later that, as president, Lyndon Johnson himself was of two minds about Vietnam. As early as 1964, he told his national security adviser, McGeorge Bundy: "The more I stayed awake last night thinking of this thing, the more . . . it looks to me like we're getting into another Korea . . . I don't think it's worth fightin' for and I don't think we can get out. It's just the biggest damned mess . . . What the hell is Vietnam worth to me? . . . What is it worth to this country?"[11]

In 1965, after increasing U.S. troop levels in Vietnam, the president told his press secretary, Bill Moyers, he might not have done the right thing: "Light at the end of the tunnel? We don't even have a tunnel; we don't even know where the tunnel is."[12] And in

1966, LBJ told Democratic senator Eugene McCarthy of Minnesota: "I know we oughtn't to be there, but I can't get out. I just can't be the architect of surrender."[13] Neither Johnson nor McCarthy could have predicted then that they would be squaring off over the war in the political arena just two years later.

By 1968, with his credibility and ego on the line, and not wanting to be seen as a loser at anything, President Johnson had greatly intensified the war in Vietnam. By then, U.S. troop strength there had reached five hundred thousand; and the bombing campaign — the aforementioned "Operation Rolling Thunder" — was vastly stepped up. Many Americans, however, were beginning to have serious doubts that the war could, or should, be won — or that the fighting was even morally justified. More than sixteen thousand Americans were killed in action in 1968 — the highest annual death toll of the war.

Candidates and Election Campaigning

As public attitudes turned against the war, so too did they turn against Johnson. Eligible to run for another term (having only served fourteen months of Kennedy's), Johnson, the sitting president, ought to have been a clear choice for the Democratic nomination. Yet it quickly became clear that the Democratic primary race would be as chaotic as the war that so consumed the nation.

The first anti-war Democratic challenger to the president in 1968 was Eugene McCarthy, an articulate intellectual who was almost unknown to the general public. In the Senate, the handsome and lanky liberal had a reputation as a backbencher with minimal clout and little interest in the legislative process. McCarthy did make terrific off-the-cuff speeches and was always available to reporters; he was an open and friendly man with an enjoyably sarcastic sense of humor, much of it aimed at his stuffier colleagues.

Lyndon Johnson's attitude towards Gene McCarthy was typical of many Washington insiders: "I always thought of Senator McCarthy as the type of fellow who did damn little harm and damn little good. I never saw anything constructive come out of him. He was always more interested in producing a laugh than a law in the Senate.[14]

At that time, New Hampshire—a tiny state with only a few electoral votes—was (and remains, in concert now with Iowa) significant for its early primary date. It routinely set a tone for the rest of the political season and drew considerable media attention. At one campaign stop in the Granite State, McCarthy expressed his views on the war with his usual no-frills eloquence: "The fact is that there is no economic justification, no economic case for the continuation of the war. There certainly is no economic justification for it. It's not militarily defensible, as we can see in the evidence being presented to us every day. And, in my judgment, it has long since passed the point in which it can be morally justified."[15]

McCarthy poured his resources into the state, and the 42 percent of the vote he won—compared to Johnson's meager lead at 49 percent—gave the McCarthy campaign a boost to national prominence.

A few days later, on March 16, Sen. Robert F. Kennedy, brother of the beloved and martyred thirty-fifth president, changed his mind and entered the race. While also a peace candidate like McCarthy, Bobby Kennedy was a dove with a high national profile, great political savvy, and access to millions of campaign dollars.

That same day in Vietnam, hundreds of innocent men, women, and children, including infants, were beaten, raped, and murdered by American soldiers, led by Lt. William Calley, near the village of My Lai, though the event would not be publicly known until the next year.

President Johnson and Robert Kennedy despised each other, as LBJ himself later admitted: "I thought I was dealing with a child. I never did understand Bobby. I never did understand how the press built him into the great figure he was."[16] Sen. Barry Goldwater witnessed the same LBJ antipathy toward Kennedy: "It would have been difficult, if not impossible, for [Johnson] to have hidden [his feelings]. Any casual conversation that Bobby's name came up [in], you could see in his face right away that he just didn't like him."[17]

When RFK threw his hat into the presidential ring, President Johnson was not surprised. He had been griping around the White House for weeks saying, "That little runt will get in . . . The runt's going to run. I don't care what he says now."[18]

In his final Senate speech, Robert Kennedy expressed serious misgivings about the war: "Are we like the God of the Old Testament that we can decide, in Washington, D.C., what cities, what towns, what hamlets in Vietnam are going to be destroyed? . . . Do we have to accept that? . . . I do not think we have to. I think we can do something about it."[19]

Johnson, no fool to political realities, recognized his plummeting popularity and the public attraction to his rival candidates. He withdrew his name from consideration at the end of the month. "I shall not seek, and will not accept, the nomination of my party for another term as your president," Johnson told the nation. Instead, he would devote the remainder of his presidency to concluding the Vietnam War and achieving a desperately needed peace.

One of the first people to meet with LBJ at the White House after the president's March 31, 1968, withdrawal speech was RFK, who called the president "a brave and dedicated man." Any idea of a new conciliatory nature in the LBJ-RFK relationship at that particular time was quickly doomed, however. President Johnson found out that the senator had pulled a fast one on him at that White House meeting, according to historian Mark Updegrove: "[LBJ] had met Kennedy in the Cabinet Room, where he had the proceedings covertly taped. Immediately afterward, he ordered them transcribed. When the tapes later came out blank, the likely result of a scrambler that Kennedy or his aide, Ted Sorenson, had carried with them, Johnson exploded . . . because he had been outflanked."[20]

Considered by many a noble gesture, Johnson's withdrawal was likely due to a full understanding that, even if he was able to secure the nomination, the election would be brutal and he stood a decent chance of losing to the Republicans in November; by choosing not to run, he could play the election like chess master, maintain control of his party, and secure a favorable legacy in the history books by locking in a Vietnam peace deal.

Former LBJ press secretary George Reedy said that the motives for President Johnson's withdrawal from the race "will probably never be fully known," but he noted that they came on the heels of McCarthy's fine showing in that early race. "At this point," Reedy disclosed, "a few people close to [LBJ] had told him verbally that things were in very bad shape and that it would take heroic efforts not only to win the election but even to assure the [Democratic] nomination."[21]

Sen. George McGovern had a similar theory: "I think the candidacy of Gene McCarthy, and then followed by Robert Kennedy in that same year, explained why President Johnson decided to not run for re-election in '68."[22]

The remainder of the Democratic primaries played out even more brutally than expected. April 4, just days after Johnson's announcement that he would not seek another term, saw tragedy befall the country with the slaying of civil-rights leader Martin Luther King Jr. In his last speech, the day before his death, King preached: "I've seen the promised land. I may not get there with you. But I want you to know tonight, that we, as a people, will get to the promised land. So I'm happy, tonight. I'm not worried about anything. I'm not fearing any man. Mine eyes have seen the glory of the coming of the Lord."

But in the wake of King's death, the nation saw no glory, nor happiness. Riots erupted around the country, and the National Guard had to be summoned to restore order. This fueled the "law and order" rhetoric of Republican partisans. As the peace and Civil Rights Movements King had so vigorously championed were in disarray, advocates for a progressive future were in mourning, and the nation at large was thrown into a state of shock.

It was at this time that Vice Pres. Hubert H. Humphrey announced he would run for president in Lyndon Johnson's stead. Though Humphrey, being closely associated with LBJ and thus with the escalated and failing war effort, started out with a popular disadvantage against Kennedy and McCarthy, he was backed advantageously by the party establishment.

The Democratic Party was split—badly. The traditional party bosses led by union leaders and big-city mayors (most notably Richard J. Daley of Chicago) threw their support to Humphrey, who also received backing from the Dixiecrats (white Southern Democrats who would rapidly shift their loyalty when segregationist third-party candidate George Wallace announced his candidacy later on). The anti-war faction—including students, intellectuals, and activists—stood strong with McCarthy, knocking on doors and organizing voters across the country. Many minority groups, including Catholics and African Americans, enthusiastically backed the brother and ally of their martyred heroes, giving Robert Kennedy a strong base of support.

Sen. Robert Kennedy rode to victory in the majority of primary states and may well have secured the party's nomination had tragedy not befallen the Kennedy family, and the nation, once more. After a rousing victory speech following his California-primary win in the early hours of June 5, the candidate and several staff members were making their way through the kitchen of the Los Angeles Ambassador Hotel on their way from the ballroom when gunfire rang out. The American nightmare of 1963 was suddenly relived: Kennedy had been shot. A young Palestinian militant, Sirhan Sirhan, had taken steady aim, and RFK's wounds would prove fatal.

In hindsight, Kennedy and McCarthy would likely have prevented each other from attaining a majority, and the rivalry would have resulted in Humphrey's nomination even if Kennedy's life had not been taken. His murder, however, set a macabre tone for the remainder of the 1968 election and beyond.

Dan Moldea, author of *The Hoffa Wars* and *The Killing of Robert Kennedy*, among other books, shares his thoughts on the political impact of RFK's slaying: "Even with his big victory in the California Democratic primary on the night he was shot by Sirhan Sirhan, Senator Kennedy did not secure the Democratic nomination for President. In fact, with 393½ delegate votes, he was still far behind Vice President Hubert Humphrey who had 561½ delegates, according to UPI. In third place was Senator Eugene McCarthy who had 258."

Politically, Kennedy's death served to further scatter Democratic support. Some of his supporters moved to the McCarthy camp, but many backed Sen. George McGovern of South Dakota, who entered the race late due to his early support for Kennedy. Though the party bosses clearly supported Humphrey, popular dissent meant that uncertainty prevailed on the left going into the convention.

The 1968 Democratic National Convention was held in late August in Chicago, where Mayor Daley's iron fist ruled the streets. Anti-war activists flocked to the city, angry citizens ready to take to the streets in a vocal stand against the war. The nation watched on live TV as the protesters were beaten, clubbed, and tear-gassed by Daley's army of police. Pre-pubescent children and the elderly alike fell victim to the brutality, as bloodied protesters chanted "The whole world is watching" and jail cells were packed.

And, indeed, the world did watch as Hubert Humphrey, having shrewdly crafted a strategy to win over delegates from non-primary states, won the nomination on the first ballot. Sen. Edmund Muskie of Maine was chosen as his running mate.

As vice president, Humphrey had remained loyal to Johnson's Vietnam policies, gaining ire from many on the left. In reality, he and Johnson disagreed on much and liked each other little. He received no blessing from Johnson, and even as his name was called in victory, the clamor and shrieks on the streets outside made clear that no one had won.

The Republicans, too, were watching the Democratic convention, secure at the sidelines with their candidate already chosen. Richard Nixon, the clear front-runner from the start (he handily won the New Hampshire primary even as the Democrats' disarray became apparent), faced down opponent after opponent, most of whom simply dropped out of the race in deference to the party's front-runner. The Republican Party had convened in Miami Beach in early August to formally nominate Nixon and select Maryland governor Spiro Agnew as his running mate.

Thus the candidates were chosen: Republican Nixon versus Democrat Humphrey — with LBJ, the chess master, ever-present just barely behind the scenes. Johnson professed neutrality in the election, and as a courtesy to both candidates agreed to keep both Humphrey and Nixon (and third-party hopeful George Wallace) informed about the progress he was making toward peace. In what would become one of history's great ironies, as the war raged on in Vietnam, it was the hawkish Richard Nixon who ran that year as the peace candidate.

The Inside View on Vietnam

After exiting the race on March 31, 1968, Lyndon Johnson did devote, as he had pledged, most of his remaining presidential days — and often nights — to trying to find a negotiated end to the carnage in Vietnam. But the odds of achieving that were overwhelmed by two effective actions by Richard Nixon. As we have seen, the Republican candidate placed a spy — Henry Kissinger — inside LBJ's delegation to the Paris peace talks. And every time Kissinger reported possible progress, the GOP nominee would turn up the heat on South Vietnam's president Thieu to resist a settlement.

After extensive "full field" FBI checks, young LBJ aide Tom Johnson received the highest possible security clearances—so high that CIA Director Richard Helms often called him to verify his own notes on super-sensitive top-secret White House meetings. So Johnson was completely in the loop on what has become known to him as the "Anna Chennault Episode." Some parts of this sordid saga have trickled out in recent decades, but Johnson knows the full story on what he terms "a *very* tightly kept secret for more than 45 years."

There are still some parts of the story that Johnson is not able to reveal. And there are still a number of documents related to the scandal that have yet to be de-classified. But he is convinced that the Nixon team's 1968 actions should have been made public at the time: "It was my personal view then, and it is my personal view now, that public announcement of this before the election would have changed the course of history—that it would have so damaged the Nixon campaign that Hubert Humphrey would have been elected President in 1968."

Tom Johnson says two of LBJ's "most intimate friends" and advisors who knew about the GOP interference with the peace talks— Clark Clifford and Abe Fortas—thought the actions were "tantamount to treason by Nixon," according to Johnson's contacts with former LBJ speechwriter and LBJ Library director Harry Middleton. (That it *was* "treason," of course, is exactly what LBJ himself—and Senate Republican Leader Everett Dirksen—came to believe.)

Tom Johnson consulted with Middleton on several other facets of the Chennault Episode, including the reasons President Johnson and Vice President Humphrey did not expose this dirty deed back then: Clifford and Fortas said LBJ agreed with them that "it was indeed treason. But, LBJ said it was not for him to reveal the information. It should be given to [Vice President] Humphrey for him to decide. So, together Clifford and Fortas told Humphrey. He said he would not use the information. 'The country has been through too much this year, and it cannot take another shock. Even if it costs me the election, I will not use it,'" Humphrey told Clifford and Fortas.[23]

Middleton says he was at a meeting in the early 1980s when Clifford and Fortas finally revealed the Chennault Episode to Lady Bird Johnson. He says he will never forget Mrs. Johnson's reaction: "Poor Hubert," she said, repeated it twice. "Poor Hubert."

There were indeed unsung heroes urging an end to the Vietnam War. Two presidential advisers in particular from the LBJ era should be recognized, at least for their prescience about war: Robert McNamara and Clark Clifford. LBJ did not heed their dissent — the depths of which we are only now learning from freshly released interviews and documents and White House tape recordings. But McNamara and Clifford — back-to-back Johnson defense secretaries — certainly did not hide their dovish views from LBJ at the time. And the American public is finally getting to know about these men's secret backstage feelings and recommendations about the war.

Clifford was one of the first of LBJ's aides to realize that the Tet Offensive was not the victory claimed by U.S. generals (and which Richard Nixon, at the time, described as a "last-ditch effort" by North Vietnam). Clifford offered his take on Tet in a 1995 interview: "It shattered the illusion that we were winning in Vietnam. The impact on the American people was enormous. The impact on Lyndon Johnson was equally profound."[24]

After taking over as secretary of defense, Clifford called a meeting of the military's top brass. He recalled the session and his subsequent disenchantment with the generals and admirals:

> I wanted to know when the Joint Chiefs thought the war would be over. They didn't know. I asked them whether or not we should send a big additional contingent of men. Yes, they thought we should. How many more men would be needed to end the war? They could not tell me . . . What is the plan . . . to win the war? There was no plan to win the war.
>
> The only plan was to keep doing what we were doing and hope that it would turn out all right. This wasn't good enough. I left those meetings totally disillusioned. I could see that we had no alternative but to get out and get out as quickly as possible. And it became my desire, at that time, to do whatever I could to persuade the President to end our participation in the war.

A tall man with a patrician bearing, known for decades as one of

Washington's "Wise Men," Clifford set up a secret cabal of doves in LBJ's White House. "A group of us began working together very well," he recalled. "We were almost conspirators. We had a little reference to how one of our group should be addressed, and the expression was, 'Is he one of us?' [Laughs.] I felt a little like I was engaging in the French Revolution."[25]

Robert McNamara preceded Clifford as defense chief—a job McNamara also held under President John Kennedy. On October 2, 1963, McNamara returned from a fact-finding trip to Vietnam and discussed with Kennedy the possible removal of all 16,000 U.S. military advisors by the end of 1965 (and taking out 1,000 by the end of '63):

> **JFK:** The advantage of taking them out [in two years] is?
> **RM:** We can say to the Congress and people that we do have a plan for reducing the exposure of U.S. combat personnel.
> **JFK:** My only reservation about this is that if the war doesn't continue to go well, it will look like we were overly optimistic.
> **RM:** We need a way to get out of Vietnam and this is a way of doing it.[26]

McNamara met up with a much more hawkish president in Lyndon Johnson—as this telling, recently released give-and-take from February 1964 displays:

> **LBJ:** I hate to modify your speech because it's been a good one. But I just wonder if we couldn't find two minutes in there for Vietnam.
> **RM:** Yeah, the problem is what to say about it.
> **LBJ:** All right. I'll tell you what I would say about it. I would say we have a commitment to Vietnamese freedom. We could pull out of there, the dominoes would fall and that part of the world would go to the communists. We could send our Marines in there and we could get tied down in a third world war or another Korean action. Nobody really understands what it is out there. And they're asking questions and saying why don't we do more. Well, I think this: You can have more war or more appeasement. But we don't want more of either. Our purpose is to train these people [the South Vietnamese] and our training's going good.
>
> I always thought it was foolish for you to make any statements about withdrawing. I always thought it was bad psychologically.

But you and the President [JFK] thought otherwise. And I just sat silent.

RM: The problem is . . .

LBJ: Then come the questions: How the hell does McNamara think when he's losing the war he can pull men out of it?[27]

By June of 1964, McNamara was really laying it on the line to President Johnson: "If you went to the CIA and said 'How is the situation today in South Vietnam?' I think they'd say it's worse. You see it in the desertion rate, you see it in the morale . . . you see it in the difficulty of recruiting people . . . you see it in the gradual loss of population control. Many of us in private would say that things are not good, they've gotten worse."[28]

By 1966, when U.S. troop strength had reached 400,000 and increased B-52 attacks had been stepped up, the war was still being lost. McNamara advised LBJ to "level off military involvement for the long haul while pressing for talks."

By the end of 1967, when troop strength rose to nearly half a million men, McNamara told the president that further "escalation threatened to spin the war utterly out of control." He warned that the "other war" — the one for the hearts and minds of the South Vietnamese people — also appeared doomed: corruption was widespread and the population was apathetic.[29]

Chapter 4
Playing the Chess Master

As publicly proclaimed and privately agonized over, Lyndon Johnson's final presidential goal—absolutely necessary to secure a favorable legacy in the public eye—was to end the bloody Vietnam War. He would leave office when his successor was sworn in on January 20, 1969, so time was short. If Johnson could wrangle the opportunity to lock in a deal before the November 1968 election, he would certainly do so.

Presidents Johnson and Thieu meet in Honolulu (Courtesy National Archives and Records Administration)

Richard Nixon knew from the start exactly what continued war meant to his political campaign: "If there's war, people will vote for me to end it. If there's peace, they'll vote their pocketbooks—Democratic prosperity."[1] A peace deal would mean Nixon's likely defeat at the polls in November; but given his high ratings and the Democrats' disarray, as long as a deal could be avoided or at least postponed, he would be ushered into the most powerful office in the world—where he could wield nearly unlimited power and push his domestic and foreign agendas into fruition.

With his natural paranoia exacerbated by the high-stakes political climate, Nixon suspected Johnson's end game was actually to boost Humphrey to power. He believed that Johnson was preparing an "October surprise"—a last-minute peace deal specifically designed to tip the scales in the Democrats' favor. In fact, Nixon was not the only one under such an impression, with many Republicans and even South Vietnamese leaders similarly suspicious.

In reality, Johnson and Humphrey were estranged, and the elder statesman held little regard for the man who had served loyally for years as his vice president. Humphrey was privately opposed to the war, and although publicly he voiced support for the president, Johnson saw this profound difference of opinion as a betrayal. Johnson even confided in advisor Clark Clifford that Nixon "may prove to be more responsible than the Democrats."[2] Furthermore, the timing of the peace talks was in large part controlled by the North Vietnamese government in Hanoi, under the influence of Russia but also enticed by Johnson and its own political calculations regarding attendance at the talks.

In early spring of 1968 at Johnson's request, spurred by a desire to better know the Republican candidate and his vision for future policy, the president and Richard Nixon met to discuss their respective views.[3] Nixon professed loyalty to the sitting president's position, even as Johnson laid out his plans for a bombing halt and subsequent peace deal. The two came to an agreement that Johnson would maintain a strong negotiating stance on Vietnam (contrary to the desire of many Democrats, including Humphrey, that the U.S.'s position be softened in the interest of peace), and Nixon would present himself publicly as supportive of Johnson's plans. Thus, as the election pressed on, Johnson and Nixon grew to be closer allies than Johnson and his own vice president.

Nixon and Johnson meet in the Cabinet Room (Courtesy National Archives and Records Administration)

Despite his reassuring words to Johnson, however, Nixon schemed. To attain the presidency, he would need some close allies — highly trustworthy, powerful, and duplicitous. He began to recruit.

Nixon's Conspirators

Nixon and Anna Chennault first crossed paths in the early 1950s when Vice President Nixon visited Taiwan. Chennault, the luxury-loving Chinese-born widow of American Air Force general Claire Chennault, a World War II hero known for his leadership of the Flying Tigers, was decidedly hawkish on foreign policy. Naturally, she bonded easily with the ambitious Republican politician, despite his early annoyances at her penchant for gossip. The two stayed in touch over the years as Vietnam rose to a major issue on the political stage. In 1960, Chennault joined the Republican Party, quickly developing into a significant fund-raiser.

Chennault, who had contacts at high levels of the government in Saigon, held staunchly pro-war views on Vietnam and believed bombing North Vietnam into submission was the best option to attain peace. She had the potential to be an invaluable asset to Nixon—thanks to the prestige associated with her friendships with Southeast Asian regional leaders (including Taiwan's Chiang Kai-shek and Ferdinand Marcos of the Philippines). Indeed, her friendship with President Thieu allowed her to meet personally with South Vietnamese leadership at least once a year. Chennault was also involved in a romantic affair with Sen. John Tower, a prominent hawkish Republican from Texas and a member of the Senate Banking Committee.

In 1967, Chennault's presence was requested by telegram to meet Nixon in New York City. She was on a trip to Asia at the time, but upon her return the two met at Nixon's swanky Fifth Avenue apartment, where Nixon requested and Chennault agreed to serve as an informal advisor on Vietnam.

"When we do things," Nixon told her, setting a conspiratorial tone, "it will be better to keep it secret."[4]

After her co-conspirators had left this world, the Dragon Lady dished the dirt with even more vitriol; "the only people who knew about the whole operation were Nixon, John Mitchell and John Tower and they're all dead. But they knew what I was doing . . . that I was getting orders to do these things. I couldn't do anything without instructions."[5]

In July of 1968, Chennault returned to Nixon's apartment for another meeting, the first of several during the campaign season, this time joined by South Vietnamese ambassador Bui Diem and Nixon campaign manager John Mitchell. A former New York bond attorney, Mitchell had met Nixon when their respective Wall Street firms merged in 1967; just a year later, Nixon had talked a reluctant Mitchell into running his presidential campaign. Ruthless and conservative, Mitchell would later be referred to as "the ultimate Nixon loyalist."

At that July meeting, Nixon announced his desire to "end the war with victory," and Chennault conveyed President Thieu's frustration about the peace talks. Thieu reportedly desired to hold the negotiations after the U.S. elections, feeling too much pressure from Johnson and believing a better deal could be reached with a new president in power.

"It was all very, very confidential," Chennault recalled later; in fact, the Nixon campaign deemed the meetings top secret. "They worked out this deal to win the campaign. Power overpowers all reason."[6]

Mitchell served as the primary campaign contact, and the clandestine meetings became a point of high paranoia for him. He lived in fear of wiretapping by the government, changed his phone number regularly, and became increasingly skittish about contacts with Chennault. Nevertheless, the two spoke almost daily, with Chennault strictly instructed to call Mitchell only from payphones. The message from the Nixon campaign was steady: in the case that Johnson announced any progress in the peace talks, Thieu must be persuaded not to participate.

Ambassador Diem was also "regularly in touch with the Nixon entourage," as he revealed years later.[7] He reported back to Saigon that he had "explained discreetly to our partisan friends our firm attitude," and that the longer Saigon held out on peace talks, the better. He also relayed to his superiors in Saigon that if elected, Nixon promised to send an emissary to meet with President Thieu and would even consider a personal pre-inauguration trip to Saigon.[8]

President Nguyen Van Thieu had traversed a rocky road to power. He was born in a deeply impoverished village in the lowlands of Vietnam (then French Indochina) and came of age during the Japanese occupation of World War II. After a stint training with the anti-French nationalist liberation army known as the Viet Minh, Thieu's disillusionment with the communist camp drove him to enlist at the Vietnamese National Military Academy, a French establishment that trained anti-Viet Minh fighters. After his commission, his reputation grew as a brave fighter and capable leader.

In the early 1960s, Thieu assisted in the coup that killed President Ngo Dinh Diem, the corrupt American-backed leader who kept thousands of opponents imprisoned at any given time. Thieu's influence grew, and in 1965 he established his own military government in South Vietnam, reigning with Vice President Nguyen Cao Ky. The tenth national leader in nineteen months, Thieu was hailed by the United States as "the best available candidate."[9]

Thieu was, if nothing else, determined to achieve victory over the communists. He was willing to use means ranging from imposing martial law to following Diem 's example of imprisoning countless political opponents. He ruled rather quietly, however—allowing the more flamboyant Ky the majority of media attention. Decidedly unsatisfied with Johnson's rhetoric and seemingly meager offers, Thieu was easily seduced by Nixon's hazy but tantalizing promises of "victory with honor."

Nixon's Manipulation

After months of intense work towards peace, in late fall of 1968 Johnson's diplomatic efforts finally began to bear fruit—or at least the appearance of such. Advisors agreed that the best way to entice all parties to the table would be a bombing halt, which would secure cooperation from the North Vietnamese. With the support of his national security team that included Commanding Gen. Creighton Abrams, President Johnson began to plan for just such an announcement.

Thieu, however, held serious doubts about the viability of any peace talks under Johnson, and his colleagues harbored personal suspicions about the electoral motivations involved. Already irked by what he felt was undue pressure from the American administration, Thieu knew Johnson would soon be out of power. He was also frighteningly aware that if the Americans withdrew from Vietnam, his regime stood little to no chance of survival in the face of communist resurgence. Humphrey, who desired withdrawal, was a dismal option in Thieu's mind. Nixon, an ally with whom he communicated through Anna Chennault and who had pledged support, would surely provide the best deal. With Nixon, South Vietnam stood a chance of survival—and even a slim chance seemed better than none.

Furthermore, the South Vietnamese were not necessarily in support of a bombing halt. Vice President Ky, in fact, was strongly opposed to such an idea. In late October he was recorded expressing that "although the U.S. wants a bombing halt in the interest of the number of votes for Vice President Humphrey, it is impossible without the concurrence of the Vietnamese.... If the U.S. unilaterally says to cease bombing of the North unconditionally, South Vietnam unilaterally should be able to carry out unrestricted bombing of the

North."[10] As a compounding factor, the South Vietnamese would not negotiate with the Viet Cong (also known as the National Liberation Front, or NLF) as equals; they demanded instead that the NLF come to the table as part of the Hanoi delegation.

An October 23 memo from the Director of National Security (DIRNSA), Lt. Gen. Marshall Carter, outlined a "disturbing" conversation between President Thieu and the South Korean Ambassador that occurred on October 18.

> [Thieu] said the U.S. can, of course, cease bombing, but is unable to block Vietnam (from bombing). Concerning the enforcement of the bombing halt, this will help candidate Humphrey and this is the purpose of it; but the situation which would occur as the result of a bombing halt, without the agreement of Vietnamese government, rather than being a disadvantage to candidate Humphrey, would be to the advantage of candidate Nixon. Accordingly, [Thieu] said that the possibility of President Johnson enforcing a bombing halt without Vietnam's agreement appears to be weak.[11]

Though negotiations seemed to be progressing, red flags indicated major obstacles yet to overcome; and Richard Nixon was determined to make these obstacles insurmountable.

For a time, Nixon maintained the promised public image: supportive of Johnson, declaring most altruistically that his support was "in the spirit of country above party" and that "the pursuit of peace is too important for politics as usual."[12] He appeared bursting with integrity and goodwill for the country, positioning himself smoothly in the public eye as almost post-partisan, and certainly pro-peace. Yet privately, Nixon stewed in paranoia and anger, convinced that Johnson was playing a game to win the election for Humphrey — playing American voters, playing the South Vietnamese, and, worst of all, playing Nixon himself.

To secure his ability to manipulate the peace talks, Nixon recruited a mole in the Johnson camp. The politically ambitious Henry Kissinger — a protégé of New York governor Nelson Rockefeller and student of realpolitik ideology, whose German Jewish family had fled from the early Nazi reign (in 1938) and resettled in America — was then a trusted advisor to Democratic president Lyndon Johnson at the critical Vietnam peace negotiations in Paris.

From Paris, Kissinger would regularly feed highly classified intelligence on the talks to Nixon, who used it in back-channel communications with the South Vietnamese to scuttle any progress. A circumspect spy, Kissinger always used public telephone booths and spoke exclusively in German to his young Nixon campaign contact, Richard Allen (whose German was even more fluent than Kissinger's). Allen, who worked out of the Nixon headquarters in Manhattan, recalls that Kissinger, from his pay phones, "offloaded almost every night what had happened that day in Paris."[13]

David Davidson, a delegate to the Paris talks, says that in using Kissinger for intelligence and advice the Nixon team had a highly professional and accurate spy: "Kissinger shared [with Team Nixon] his analysis of what was happening with [the talks]. And he was probably by far the most brilliant mind available to them, and the most sophisticated analyst."[14]

Henry Kissinger did not have to be begged, nor did he accept cash-filled envelopes, to become Nixon's 1968 Paris spymaster. Indeed, as Allen later observed, the esteemed intellectual had "on his own, volunteered information to us" on the negotiations. This account is congruous with that of Nixon biographer Stephen Ambrose, who writes that Kissinger "approached John Mitchell . . . and said he was eager to pass on information to the Nixon camp, if his role could be kept confidential."[15] Thus, as parties began to meet in Paris in preparation for full-blown negotiations, Nixon was fully informed and one step ahead even of the chess master, Johnson.

At first, to convey his information from Paris, Allen briefed Nixon personally at the candidate's Fifth Avenue apartment. He would also summarize each Kissinger phone call from Paris in writing—with copies to both Nixon and John Mitchell.

In many memos, Allen stressed the importance of keeping Kissinger's involvement "absolutely confidential." Years later, Allen ruefully conceded to Kissinger biographer Walter Isaacson, "I became a handmaiden of Henry Kissinger's drive for power."[16] In a separate interview, Allen offered some backhanded praise for Kissinger's chutzpah: "It took some balls to give us those tips" because it was "a pretty dangerous thing for him to be screwing around with national security."[17]

At a key point in the talks, Kissinger dispatched an urgent

warning to the Nixon forces that "something big was afoot" in Paris.

On October 16, Chennault flew to Kansas City to meet with Nixon. It was the same day that Johnson briefed the candidates on his plans for Vietnam, and just weeks out from Election Day. Chennault penned a statement supporting a long-term approach to the war, cautioning against hasty, ill-though-out deals, but urging discretion in Nixon's statements on the topic. The crafty operative knew how high the stakes were, and she knew that part of her job was to ensure that cooler heads prevailed — at least, when coolness served her interests.

Nevertheless, as tensions rose on either side, the agreement between Nixon and Johnson by which Nixon would support Johnson publicly began to waver. Nixon even flirted with revealing his plan to the public, describing his co-conspirators as "the enemy," though not quite acknowledging direct dealings: "Let's not destroy the chances for peace with a mouthful of words from some irresponsible candidate for President of the United States," he told the crowd at a campaign event in Evansville, Illinois. "Put yourself in the position of the enemy. He is negotiating with Lyndon Johnson and Secretary Rusk and then he reads in the paper that, not a senator, not a congressman, not an editor, but a potential President of the United States will give him a better deal than President Johnson is offering him. What is he going to do? It will torpedo those deliberations . . . The enemy will wait for the next man."[18]

(In mid-October 1967, Nixon and Johnson had had their first public spat over Vietnam. Johnson took a diplomatic trip to Southeast Asia, and Nixon used the opportunity to criticize him in a newspaper column. "He is the first president in history who has failed to unite his own party in a time of war," wrote Nixon. He also posed the query, "Is this a quest for peace or a quest for votes?"[19]

Johnson responded, as Johnson often did, with rage far exceeding proportionality to what Nixon had expressed, labeling Nixon "a chronic campaigner" who "doesn't serve his country well" by making such statements "in the hope that he can pick up a precinct or two." He also alluded to a stinging statement President Eisenhower had made about Nixon more than a decade prior: "that if you would give him a week or so, he'd figure out what Nixon was doing."[20]

Nixon quickly and coyly rolled back his stance, accusing Johnson of a "shocking display of temper." He took the position of bigger man and stated diplomatically, "Now President Johnson and I can disagree . . . but let's disagree as gentlemen."[21])

Now in election year 1968, GOP candidate Nixon displayed similar political smarts in dealing with LBJ on Vietnam. On October 25, Nixon made another public statement: "In the last 36 hours I have been advised of a flurry of meetings in the White House and elsewhere on Vietnam. I am also told that this spurt of activity is a cynical last minute attempt by President Johnson to salvage the candidacy of Mr. Humphrey." After deliberately planting this seed, he craftily established the appearance of rebuffing such a claim, adding, "This I do not believe."[22]

Nixon, fearing that Johnson was playing him, was now playing Johnson; and Johnson, a seasoned political animal, was surely playing back.

Secrets Revealed

Time was growing short for Johnson to secure his legacy as he grappled with the South Vietnamese and pushed the peace talks forward. A later memo written by Walt Rostow reported:

> From October 17 to October 29 we received diplomatic intelligence of Saigon's uneasiness with the apparent break in Hanoi's position on total bombing cessation and with the Johnson administration's apparent unwillingness to go forward. This was an interval, however, when Hanoi backed away from the diplomatic breakthrough of the second week of October. Only towards the end of the month was the agreement with Hanoi re-established. As late as October 28, Thieu, despite the uneasiness of which we were aware, told Amb. Bunker he would proceed, as he had agreed about two weeks earlier.[23]

An October 27 memo from DIRNSA to the White House, heavily redacted but apparently relaying an intercepted message from Bui Diem to Thieu, states:

> In accordance with . . . instructions . . . continuing my conversations

to try to gain a clear-cut attitude . . . The longer the situation continues, the more favored, for the elections will take place in a week and President Johnson would probably have difficulties in forcing . . . hand . . . still in contact with the Nixon entourage which continues to be the favorite despite the uncertainty provoked by the news of an imminent bombing halt.[24]

The next day another memo from DIRNSA expounded on a speech made by President Thieu. "Thieu said that it appears that Mr. Nixon will be elected as the next President, and he thinks it would be good to try to solve the important question of the political talks with the next president (no matter who is elected)."[25] That said, Humphrey's recent statement that "Vietnam does not have the right to reject a decision to halt the bombing" had infuriated many South Vietnamese and caused, in DIRNSA's words, "a temporary aggravation" and some anti-American protests. As for Thieu's reliability in going forward with the peace talks, "On the U.S. side, rumors are spreading that one cannot predict what President Thieu is going to do and is adopting a much too stubborn attitude."[26]

Vital news reached the White House on October 29. Thieu was not, as it had for a time appeared, committed to the peace talks—in fact, it seemed he was backing out of the negotiations set to occur in Paris, obfuscating to avoid any promises of Saigon's attendance.

In the early hours of that day, Johnson's undersecretary of state for political affairs, Eugene Rostow (brother of Walt Rostow, Johnson's national security advisor and later purveyor of the X Envelope), received a tip from a source on Wall Street that a close Nixon ally was discussing plans to block a Vietnam peace deal.[27] As Wall Street investors are wont to do, this particular supporter of Nixon was sharing information with colleagues to better inform their stock market investments, which were sensitive to matters of guns or butter.

Rostow's memo stated that, according to his source, Nixon "was trying to frustrate the president by inciting Saigon to step up its demands and by letting Hanoi know that when he took office 'he could accept anything and blame it on his predecessor.'"[28]

In a more detailed memo later that day, Eugene Rostow stated that "the speaker said he thought the prospects for a bombing halt or a cease-fire were dim, because Nixon was playing . . . to block."

He added:

> Part of [Nixon's] strategy was an expectation that an offensive would break out soon, that we would have to spend a great deal more (and incur more casualties)—a fact which would adversely affect the stock market and bond market. . . . These difficulties would make it easier for Nixon to settle after January . . . he would be able to settle on terms which the President could not accept, blaming the deterioration of the situation between now and January or February on his predecessor.[29]

The New York source who spoke to Rostow was later revealed to be Alexander Sachs, a board member of the investment firm Lehman Bros. and former advisor to Pres. Franklin D. Roosevelt. His observations showed that Nixon was not only determined to block a peace deal but intent on worsening the situation in Vietnam in order to personally benefit.

This exchange provides evidence that Nixon fully expected an upsurge in violence, and that he was entirely willing to make such a trade for his political victory. It also showed—not only in hindsight, but to the Johnson White House for the first time—that Nixon was lying through his teeth about supporting the president's plans for peace.

As Walt Rostow wrote later in a 1973 memorandum for the record, "the diplomatic information previously received plus the information from New York took on new and serious significance."[30] Finally understanding the origin of Thieu's obfuscation, Johnson stated, "It all adds up."[31]

The White House was just beginning to unravel Nixon's sabotage, and only days remained until the election.

Chapter 5

"This is Treason"

Just one week before the election, the White House finally discovered that Nixon was somehow involved in discouraging South Vietnam from attending the Paris peace talks painstakingly orchestrated by President Johnson. The administration was thrown immediately into controlled chaos, simultaneously attempting to contain the damage while investigating exactly what Nixon had been up to.

As John Mitchell had feared, he and the other conspirators were placed under surveillance. Johnson ordered FBI wiretaps and physical stakeouts of the South Vietnamese Embassy, and after Chennault's presence was detected there she too was placed under watch. The NSA was already intercepting and deciphering cable traffic to and from the embassy, and the CIA had bugged Amb. Bui Diem's office and personal living space there, as well as President Thieu's office in Saigon.[1]

On October 31, Johnson made a conference call to all three presidential candidates (Nixon, Humphrey, and third-party candidate Wallace) to inform them of an impending bombing-halt announcement. It was a courtesy to the candidates so that each could prepare talking points and strategies given the changing political climate. It was also an opportunity for the chess master. During this conversation, Johnson made sure to include some loaded hints to let Nixon know he was aware of the candidate's efforts to undermine the peace process. Nixon joined Humphrey and Wallace — neither of whom was yet aware of any foul play — in assuring Johnson of their full support.

Behind the scenes, the Nixon camp was also thrown into panic. Mitchell feigned an internal investigation, but the pool of conspirators had been tiny, so he was able to report that no one on the Nixon staff had been privy to any untoward efforts or communication with the South Vietnamese.

Utterly spooked and certain of surveillance, Mitchell became difficult for Chennault to contact. When vitally necessary to ensure Thieu's continued cooperation, Nixon's campaign manager reached her on a safe line to deliver a message: "Anna, I'm speaking on behalf of Mr. Nixon. It's very important that our Vietnamese friends understand our Republican position, and I hope you made that clear to them." Seeking reassurance, he asked, "They really have decided not to go to Paris?"[2] Chennault confirmed this.

Indeed, the sabotage appeared to have worked—though the White House persisted in attempts to keep the information quiet and roll back the damage. Thieu had never truly desired negotiations without significantly greater concessions than the existing administration was willing to provide. But Johnson was a powerful political master, capable of convincing even his staunchest opponents to support him if given the proper incentives. National security advisor Clark Clifford, deeply involved in the events, thus later analyzed the situation and concluded that Nixon's actions were "probably decisive in convincing President Thieu to defy President Johnson."[3]

On October 31, despite the unraveling plot, Johnson declared a full bombing halt of North Vietnam as a sign of goodwill and what he hoped would be a major step towards serious peace talks.

The same day, Johnson phoned Everett Dirksen, the Senate's top Republican. Dirksen had played a key role in helping pass the Civil Rights Act, and despite their rival party affiliations, the two men were confidantes.

Johnson revealed to Dirksen part of what had transpired, including that he considered Nixon's actions a betrayal. "I played it clean," bemoaned the president. "I told Nixon every bit as much, if not more, as Humphrey knows. I've given Humphrey not one thing."

He continued, "I really think it's a little dirty pool for Dick's people to be messing with the South Vietnamese ambassador and carrying messages to both of them. And I don't think people would approve if it were known."

Dirksen concurred.

"We have a transcript where one of his partners says he's going to frustrate the President by telling the South Vietnamese that, 'just wait a few more days,'" the president said. "He can make a better peace for them, and by telling Hanoi that he didn't run this war and didn't get them into it, that he can be a lot more considerate of them than I can because I'm pretty inflexible. I've called them sons of bitches." (Johnson, in fact, called many people sons of bitches, or worse.)

"The fellas on our side get antsy pantsy about it," said Dirksen, reiterating Republican concerns. "They wonder what the impact would be if a ceasefire or a halt to the bombing will be proclaimed at any given hour, what its impact would be on the results next Tuesday."

Johnson assured Dirksen that he would never play politics with the war, and the conversation ended. Johnson hoped that Dirksen, as the top-ranking Republican in Congress, might have some sway over the wayward presidential candidate.[4]

The next morning, Johnson called another close contact in the Senate, Democrat Richard Russell, chairman of the Senate Armed Services Committee. Johnson told Russell that Nixon was engaging in scurrilous behavior with the South Vietnamese.

"Folks messing around with both sides . . ." said Johnson. "Hanoi thought they could benefit by waiting and South Vietnam's now beginning to think they could benefit by waiting, by what people are doing. So [Nixon] knows that I know what he's doing."

Johnson also expressed hope to Russell that the conspirators were giving up. "This morning they're kind of closing up some of their agents, not so active."[5]

Nixon, however, was far from conceding. The election was a few days off, and he was still determined to ride his sabotage to victory.

On November 2, three days before the election, the most incriminating evidence yet of Nixon's sabotage reached the White House by way of an FBI intercept. Chennault had contacted Amb. Bui Diem with a message from "her boss," who had just contacted her from New Mexico. The message: "Hold on, we are gonna win."[6]

In Albuquerque, New Mexico, that day, Republican vice presidential candidate Spiro Agnew made a high-profile campaign appearance. Records show that an Agnew aide made five consecutive phone calls from the Albuquerque airport, corresponding exactly with the time frame that Chennault called Diem with the message to "hold on."[7]

Clearly the Nixon campaign was far from backing down. Johnson also learned that Chennault had an exclusive invitation to watch the election returns with Nixon himself in New York. FBI surveillance was ordered for the lady's trip north,[8] and Johnson doubled down to secure his much-awaited peace talks, for which he had sacrificed a second term and so much more.

FBI director J. Edgar Hoover, however, was friendly with Chennault and warned her that she was under surveillance; he assured her, however, that the FBI was simply "making a show."[9]

Before November 2 came to a close, another devastating blow to Johnson arrived along with proof that Nixon's plot had worked. Thieu informed American ambassador Ellsworth Bunker that South Vietnam would not participate in the peace talks and made a public speech reinforcing the refusal, though he claimed in the speech that the primary sticking point was the representation of the Viet Cong by the North Vietnamese delegation at the talks, which he would not abide.

Adding insult to injury, eleven South Vietnamese senators defied months-old and oft-reinforced U.S. requests that Vietnamese government officials remain neutral in the American election and sent Nixon a telegram hailing his candidacy. The senators "keenly awaited [Nixon's election] for the safeguard of South Vietnam."[10]

Johnson spoke with Senator Dirksen again on the night of November 2, with the goal of urging Dirksen to intervene more forcefully with the Republican candidate. "I think it would shake America if a principal candidate was playing with a source like this on a matter of this importance," said Johnson. "I don't want to do that. They ought to know that we know what they're doing. I know who they're talking to. I know what they're saying."

"We've had 24 hours of relative peace," said Johnson, referring to the bombing halt that began the previous day. "If Nixon keeps the South Vietnamese away from the conference, well, that's going to be his responsibility. Up to this point, that's why they're not there. I had them signed on board until this happened."

"I'd better get in touch with him, I think," conceded Dirksen, reluctant to involve himself in what was clearly a growing scandal.

Johnson added: "They're contacting a foreign power in the middle of a war. It's a damn bad mistake. And I don't want to say so. . . . You just tell them that their people are messing around in this thing, and if they don't want it on the front pages, they better quit it."

Dirksen agreed to warn Nixon, but before the discussion ended, Johnson dropped a profound accusation. "They oughtn't be doing this. This is treason."

The president of the United States, a Democrat, had, in a relatively calm conversation with a high-powered GOP colleague, accused the Republican presidential candidate of the highest crime possible against his country. And Dirksen, agreed — declaring, "I know."[11]

Dirksen did indeed speak with Nixon, warning him of Johnson's knowledge, anger, and threats to go public; Nixon subsequently telephoned Sen. George Smathers, a conservative ally from Florida, to discuss concerns that Johnson would reveal what he had now dubbed "treason."

On behalf his friend, Smathers called President Johnson on November 3 to deny Nixon's involvement. A memo detailing the phone call reads:

> Senator Smathers called [the White House] to report on a call he got from Nixon. Nixon said he understands the President is ready to blast him for allegedly collaborating with Tower and Chennault to slow the peace talks. Nixon says there is not any truth at all in this allegation. Nixon says there has been no contact at all. Tonight[12] on *Meet the Press* Nixon will again back up the President and say he (Nixon) would rather get peace now than be President. Also tomorrow night, Nixon will say he will undertake any assignment the President has for him whether that be to go to Hanoi or Paris or whatever in order to get peace. Nixon told Smathers he hoped the President would not make such a charge.[13]

Nixon spoke directly with Johnson later that day. "I just wanted you to know that I got a report from Everett Dirksen with regard to your call," he blustered to the president. "I just went on *Meet the Press* and I said . . . that I had given you my personal assurance that I would do everything possible to cooperate before the election and, if elected, after the election and if you felt . . . that anything would be useful that I could do, that I would do it, that I felt Saigon should come to the conference table."

Johnson was not convinced by Nixon's denials or his appearance on the venerable weekend news program. The candidate continued, "I feel very, very strongly about this. Any rumblings around about somebody trying to sabotage the Saigon government's attitude, there's absolutely no credibility as far as I'm concerned."[14]

Nixon again promised to take any action Johnson and Secretary of State Dean Rusk saw fit. Johnson, however, would not be swayed. White House aide Joe Califano recounted later that "Johnson was certain in his own mind that Nixon betrayed his country. . . . Nixon's denials did nothing to undermine the President's conviction . . . it was horrendous . . . at last now, in the final hours of the election, Johnson desperately wanted Humphrey to win."[15]

Debating Disclosure

Though Humphrey had left the Democratic Convention in Chicago with a twenty-two point disadvantage in the polls, in the closing weeks of the campaign he had recovered nearly all of that. He made a point to delineate his proud civil rights record from Nixon's less-than-stellar one, and on September 30, in an appearance in Salt Lake City, Humphrey finally broke with LBJ on the war:

> As President, I would stop the bombing of North Vietnam as an acceptable risk for peace because I believe it could lead to success in the negotiations and thereby shorten the war. In weighing that risk, and before taking action, I would place key importance on evidence — direct or indirect — by word or by deed of Communist willingness to restore the Demilitarized Zone between North and South Vietnam. If the government of North Vietnam were to show bad faith, I would reserve the right to resume the bombing.[16]

Humphrey also held out the possibility of a subsequent withdrawal of all U.S. troops from South Vietnam during his first year as president. As the campaign season waned, the race was neck-and-neck, and Humphrey was buffered by a late-gaining surge.

Years later, Humphrey campaign manager Larry O'Brien observed: "The Vietnam speech in Salt Lake City turned the corner. The [Edmund] Muskie [vice presidential] candidacy was a major plus in the campaign. We were able to play catch-up ball, not nearly all we would like to. We did stay in the fight with Nixon, pretty evenly matched in terms of media exposure and campaign effort over the last two or three weeks of the campaign."[17]

South Vietnamese leaders were steamed: A classified CIA cable quoted President Thieu as describing LBJ's bombing halt as a "betrayal comparable to the U.S. abandonment of Chiang Kai-shek as a result of Yalta, Tehran and Casablanca conferences."

President Johnson, too, was not happy with his vice president's Salt Lake City move. As Johnson aide Joe Califano put it later, "the cooling relationship between Johnson and Humphrey dropped into a deep freeze."[18]

Yet, once the White House learned of Nixon's sabotage and it became clear the damage was very serious, the primary question on the minds of those in the know was whether or not to make the Republican candidate's actions public. With the election just a few days away, the direction of the country's leadership was at stake; but so was the American public's faith and trust in that leadership.

President Johnson personally briefed a Humphrey aide on Nixon's duplicity. When the candidate himself was in turn informed, Humphrey incongruously lost his temper. "By God," he raged on his campaign plane, "when we land I'm going to denounce Thieu. I'll denounce Nixon. I'll tell about the whole thing!" He pondered furiously, "What kind of guy could engage in something like this?"[19]

Certainly not a candidate for president of the United States.

And yet, Nixon had engaged in such activity, and Humphrey's political instincts, despite the initial outburst, drove him to carefully reconsider his decision to reveal what he now knew. Aides warned him that it might be perceived as a cheap political ploy were he to go public so soon before election day, and ultimately Humphrey was concerned he did not have the hard evidence to prove to the American public that it was anything but rumor.[20]

Norman Sherman, Humphrey's press secretary, later recalled: "I begged [Humphrey] to let me tell all of this to the press. I was certain that Americans, of both parties, would be outraged and that we would get the final boost we needed. I told him that, if it rebounded against us, he could dramatically fire me as the unauthorized leaker and regain the high ground and his virtue as he said a muted goodbye to me." But, Sherman lamented, "Humphrey would not disclose any of this."[21]

Decades later, Sherman also remembered the words of journalist and author Teddy White in White's revised book about the 1968 election: "Fully informed of the sabotage of the negotiations and the recalcitrance of the Saigon government, Humphrey might have won the Presidency of the United States by making it the prime story of the last four days of the campaign. He was urged by several members of his staff to do so. And I know of no more essentially decent story in American politics than Humphrey's reluctance to do so."[22]

So Hubert Humphrey remained silent and rode out the twilight of his campaign, leaving the decision on whether to go public for President Johnson.

On November 4, election eve, a reporter for the *Christian Science Monitor*, Saville Davis, was identified by FBI surveillance as having been at the South Vietnamese Embassy. Davis had called the embassy for an appointment with Amb. Bui Diem and was informed that Diem was busy. Davis then went to the embassy to wait the ambassador out.

The reporter wanted to check a story received from a colleague in Saigon containing "elements of a major scandal which also involves the Vietnamese Ambassador and which will affect presidential candidate Richard Nixon if the *Monitor* publishes it," according to a memo, which continued: "Time is of the essence inasmuch as Davis has a deadline to meet if he publishes it. He speculated that should the story be published, it will create a great deal of excitement."[23]

A cable reported, "Davis said they are holding out of the paper a sensational dispatch from Saigon correspondent, the first paragraph of which reads: 'Purported political encouragement from the Richard Nixon camp was a significant factor in the last-minute decision of President Thieu's refusal to send a delegation to the Paris peace talks—at least until the American Presidential election is over.'"[24]

Three of Johnson's top advisors, Dean Rusk, Walt Rostow, and Clark Clifford, discussed whether or not to go public. "Some elements of the story are so shocking in their nature," Clifford judged, "that I'm wondering whether it would be good for the country to disclose the story and then possibly have a certain individual [Nixon] elected. It could cast his whole administration under such doubt that I think it would be inimical to our country's best interests."[25]

Rostow's November 4 memo to Johnson following a meeting among himself, Clifford, and Rusk concluded that while the advisors agreed Nixon had certainly been involved in the sabotage, it was unwise to release the information.

> Even with these sources, the case is not open and shut. On the question of the "public's right to know," Sec. Rusk was very strong in the following position: we get information like this every day, some of it very damaging to American political figures. We have always taken the view that with respect to such sources there is no public "right to know." Such information is collected simply for the purposes of national security.[26]

The three advisors thus agreed on three points: "(A) Even if the story breaks, it was judged too late to have a significant impact on the election. (B) The viability of the man elected as president was involved as well as subsequent relations between him and President Johnson. (C) Therefore, the common recommendation was that we should not encourage such stories and hold tight the data we have."[27]

Robert McCloskey, the State Department aide Davis had approached for comment, was instructed to tell the journalist, "Obviously I'm not going to get into this kind of thing in any way, shape, or form."[28] He repeated those words verbatim to the journalist, and Davis conceded that his newspaper would not print the story in the form in which it was filed, but might go ahead with a story explaining that Thieu, of his own accord, had decided to refuse peace talks until after the election—a fact that was readily apparent to anyone already reading the news.

Despite the perfect opportunity to discreetly uncover the sensationally true story of Nixon's perfidy, Lyndon Johnson and his staff kept mum. "You couldn't surface it. The country would be in terrible trouble," recalled aide Henry McPherson.[29] And of course, there was always "national security" to consider: after all, Johnson had used FBI and NSA surveillance on both American citizens and foreign diplomats to uncover the plot—a fact that would not be taken lightly should it be discovered.

Democracy is, of course, a mutual agreement between citizens and their representatives deeply rooted in trust; and trust is what the Johnson administration decided to maintain. Had the American people found out what Nixon had done, their trust in political leaders would lie in tatters for years to come, possibly in perpetuity.

The result was the election of Richard Nixon, whose later actions in orchestrating the Watergate cover-up would shatter the trust of the American people just as his "treason" would have had it been revealed in the waning days of the 1968 campaign—and the two events, as will be shown, were directly related. It was thanks to Johnson's secrecy, and Humphrey's insecurity, that the most high-profile criminal of the twentieth century would hold the highest office in the land for a full five years before finally—deservingly—falling from grace.

Chapter 6
Covering Nixon in '68

I was wrong to think there might be a "New Nixon" when he gave me a brief radio interview in a New Hampshire parking lot in March 1968. During the rest of the state primaries, and in the general election campaign, Richard Nixon was not as press-friendly as that early personal experience might have indicated. Maybe I'd just caught the candidate in a rare expansive mood. More likely, he was using me as a guinea pig to try out his new secret Vietnam peace plan pitch for more important audiences.

Author Don Fulsom with Pres. Richard Nixon (Courtesy National Archives and Records Administration)

As it turned out, the 1968 Nixon was still the unscrupulous press-hating politician of old—tanned and freshly shaved, however, and now sporting the angelic wings of a dove. His savvy image-makers had transformed the sore loser of 1962 to a more calm, thoughtful, and statesmanlike figure.

Unlike the tumultuous Democratic convention in Chicago—where police had rioted against anti-war protestors in the streets—the Republican convention in Miami Beach was, for the most part, orderly and peaceful. Having been victorious in every primary he'd entered, Nixon won the nomination on the first ballot. It was more of a coronation than a convention.

Behind the scenes, Nixon made a Miami Beach compromise on a certain issue with liberal Republican Nelson Rockefeller. The two men who shook hands on the deal were Nixon aide Richard Allen and Rockefeller aide Henry Kissinger. That handshake, held in a public place, was almost seen by a reporter at the convention. But Allen introduced himself to the reporter with a fake name, claimed to be one of Kissinger's students, and quickly exited the scene.[1]

Allen and Kissinger would collaborate again when Kissinger was Nixon's spy at the Paris peace talks. As earlier noted, using presumably untapped random pay phones in Paris, Kissinger would provide a steady flow of sensitive information on the talks to Allen—who would pass them along to GOP candidate Nixon.

Even Nixon himself has confirmed that Kissinger was his mole in Paris. In his memoirs, the ex-president declared: "During the last days of the campaign . . . Kissinger was providing us with information about the bombing halt."[2] And in 1983, Allen—who would later serve as Pres. Ronald Reagan's national security advisor—confirmed this, saying, "Henry was in active contact with us about what was going on in Paris throughout this period."[3] Kissinger had denied accounts of his spying for Nixon from Paris as "a slimy lie."

Also in 1983, no fewer than four former Humphrey aides claimed that during the 1968 campaign, Kissinger had offered them Rockefeller files that were derogatory of Nixon and then took back the offer. When asked about such claims, Kissinger said he had "no recollection" of making such a proposal. Humphrey aide Ted Van Dyk remembered things differently. In late October 1968, when the Democratic candidate was rising sharply in the polls, Kissinger sent a letter to Humphrey expressing his "distaste" for Nixon, his high regard for Humphrey, and his willingness to serve in a Humphrey administration. "I remember thinking to myself," asserted Van Dyk, "here's another letter from another academic looking for a job. I laughed and threw it in the 'out' box." When informed of this account, Kissinger responded, "That's a total lie, a goddamned lie. Let them produce such a letter."[4]

On August 8, in his acceptance of the Republican presidential nomination in Miami Beach, Nixon spoke from a high platform that resembled the bow of a large Navy ship. (He was an ex-sailor, after all.) And he castigated the Johnson-Humphrey administration on the Vietnam War:

> We all hope in this room that there is a chance that current negotiations may bring an honorable end to that war. And we will say nothing during this campaign that might destroy that chance. But if that war is not ended when the people choose in November, the choice will be clear . . . if after all this time and all this sacrifice and all of this [Republican] support there is still no end in sight, then I say the time has come for the American people to turn to new leadership — not tied to the mistakes and the policies of the past.

In his speech, Nixon also played the race card — blaming the courts for "weakening the peace forces as against the criminal forces" and pledging to end the plague of "unprecedented racial violence."[5] It was an obvious bid for white Southern votes that might otherwise go to third-party candidate George Wallace, the segregationist governor of Alabama.

Nixon so easily captured the GOP nomination because, as ex-United Press reporter and LBJ press secretary George Reedy later observed, he had rightly anticipated that 1968 might well be his final opportunity to try again for the White House: "For eight years, Richard M. Nixon had been plodding the Republican fund-raising circuit — appearing at party dinners, showing up when no one else would, placing in his political debt virtually every GOP leader in the United States."

Reedy concluded that, while Republican rank and file convention delegates "were not overly enthusiastic" about Nixon, "his troops were too well organized. He had figured that 1968 was his 'last main chance' year and he was ready when no one else was prepared."[6]

Nixon and Spiro Agnew

The only real news out of the 1968 GOP convention was Nixon's surprise pick of an almost unknown governor—Spiro Agnew of Maryland—to be his running mate. Only many years later did we learn that a possible reason may have been a huge secret payoff to Nixon from the Greek military government—something else that Larry O'Brien knew about Nixon, thanks to Greek journalist Elias Demetracopoulos. Historian Stanley Kutler explains how the "Greek Connection" apparently worked:

> According to Demetracopoulos, the Greek KYP—the intelligence service which had been founded by the CIA and subsequently subsidized by the agency—had transferred three cash payments totaling $549,000 to the Nixon campaign fund. The conduit was Thomas Pappas, a prominent Greek-American businessman with close links to the CIA, the Colonels (Greek military brass), and the Nixon campaign.[7]

Pappas was "widely regarded as the man who had persuaded Nixon and Mitchell to put Agnew on the ticket, although Agnew later claimed that he disliked the businessman," according to Kutler. The historian got confirmation of the Greek Connection from "an authoritative KYP official" in 1987.[8] Demetracopoulos is now a senior citizen living in Washington, DC. He has helped this author in many ways over decades of friendship. But he has never revealed his source for his Greek Connection evidence.

Agnew was forced from office in November 1973. And it was President Nixon who greased the skids for the vice president he had grown to passionately dislike. Nixon exerted heavy pressure through his final chief of staff Alexander Haig—who regularly met with top Justice Department prosecutors during weeks of efforts to get Agnew to step down.

Facing criminal charges that he had taken cash payoffs from Maryland contractors, Agnew finally agreed to plead no contest to income tax evasion. He got a suspended sentence and was assessed a modest fine in return for his resignation. In his memoirs, Agnew charged that Haig had made a threat "that made [him] fear for

[his] life.[9] An aide to Atty. Gen. Elliot Richardson later confirmed that White House negotiators "wanted the guy out of there. They wanted resignation without anything. They just wanted him out."[10]

Agnew never spoke with Nixon again. He refused to take Nixon's phone calls, but he did put aside twenty years of resentments and showed up for the thirty-seventh president's funeral in Yorba Linda, California, in 1994.

The Campaign Behind the Campaign

In a post-convention phone conversation, after President Johnson had briefed Nixon on Vietnam developments, the Republican nominee tried to drive a wedge between LBJ and Humphrey over Vietnam:

> **RN:** "Can you keep . . . your vice president and others, keep them firm on this? The hell with the god damned election. We must stand firm on this!
>
> **LBJ:** Very frankly, I don't know. That's the honest answer. I just plain don't know . . .
>
> **LBJ:** You [Nixon] can have every reason to be proud of what your platform is.
>
> **RN:** I won't take any advantage of you.
>
> **LBJ:** I know that (or) I wouldn't be calling you. I'm going to keep you informed . . .[11]

This conversation took place on August 20. Not long afterward, Nixon again secretly tried to ingratiate himself with President Johnson on Vietnam. Stanley Kutler reports that Nixon secretly met with televangelist Billy Graham in Pittsburgh on September 8 and asked him to carry a message to LBJ: that Nixon would do nothing to embarrass the ex-president, and above everything else, if elected, he would give Johnson his proper share of the credit when the war was ended. Graham carried out the mission and was able tell Nixon that LBJ was "touched" by Nixon's gesture—but that he would continue to "loyally support" Humphrey. The president added that if Nixon were elected in November he would "do all in [his] power to cooperate with him."[12]

Reporters following Nixon around were completely in the dark on this Nixon tactic—as we were on just about all aspects of the campaign behind the campaign. Nixon and his gang excelled at keeping secrets and erecting smokescreens and mirrored hallways. Though several reporters—Jack Anderson and Saville Davis, chief among them—did get an inkling of Nixon's nefarious backstage activities, including what LBJ termed "treason," I'm sorry to say I was not one of them.

Nixon saved his most savage Vietnam one-liner until October 9, 1968, when he declared: "Those who have had a chance for four years and could not produce peace should not be given another chance."[13] LBJ did not learn of Nixon's backstage sabotage of the Paris talks until October 29 or he might have crafted a proper retort.

Behind Closed Doors

The man most responsible for making the 1968 Nixon campaign's planes, trains, and automobiles run on time was John Ehrlichman, an acerbic, veteran advance man who was given the title of tour manager. (Dave Shields was in charge of luggage, and, as Ehrlichman once remarked, Dave "knew every suitcase by its first name." He hardly ever lost a bag.)

The candidate and his entourage flew around the country in three chartered 727s from United Airlines. The planes were named after Nixon's daughters and his son-in-law, David Eisenhower. They were the *Trisha*, the *Julie*, and the *David*. Nixon and his family traveled aboard the *Trisha* while the *Julie* carried important television and newspaper reporters.

The *David* was the most fun to be on. Informally, it was called the Zoo Plane because its main cargo were the "animals" who toted around heavy television equipment, the most unimportant reporters—like yours truly—and many of the candidate's Secret Service agents. Heavy partying, pillow fights, and rolling oranges and other objects up and down the aisles on takeoff and landing were standard practices on the *David*.

On the *Trisha*, the candidate and his chief handler, Bob Haldeman, sat in the forward cabin. Nixon's wife, Pat, sat in the staff section, usually reading a book or a magazine. The couple's daughters, Trisha and Julie, and son-in-law sat in the next cabin back. This was not a tight-knit family. As Ehrlichman recalls, they had to be brought together every time the *Trisha* touched down: "As the plane landed at each campaign stop the girls and David would walk forward, collecting Pat at her seat, assembling their coats and campaign smiles. When they arrived in the front cabin to line up behind him, Nixon would greet them, the airplane door would open and they would walk out to stand as a family, waving and smiling to the airport crowd."

Ehrlichman noted that Nixon treated his wife as a "limited partner, skilled at giving interviews to local women's-page editors, an indispensable auxiliary in receiving lines and on stage at rallies, but not a heavyweight." The tour manager added: "Nixon's attitude toward his family naturally became the attitude most of his staff took toward them. Pat Nixon's suggestions and complaints were tolerated without being much heeded by Haldeman and the rest of us."[14] Haldeman had the least respect for Mrs. Nixon—referring to her as "Thelma," her given name, behind her back.

In the fall campaign, Nixon was far more cautious than he had been as the 1960 Republican standard-bearer. He had learned from his poor 1960 appearances in the TV debates against his more telegenic opponent, Sen. John F. Kennedy. (Most people who listened to the debates on the radio thought Nixon had won.) The GOP nominee refused to debate Humphrey, held no press conferences, and kept his campaign as TV-centric as possible.

Television ads were especially critical to the Nixon campaign. Referred to by Nixon's handlers as "The Living Room Campaign," the commercials targeted families gathered around their sets to view popular prime-time shows. The heavily funded barrage of Nixon TV spots frequently featured the Republican candidate at his most dovish.

All of his live TV question-and-answer sessions took place before carefully screened, local, pro-Nixon audiences. In especially chilly studios (to keep the sweat on Nixon's upper lip to a minimum), these Nixon admirers lofted softballs to the solitary authoritative-sounding man standing—without a podium—behind a lone mic stand at center stage. For the most part, the national press was not even allowed in the same room during the candidate's hokey "Man in the Arena" performances. In many instances, we had to watch the event on TV sets set up in a nearby press center.

The Nixon campaign that year must have been one of the most efficiently run in the history of American politics. The candidate was always on time, and his schedule was purposely light because of his penchant for exploding under pressure. (As one example, at his infamous "last press conference" after losing the California governor's race in 1962, a bitter, hung-over, and trembling Nixon scolded the press and announced they would not have him to "kick around anymore" because he was retiring from politics.)

So, for Nixon—and for the national press trailing him around the country at snail's speed—there was no heavy lifting. The candidate's press people, led by the young and affable Ron Ziegler, even pretended to like the press. They went out of their way to be polite and helpful—as long as you didn't ask too often about why Nixon seemed to be hiding from the press and from Hubert Humphrey. (When Nixon took Florida vacations, a small plane usually buzzed his waterside retreat trailing a sign asking, "Afraid to Debate Humphrey?")

Just how efficient and reporter-friendly was the 1968 Nixon campaign? As a reporter following Nixon, you placed your luggage outside your hotel room door in the morning and it would wind up inside your hotel room at the next campaign stop that night. The hotels were always first-class. There were even frequent rest and recreation trips to Key Biscayne, Florida—where the candidate went to tan up for TV and frolic with his longtime best buddy, Bebe Rebozo. (After a few drinks, they enjoyed playing "King of the Pool," a child's game in which—according to a Nixon aide— "Nixon mounted a rubber raft in the pool while Rebozo tried to turn it over. Then, laughing and shouting, they changed places and Nixon tried to upset Rebozo."[15])

When Nixon took breaks at his Manhattan apartment, the national press was put up at either the Pierre or the equally posh Plaza. In other words, we were spoiled. We didn't fully realize it at the time, but one of the main reasons is that Nixon did not wear well under any kind of stress—even the stress that goes into preparing for a debate or a real press conference. Had we known, perhaps we would have questioned more loudly whether this man was fit to serve as commander in chief.

Reporters covering Humphrey, by contrast, were frazzled by his high-energy, wide-ranging, day-and-night effort to gain the White House. In trying to sell what he called "the politics of joy," the Happy Warrior was hardly ever on time. It was hard for the exuberant Humphrey not to add another rousing line or two to his speeches or to say no to just one more handshake or autograph or photo opportunity or impromptu press conference. The press covering his campaign got no special favors—they might even have had to carry their own bags from time to time.

The Humphrey campaign is described by historian Stanley Kutler as "perhaps the last traditional campaign in American presidential elections, featuring large rallies of the party faithful whom he addressed with hortatory stem-winders, desperately trying to create a bandwagon psychology." Kutler observes that it was the Nixon campaign that "broke new ground" with a "made-for-media" campaign, "largely avoiding longwinded orations, relying instead on clever thirty- or sixty-second commercials" and on the Man in the Arena TV format.[16]

Neither Humphrey nor Nixon committed any major gaffes during the campaign—though the latter, in retrospect, wished he had broken with LBJ's Vietnam policies much earlier. In a letter to a friend afterwards, Humphrey lamented: "I ought not to have let a man who was going to be a former president dictate my future."[17]

Nixon kept his alcohol and pill consumption to a minimum during the 1968 campaign, and—at least in public—he was able to control his infamous temper. The GOP nominee only put his foot in his mouth once, but almost no one—except for the reporters covering him—really noticed. Because his verbal gaffe was so minor, as well as too indelicate to explain to our reading, listening, and viewing audiences, we let it go. Jim McManus, then a reporter for Westinghouse Broadcasting, recalls that Nixon's miscue was apparently inadvertent:

> [It was] the night we spent in Burbank . . . when Nixon answered phoned-in questions. You know he hated to sweat on camera. So he had the [NBC-TV] studio AC'd down to about 60 degrees. We

warmed suddenly when [Nixon] took a call and then said, like a good city boy: "Well, now that gets us right down to the nut cutting!" Clearly Nixon did not know that that formulation dealt with removing the gonads from various farm animals.[18]

Neither did most of the TV audience that tuned in for that particular event.

Because Richard Nixon's sabotage of the Vietnam peace talks was a stealth campaign that went undetected by reporters on both the Nixon and Humphrey campaigns — and by those covering the Johnson White House — it has become one of the most underreported political, diplomatic, and military stories of our time. And if the X Envelope had not been opened earlier than scheduled, we would still not know that Richard Nixon gained the Oval Office by playing politics with peace.

Chapter 7
The Humphrey Campaign

Pres. Lyndon Johnson was incensed at Vice Pres. Hubert Humphrey for abandoning him on Vietnam. He told a top advisor he doubted Hubert's ability to succeed him. And LBJ bellowed to an old friend, "You know that Nixon is following my policies [in Vietnam] more closely than Humphrey."[1]

When Hubert finally convinced the president to hold a one-on-one reconciliation meeting, the vice president showed up late at the Oval Office, and LBJ refused to see him. It was Humphrey's turn to let off steam. "That bastard Johnson," he reported on the incident to an aide, "I saw him sitting in his office. . . . [LBJ assistant] Jim Jones was standing across the doorway, and I said to him: 'You tell the President he can cram it up his ass.' I know Johnson heard me."[2]

According to Jones, LBJ—after dropping out of the 1968 race—initially rooted for New York governor Nelson Rockefeller to be the next president. "I think he felt that [Hubert Humphrey] was maybe too nice to be president. He thought Rockefeller was the most talented."[3]

Even in his laid-back retirement in Texas, Lyndon Johnson—wearing his hair long, peacenik style—had not taken a kinder, gentler view of Humphrey. During a visit to the LBJ Ranch, former Senate aide Bobby Baker heard Johnson unleash a cruel anti-Hubert rant:

> I often think it's a good thing that Hubert Humphrey never got to be President—for his own good and the good of the country. He can't say no to anybody about anything, he hasn't got much more spine than a small girl, and he runs his mouth ninety miles an hour without thinking about what he's saying.

Baker was so uneasy with the ex-president's acidic take on Humphrey—whom Baker "had always considered with affection"—that he quickly changed the subject.[4]

One of the saddest-if-true stories of the 1968 Democratic campaign is that President Johnson may have been bugging Vice President Humphrey's phones. "The speed with which Johnson had information about Humphrey's presidential campaign" suggested such bugging, according to historian Robert Dallek. LBJ could have used such information, Dallek speculates, to "gain advance notice and a chance to dissuade him should Humphrey decide to break away on the war."[5]

Amazingly, as president—as we have only recently learned—Lyndon Johnson even considered stabbing his political partner in the back at the 1968 Democratic convention in Chicago. In a series of phone calls from his Texas ranch to Mayor Richard Daley and others in Chicago, the president started clandestinely counting convention votes. He wanted to know whether he had enough to jump back into the race and defeat his vice president.

LBJ contemplated a dramatic surprise flight from Texas to Chicago to put his name forward as an alternative to Humphrey. Johnson's finagling might have ultimately led to Marine One landing on the top of the Hilton Hotel to avoid anti-war protestors. That option was actually discussed.

But Johnson scuttled the idea of reentering the race when the Secret Service told him it could not assure his safety in the riot-prone convention city.[6] His protectors were rightly opposed to almost anything that would even slightly endanger him. They were especially antsy because of a spate of assassinations in the sixties—those of Jack and Robert Kennedy and Martin Luther King Jr.

Not aware that Johnson was secretly working the long-distance phones to gauge his chances at drumming up a convention coup, Humphrey's handlers were actually delighted that the president had planned not to be in Chicago in the summer of 1968. Years later, Humphrey press secretary Norman Sherman recalled: Johnson "didn't feel he *could* come. I guess we didn't feel he *should* come. It would have caused more chaos than we needed."[7]

Personal safety was certainly a concern for anyone attending the Chicago conclave. Luckily, everyone I knew made it in and out of the city in one piece, mainly by keeping off the streets. I was either safely inside the well-guarded convention hall, co-anchoring UPI's radio coverage, or safely inside the Hilton Hotel. (My employer, United Press International, was the wire service rival of the Associated Press back then. It had more than one thousand domestic radio stations and networks as subscribers to its audio feeds, including NPR, and live newscasts and news programming.)

From my eleventh-floor hotel room one night, I looked down on a horrible sight: Mayor Daley's police attacking anti-war demonstrators. I was able to broadcast regular live blow-by-blow accounts of the street violence from a comfortable distance while noshing on a cold room service meal. Protestors exploded some stink bombs in the lobby. And a few whiffs of police-fired tear gas filtered into open hotel windows on lower floors. That's the closest I came to the riots.

The Democratic presidential nominee-to-be was also on an upper floor of the Hilton, his headquarters hotel. Hubert Humphrey viewed the same police riots with dismay: for one thing, the politically savvy candidate knew that TV replays of the street violence would preempt coverage of important convention proceedings — including his acceptance speech. But he did not shed tears over the bloody scene below, contrary to some news reports at the time.

Not only from the Hilton's windows, and on constant TV replays, but also on live TV could viewers see the helmeted police, many on horseback, striking individuals of all ages with batons, seemingly at random. They sprayed mace as well as tear gas into the crowd. It was one frightening scene. What a way to open a convention — brownshirts-in-blue pummeling those exercising their right of free speech and assembly. This horrible precedent foreshadowed the most disastrous convention in United States history — a convention that would go on to nominate a man who preached, of all incongruous things, the "Politics of Joy."

It wasn't just Mayor Daley's cops who acted like Nazi brownshirts. The mayor himself displayed a thuggish attitude inside the barbed wire-protected convention hall. His security force dealt harshly with unruly delegates and slugged CBS reporter Dan Rather in the belly. CBS convention anchor Walter Cronkite denounced the brutality.

From the podium, Sen. Abraham Ribicoff of Connecticut denounced "Gestapo tactics in the streets of Chicago." Daley became livid, his facial veins and arteries appeared ready to burst.

The mayor shook his fist at Abe from the convention floor and called him a "fucking Jew bastard." Daley held his hands over his mouth when uttering the line—so you couldn't read his lips if you were watching on TV.

Humphrey won the nomination on the first ballot—easily outdistancing two anti-war senators, Eugene McCarthy and, in third place, George McGovern.

As the convention drew to a close, my UPI radio colleague Bill Greenwood and I decided to leave Dodge City on the first available flight back to DC. I frankly feared being recruited for potential post-convention riot coverage. "Let's go before they know we're gone," I suggested when pitching my cowardly plan. "Now that the main event is over, the possible residual riots will just be a local story. This is something the Chicago bureau is much better qualified to cover," I rationalized as a mask for fright.

Bill was easy to persuade. After all, both of us had been roughed up in separate incidents during our ill-advised attempts to try to cover rioting in black sections of DC after Martin Luther King's murder. We felt we'd paid our riot duty dues.

Hubert Humphrey's split with Lyndon Johnson on Vietnam took place on September 30 in Salt Lake City. The nationally televised speech was a masterstroke:

> As President, I would stop the bombing of North Vietnam as an acceptable risk for peace because I believe it could lead to success in the negotiations and thereby shorten the war. In weighing that risk, and before taking action, I would place key importance on evidence—direct or indirect—by word or by deed of Communist willingness to restore the Demilitarized Zone between North and South Vietnam. If the government of North Vietnam were to show bad faith, I would reserve the right to resume the bombing."[8]

Humphrey also held out the possibility of a subsequent withdrawal of all U.S. troops from South Vietnam during his first year as president. It was a genuine and non-secret plan for an end to the war.

Internal Humphrey campaign tussles over tactics and leadership hurt the Democrats as much as the Johnson-Humphrey rift over Vietnam. Top Humphrey campaign advisor Bill Connell now reveals that—on the eve of the Salt Lake City speech—DNC Chairman Larry O'Brien urged the candidate *not* to break with the president. "Had he listened to O'Brien . . . Humphrey would have gone down to an ignominious defeat. And there would have been no need for the Nixon/Kissinger act of treason. But [the Nixon campaign] had the shit scared out of them in the last days, and they were willing to do anything to blow up the Humphrey surge of the previous three weeks—including a betrayal of their own country and its servicemen in Vietnam."[9] Connell says he and fellow Humphrey advisor Jim Rowe "fought hard for the balanced, forceful and precise statement that Humphrey finally decided upon" in the Salt Lake City address.

In the Nixon camp, there was serious consternation that Humphrey's keen political move contrasted too sharply with their own man's still-hidden blueprint "to end the war and win the peace." (The wonderful ambiguity of this artful phrase is usually credited to Nixon speechwriter William Safire.) And Nixon used the same old alibi for not revealing his own Vietnam plan, the same one he used during my brief encounter with him in the March 1968 New Hampshire primary: To do so might hurt the peace talks, he continued to claim. (The very talks he was secretly sabotaging!)

A key 1968 Nixon campaign (and later White House) official, Tom Charles Huston, has now confirmed the campaign's use of back-channel political efforts to keep Saigon from the bargaining table. In an interview with the Nixon Library released in 2014, Huston said Nixon campaign manager John Mitchell "was directly involved" in the anti-peace conspiracy—and that it was "inconceivable to [him]" that Mitchell "acted on his own initiative." Huston says neither Nixon nor President Johnson desired to push the issue: "I think there was an implicit understanding between two very politically sophisticated people, who had been in the arena for a very long time, to say 'Hey, look, this thing is over, you know, neither of us is going to gain anything by stirring up this pot.'"[10]

The Huston oral history interview was conducted by former Nixon Library head Tim Naftali, a hero to those wishing more truthfulness in Nixon Library exhibits. (Before being forced out of his job by Nixon loyalists, Naftali cleaned up the totally dishonest Watergate exhibit and made other exemplary decisions).[11]

Huston's comments on Nixon's alleged perfidy are also important in another respect: until now, this arguably treasonous act has remained undefended even by Republicans—until Huston's contention that the interference in the peace talks made no difference because Saigon didn't need Nixon to tell them they'd do better by waiting. Huston adds: "But there is little doubt that in typical Nixonian fashion, he wasn't going to leave anything to chance."[12]

After Humphrey's Vietnam divorce from LBJ, anti-war demonstrators stopped showing up and shouting "Dump the Hump" at his political rallies. The tuba-heavy local marching bands that pumped out the addictive "Minnesota Rouser" to herald the candidate's arrival seemed more on key, as did the campaign itself. The Happy Warrior was his old, ebullient self—and he drew bigger, more enthusiastic crowds. Donations shot up. (Nixon's 1968 campaign pockets, however, proved to be far deeper than Humphrey's. The GOP nominee spent an estimated $20 million to Humphrey's $5 million.) The polls narrowed. Behind the scenes, Richard Nixon intensified his efforts to keep Saigon's representatives away from Paris.

Backstage on the Democratic side, there was a rough intra-party struggle over major campaign issues. A loyal top Humphrey staffer since 1955, Bill Connell broke with the candidate on the value of adding Larry O'Brien as a strategist and head of the Democratic National Committee: "I was furious with [O'Brien] for his constant assurances to the press corps that he was only marking time, that the game was up and the defeat of Humphrey was inevitable." (Such assurances must have been off-the-record and did not leak at the time.)

O'Brien was, however—as Connell observes—keen on moving into a high-end private sector spot. He had already agreed to become the top Washington lobbyist, at $15,000 a month, for one of the world's richest and most influential men, Howard Hughes.[13]

Humphrey persuaded O'Brien to enlist in the campaign before he officially took the job with Hughes. The candidate himself reportedly even phoned Hughes—by then a drug-addled hermit with only limited periods of rationality—for permission to temporarily borrow Larry. Yet Connell thinks O'Brien, the premier Democratic political operative of his day, did not deserve to be so intensely courted:

> To my knowledge, [O'Brien] did not contribute any effort to the single-handed Humphrey campaign that drove [Humphrey's] poll numbers up from 22 points down at the end of the Chicago convention in late August to a dead heat at the end of October.

Another key advisor on the Humphrey campaign plane was Norman Sherman, the vice president's press secretary. As previously noted, Sherman implored the vice president to let him leak the story of Nixon's anti-peace actions. But Humphrey rejected that scheme, as well as the idea that he himself should expose Nixon's meddling. For Humphrey, the reason he did *not* was simple, according to Sherman:

> He felt that if Nixon won, the actions which others called treason, would make it hard to govern. If I can use technical terms, the fucking liar [Nixon] said, at some point, that he knew nothing of sweet Anna's messing around. What is really ironic is that Nixon soon after asked Humphrey to be his Ambassador to the United Nations.

Sherman also acknowledges there was some concern on the Humphrey plane "about whether he, as vice president, should have been told [about the sabotage]."[14]

Reaction to Nixon's Treason

As for the LBJ-Humphrey divide, Humphrey's press secretary opines that Johnson, "even by the immediately pre-election days . . . must, I think, have remained ambivalent about Humphrey. That doesn't preclude his telling Humphrey about Nixon-Chennault, but I think the facts must have come from someone else."[15]

Despite the Vietnam-created "deep freeze" in the LBJ-Humphrey relationship, Republican candidate Richard Nixon's Vietnam perfidy brought the top two Democrats together at the end of the 1968 race—at least on that grave subject. Each had the lowest possible opinion of Nixon and his anti-peace actions. Their inner-circles agreed, as a little sampling will show:

The aforementioned Bill Connell, a top Humphrey advisor on the campaign trail, now says the 1968 election turned out to be "one of the most fateful acts of treason in our short history, as it gave us five more years of a disastrous war, 20,000 more military deaths, a Presidency so awful that he was driven out of office, and was the stage for a 30-year assault on the working class and the poor that has brought us to the oligarchy that we all now recognize."

Neither of us knowing the answer to this critical question when we first communicated, Connell was certain that Larry O'Brien knew about Nixon's seamy pre-election anti-peace maneuvers: "Indeed, he was chairman of the Party, and it was inevitable that he would have heard the news about the Nixon/Kissinger/Dragon Lady caper within 24 hours of the time we heard about it on the Humphrey plane."

Now ninety, Connell concludes that the "Nixon/Kissinger subversion of their nation's commander in chief was surely the greatest criminal act of any major figure in our nation's history." As for Kissinger, he thinks Benedict Arnold was a "piker" compared to Nixon's secret mole at the 1968 peace talks. "It's a crying shame," he adds, "that Kissinger is not spending his time picking his feet in prison for life."[16]

As president, at a time when he was on the outs with Kissinger, even Nixon, of all people, used Kissinger's 1968 double-agent activities in Paris against him. In January 1972, when Nixon was thinking of firing his national security adviser, he told aide Bob Haldeman, "Maybe we've got to bite the bullet now and get him out. The problem is, if we don't, he'll be in the driver's seat during the campaign, and we've got to remember that he did leak things to us in '68, and we've got to assume he's capable of doing the same to our opponents in '72."[17] In other words, Nixon seemed to be saying, "Henry is potentially politically dangerous. If we keep him around, he could do to us what he did to the Democrats in '68."

Interviewed by the BBC in the 1990s, LBJ advisor Clark Clifford said he was "outraged" by Nixon's actions "because by delaying the peace talks, that permitted the war to go on. It was possible that, had the peace talks made some progress, that there might even be a temporary armistice. That had been considered as a possibility — and the fighting, and more importantly the dying, could have been stopped. Possibly. But by delaying the peace talks, the war was permitted to go right on. And I felt it was an enormous disservice to our country."

In another '90s interview with the BBC's Charles Wheeler, President Johnson's assistant secretary of state William Bundy stated, "I'm categorical that Nixon was involved. I'm categorical on it. There is no question that Nixon set this up—got this operation underway."[18] LBJ aide Tom Johnson describes Nixon's actions as "reprehensible" and believes "Nixon would not have been elected if the public had learned of the efforts to sabotage, or at least to delay, the peace talks until Nixon was president."[19] Key Johnson assistant Joe Califano says LBJ felt the Republican candidate was "a man so consumed with power that he would betray the country's national security interests, undermine its foreign policy, and endanger the lives of its young soldiers to win office."[20] President Johnson, of course, thought Nixon was guilty of treason.

DNC Chairman Larry O'Brien later recalled that, in the campaign's final days, Hubert Humphrey confided to him that he had "sufficient evidence to consider going public [to expose Nixon's sabotage] . . . but he was wavering and leaning toward leaving it alone."[21]

As the Director of Communications for the DNC, John Stewart worked out of Washington during the 1968 campaign. Without knowing that O'Brien *was* aware of Nixon's underhanded actions, Stewart correctly theorized his boss must have been in the know:

> O'Brien was deeply involved in the 1968 campaign and HHH vetted most major decisions through O'Brien. HHH in the final weekend of the campaign faced the agonizing decision about what to do about Nixon's actions . . . and decided against going public. . . . I can't imagine a scenario where O'Brien would be unaware of this dramatic development."

Stewart even sees a possible connection between Nixon's 1968 interference with Vietnam peace efforts and Watergate four years later: "Fear of disclosure of the Chennault affair could well be the motivating factor that explains [the 1972 break-in]," he posited.[22]

High-ranking Humphrey partisans from the 1968 campaign remain, to this day, unforgiving toward Richard Nixon—convinced that he both stole a U.S. presidential election and simultaneously thwarted peace in Indochina. Hubert Humphrey himself, however, showed the kind of compassion for his sinister 1968 Republican rival that reinforces his reputation for decency and bipartisanship.

In January 1978, a seriously weakened and bedridden Humphrey telephoned the disgraced Nixon. The ex-president was still in self-imposed purgatory in California after the Watergate scandal had forced him to quit the presidency in August 1974. Humphrey advisors Norman Sherman and John Stewart recently revealed the little-known story behind that final Humphrey-Nixon conversation:

> Humphrey was direct: "Dick, I'm not going to be around much longer. There is going to be a memorial service for me in the Capitol Rotunda. I want you to attend that service." Nixon said no, he just couldn't return to Washington. But Humphrey persisted: "You must attend." Nixon finally relented. And he stood with Presidents Jimmy Carter and Gerald Ford and other political luminaries at the memorial service. [23]

Just why did Hubert invite Dick to his funeral? Sherman and Stewart quote Humphrey as telling his wife, Muriel, "No former president should live in exile from the nation's capital."[24]

Five days after his invitation to Nixon, the Happy Warrior died from bladder cancer at his home in Waverly, Minnesota.

Chapter 8

"Treason" Takes the White House

On November 5, 1968, Richard Nixon won the office of president of the United States, which he had for so long coveted. He received just half a million more votes than Democrat Hubert Humphrey (0.7% of the popular vote), but trounced Humphrey in the Electoral College with 301 delegates to 191. Humphrey carried just thirteen states (plus the District of Columbia) to Nixon's thirty-two. Third-party segregationist candidate George Wallace received 13% of the popular vote and forty-six delegates in the Electoral College (carrying just five states, all in the Deep South).

The intrigue over Nixon's interference with the peace negotiations was far from over, and ten weeks separated Nixon from his inauguration on January 20. Johnson, now a lame duck in the Oval Office, still pushed for a peace deal, and as he would soon find out Anna Chennault remained actively involved behind the scenes.

On November 7, two days after the election, an unidentified man in contact with the assistant armed forces attaché of the South Vietnamese Embassy, Maj. Bui Cong Minh, sparked the interest of the White House. A memo to President Johnson from Walt Rostow stated: "The unidentified man inquired as to how the peace talks were coming, and Major Minh expressed the opinion that the move by Saigon was to help presidential candidate Nixon, and that had Saigon gone to the conference table, presidential candidate Humphrey would probably have won."[1]

That same day, the FBI intercepted a conversation between Anna Chennault and the South Vietnamese Embassy. Chennault told Ambassador Diem's secretary that she had been "talking to 'Florida,' and has to make a few calls before she can move."[2] Notably, President-elect Nixon had jetted off to Florida after the election for some much-needed relaxation. The "Florida" mentioned by

Chennault was most certainly Nixon himself.

The FBI also reported on a November 7 conversation with Diem himself, discussing Nixon without directly using his name:

> Chennault stated the person she had mentioned to Diem who might be thinking about "the trip" went on vacation this afternoon and will be returning Monday morning at which time she will be in touch again and will have more news for Diem. Chennault continued that "they" are still planning things but are not letting people know too much because they want to be careful to avoid embarrassing "you," themselves, or the present U.S. government.[3]

Chennault also noted that she and Senator Tower planned to meet with Diem on Monday.

The next day, November 8, Rostow wrote to Johnson a note accompanying the cable reports of Chennault's contact with Diem: "I think it's time to blow the whistle on these folks."[4] Rostow, Rusk, and Clifford had previously agreed that the public had no right to know and the dealings of candidate Nixon should be kept under wraps; in the closing days of the election, Johnson had heeded their advice. At last now, and yet too late, the White House began to regret its decision to hold its cards so closely—a decision that played a crucial role in Richard Nixon's victory.

As President Johnson began reconsidering his silence, he received a phone call from Nixon. The President-elect was calling from Key Biscayne, Florida, and Johnson saw the opportunity to get his legacy back on track toward peace—and a favorable place in the history books.

Johnson began speaking about the South Vietnamese. "Now they've started that [boycott of the peace talks] and that's bad. They're killing Americans every day. I have that [Nixon's underhanded moves] documented. There's not any question but that's happening." There would be no beating around the bush in this phone call. "That's the story, Dick, and it's a sordid story. I don't want to say that to the country, because that's not good."[5]

Johnson—intentionally ditching subtlety—was threatening to blow the whistle on Nixon's actions if Nixon did not right his wrongs. Nixon promised the president that he would contact the South Vietnamese and urge them to reconsider attending the peace talks.

Thus, as Rostow recalled, Johnson "actively sought and obtained Nixon's cooperation . . . in delivering the word that the President-elect wished the South Vietnamese to proceed in moving toward a negotiation with Hanoi."[6]

When Chennault learned of this new turn, she was floored. The man she had helped double-cross his country, president-elect Richard Nixon, was now double-crossing her by urging Saigon to attend the negotiations.

"What makes you change your mind all of a sudden?" Chennault asked co-conspirator John Mitchell.

"Anna, you're no newcomer to politics," Mitchell replied. "This, whether you like it or not, is politics."[7]

Chennault was furious, and despite the Nixon camp's best attempts to get her on board with the new plan and encourage her friend Thieu to reconsider the talks, she refused to be the catalyst that brought the South Vietnamese to Paris. Nixon had what he wanted — the presidency — but Chennault and her Asian allies were quickly losing sight of what they had been promised: victory with honor, should such a thing exist in war.

At a political fundraiser later, Nixon thanked Chennault profusely for her efforts in the election.

"I've certainly paid dearly for it," she replied stoically.

"Yes, I appreciate that," Nixon told her. "I know you're a good soldier."[8]

Yet the Dragon Lady kept her silence. With friends in such high places — friends that might become enemies at any moment — Chennault feared for her safety, and indeed still held out hope that the war would end on terms she could abide; as a political player on the international scene, she held a great deal of power in her own right.

South Vietnam Reacts

Less than a week after the election, on November 11, President Thieu spoke at a formal dinner of South Vietnam's "betrayal" by the United States, referring to the administration's push for talks with the Viet Cong to go forward. Thieu "held forth expansively"[9] (according to a White House memo), expounding on his stance that two-party talks—that is, negotiations requiring the Viet Cong to be included as part of Hanoi's delegation, and not as their own separate delegation—were the only acceptable proposal.[10]

Thieu also informed his guests that during the U.S. election campaign he had sent two secret emissaries to the United States to contact Richard Nixon. The South Vietnamese president speculated that President-elect Nixon would let Johnson attempt to resolve the diplomatic impasse, understanding that any solution by Johnson would make Nixon's post-inauguration task far easier.

While the South Vietnamese minister of information confirmed two days later contact between the Vietnamese Embassy and Nixon staffers, he held that "a person of the caliber of Nixon would not do such a thing."[11]

Two reporters had caught whiffs of a story—Drew Pearson and Jack Anderson, the latter of whom would later be a prime target of President Nixon's "enemies list." They authored an article in the Sunday, November 17, issue of the *Washington Post* entitled "Washington-Saigon Feud: Details Leak Out of Backstage Fight Between U.S. and South Vietnam." Pearson and Anderson noted that the South Vietnamese "began throwing up procedural objections" just as the Paris negotiations were beginning to make headway. "The President [Johnson], meanwhile, learned that Saigon's Ambassador Bui Diem had been in touch secretly with Richard Nixon's people. There were unconfirmed reports that South Vietnamese leaders had even slipped campaign cash to Nixon representatives. These reports made Mr. Johnson suspicious that the South Vietnamese were trying to sabotage the peace negotiations in the hope that Nixon would win the election and take a harder line."[12]

The final blow-up, it appears, was spurred by American ambassador Averell Harriman's frustration at South Vietnamese refusals to let the Viet Cong flag be displayed at the negotiations. Harriman verbally exploded at Saigon's chief observer, Pham Dang Lam, and word of this conflict reached Saigon just in time to interrupt a joint American-Vietnamese announcement of a bombing halt. This postponed the bombing halt, but Johnson's desire to move forward unilaterally, if necessary, created a rift that could not be healed.

Also in mid-November, the *Chicago Daily News* published a story on the sabotage. "Saigon boast: 'We helped elect Nixon,'" ran the headline.

> Their reasoning is that by sabotaging President Johnson's attempt to call a bombing halt two weeks before the elections they eliminated the support this would have brought for Vice President Hubert H. Humphrey . . .
>
> To many American officials here it is offensive that the government for which Mr. Johnson literally gave up the Presidency and sacrificed his political career should treat him in this way.
>
> These officials predict, with grim satisfaction, that the Saigon government will be unpleasantly surprised with the man they think they helped put in the White House.[13]

Efforts for peace pushed forward in spite of the growing divide and scattered whispers in the media of foul play. On November 28, at Nixon's apparent urging, the South Vietnamese announced they would attend the Paris negotiations after all. Procedural disputes, once again, delayed commencement of the talks—possibly as a cover for stalling until Nixon, just weeks away from taking the oath of office, assumed the presidency.

Chennault, though estranged from her former allies Nixon and Mitchell, remained on the scene. A December 10 "eyes only" memo from Rostow to LBJ noted simply: "The Lady is still operational."[14] Several cables detailing Chennault's activities accompanied the note.

On December 9, Chennault contacted Nguyen Hoan, counselor at the Vietnamese Embassy, regarding Nixon's choice for secretary of defense. She told Hoan that her "very good friend," Melvin Laird of Wisconsin, would be appointed to the position and advised him "not to be too concerned about the press's references about a coalition government."[15]

As Lyndon Johnson's presidency came to a close, peace remained out of his reach. His Grand Bargain had escalated the Vietnam War to the point where he lost control; his power was too concentrated and his legacy tarnished with the blood of fallen Americans and brutalized innocents. His final Hail Mary, sacrificing a second term to devote his efforts to diplomacy, had failed. The Great Society stagnated under a dark cloud of war.

7 (INFORMATION

THE WHITE HOUSE
WASHINGTON

15

LITERALLY EYES ONLY

~~SECRET~~   Tuesday, Dec. 10, 1968
                             10:00 a. m.

MR. PRESIDENT:

────────────────── The Lady is still operational. ──────────

                              W. *alt* Rostow

~~SECRET~~ attachment

*Keep all these in
one file for ready
reference —*
                    L

PRESERVATION COPY

DECLASSIFIED
E.O. 12958, Sec. 3.6
NLJ 00-233
By cb   , NARA Date 8-31-00

REFERENCE FII F

COPY LBJ LIBRARY

Document 15 of the X Envelope, declaring "The Lady is still operational"
(Courtesy LBJ Presidential Library)

As Johnson prepared for retirement, he began to gather the documents relating to Richard Nixon's sabotage of the much-sacrificed-for peace talks. This story, Johnson knew, deserved a record—even if it had to remain secret, possibly forever. He entrusted the folder to Walt Rostow and called it the "X Envelope."

Navigating the Press

On the third day of January 1969, two weeks out from Inauguration Day, a reporter with the *St. Louis Post-Dispatch* named Tom Ottenad contacted Rostow to inquire about a story. The sabotage had been masterfully and almost entirely kept under wraps, but whiffs of intrigue were spreading.

"It has to do with the last period of the Presidential campaign about the time of Johnson's announcement of the bombing halt and steps to broaden the Paris talks," Ottenad began. "I've been told that during that period some Republican contacts were made with South Vietnamese officials urging them to go slow in the hope that, from their standpoint, they might get a better shake under Nixon than they would otherwise, and that these contacts—contacts of this type—were made by Mrs. Chennault. We have established this from a number of sources, and it's not really about that as such that I was inquiring, but rather about another aspect of it. I was told also that this activity had come to the attention of the Administration, and I wondered—I wanted to ask you—if that is in fact correct."

"I have not one word to say about that matter," replied Rostow.

"Not even on a background or completely non-attributable basis?" pushed Ottenad.

"On no basis whatsoever."

The two further established that Rostow would remain mum.

"May I ask about a different but somewhat related matter—because I don't know whether you will say the same thing to that or not; if it is, of course, I'll drop the business right there," the reporter continued. "The other matter I've been told of is about this same time. Contacts were made indirectly by South Vietnamese officials with the Nixon camp asking—unsuccessfully, as it turned out—asking for an opportunity to meet with Nixon or one of his aides and hinting that South Vietnamese would not take action on the question of going to Paris until after the election. My question: Did that ever come to your attention."

"I have nothing whatsoever to say about it," Rostow replied.

Ottenad acknowledged he could tell from Rostow's tone he would get nowhere with this line of questioning. He left Rostow with the offer, "If you find at any time that is no longer the case, I would appreciate an opportunity to talk with you about it."

"Right," said Rostow. "Thank you."[16]

Rostow immediately forwarded a transcript of this phone call to Johnson, with an accompanying eyes-only memo stating: "The Lady is about to surface."[17]

Ottenad's article appeared in the *Boston Globe* on January 6 with the title "Was Saigon's peace talk delay due to Republican promises?" The first several paragraphs of the article set out, in stark, straightforward terms and for the most part accurately, what had transpired in the final days of the election:

> WASHINGTON—A well-known top official of committee working for the election of Richard M. Nixon secretly got in touch with the representatives of South Vietnam shortly before the presidential election.
>
> It was in connection with an apparent effort to encourage them to delay in joining the Paris peace talks in hopes of getting a better deal if the Republicans won the White House. . . .
>
> [The South Vietnamese government's] action is credited by some political experts, including some of Nixon's staff, with cutting the loss of votes that his aides believe he suffered in the election from the last-minute peace move.[18]

The article continued on for numerous column inches, including denials by the South Vietnamese that their decision was based on "internal politics" and further denials from the Nixon camp that the candidate had been directly involved. Chennault, for her part, "refused to give much information," taunting Ottenad to "come back and ask me that after the inauguration . . . I know so much and can say so little."[19]

For the most part, the media failed to catch on to the story of Nixon's maneuverings. In the summer of 1969, Theodore White published the third volume in his *Making of a President* series, focusing this time on the 1968 election. White wrote of Anna Chennault's contact with the Vietnamese but was apparently unaware that Nixon was directly involved; he reported instead that the Nixon campaign was furious when Chennault's behavior became known.

The publication of White's book led to a brief and cursory media flurry during which several articles appeared in newspapers around the country discussing, in one form or another, the failure of the peace talks.

The Associated Press circulated an article discussing the story published by White. It appeared on July 9 on page one of the *Austin Statesman* as "Did HHH's 'Fair Play' Cost Election?" and under the title "White Reports Nixon Backer Tried to Block Peace Talks" in Washington DC's *Evening Star*. The article discusses White's claims but fails to question the author's understanding that Nixon was an innocent bystander to his supporter's energetic efforts to sabotage the negotiations.

> White says, "What could have been made of an open charge that the Nixon leaders were saboteurs of the peace one cannot guess; how quickly it might, if aired, have brought the last 48 hours of the American campaign to squalor is a matter of speculation. . . .
>
> "I know of no more essentially decent story in American politics than Humphrey's refusal to do so; his instinct that Richard Nixon, personally, had no knowledge of Mrs. Chennault's activities; had no hand in them; and would have forbidden them had he known; Humphrey would not air the story."[20]

Two days later, the *Austin-American* ran a piece, "Humphrey Agrees With 'Sabotage' Charge." The article began: "Hubert H. Humphrey acknowledged Thursday that he knew a supporter of Richard Nixon was trying to 'sabotage' the Paris peace talks but turned down the chance to make the information an issue in the 1968 presidential campaign." Humphrey described White's claims as "accurate." The article continued:

> White said the 1968 Democratic presidential candidate refused to use the information because he did not believe Nixon knew of what had been done.
>
> Asked if he agreed with White that publicizing the incident might

have won him the presidency, Humphrey said: "I don't know what the results would have been. It's no good musing over that sort of thing. It's all in the past."

White says Mrs. Chennault learned through gossip, rumor and speculation of the October negotiations preceding the bombing halt and the Paris talks.[21]

The *New York Times* published an article on July 23 titled "Mrs. Chennault Denies Seeking Peace Talk Delay," which addressed White's claims and Chennault's response. Chennault was quoted at a news conference as saying, "This is an insult to my intellect and the integrity of the South Vietnamese Government," and urging support for the new president. She added elusively, "Some day when the right time comes, all the facts will be made known."[22]

That day would not come in the year 1969, or even for several more decades. Thus, without the American people finding out how he had manipulated Johnson's diplomatic efforts for his own political gain, Richard Nixon took office. He was sworn in

Richard M. Nixon takes the oath of office as president of the United States, January 20, 1969 (Courtesy National Archives and Records Administration)

Johnson shaking hands with the newly inaugurated President Nixon (Courtesy National Archives and Records Administration)

on January 20, 1969, with opening remarks made by Sen. Everett Dirksen, whose influence had failed to hinder Nixon's anti-peace efforts.

Nixon's inaugural address was lofty and eloquent, the rhetoric focused around peace, sacrifice, and communal effort. "For the first time," he declared, "because the people of the world want peace, and the leaders of the world are afraid of war, the times are on the side of peace."

The new president continued:

> What kind of nation we will be, what kind of world we will live in, whether we shape the future in the image of our hopes, is ours to determine by our actions and our choices.
>
> The greatest honor history can bestow is the title of peacemaker. This honor now beckons America—the chance to help lead the world at last out of the valley of turmoil, and onto that high ground of peace that man has dreamed of since the dawn of civilization.
>
> If we succeed, generations to come will say of us now living that we mastered our moment, that we helped make the world safe for mankind. . . .
>
> We are caught in war, wanting peace. Division tears us, wanting unity. We see around us empty lives, wanting fulfillment. We see tasks that need doing, waiting for hands to do them. . . .
>
> When we listen to "the better angels of our nature," we find that

they celebrate the simple things, the basic things — such as goodness, decency, love, kindness. . . .

Let this message be heard by strong and weak alike: The peace we seek to win is not victory over any other people, but the peace that comes "with healing in its wings," with compassion for those who have suffered, with understanding for those who have opposed us; with the opportunity for all the peoples of this earth to choose their own destiny.[23]

These words would ring in stark contrast to what would unfold over the coming years of Richard Nixon's presidency. It was division and discord that would mark his tenure, and far from healing the country, Nixon would utterly redefine the American public's view of its leaders. Dark years were coming: "treason" had taken the White House.

Chapter 9
Nixon's War

On November 11, 1968, the traditional stakeout site on the blacktop driveway outside the West Wing of the White House was jam-packed. A dozen TV cameras, backed by light stands, formed a semicircle facing a long row of disorganized microphones, clamped and duct-taped together on metal stands some twenty feet away. The mics faced the entrance to the West Wing door. Reporters, technicians, stepladders, audio mixers, still and TV photographers vied for space and prized viewing and listening spots.

The media throng awaited word on Pres. Lyndon Johnson's first face-to-face meeting with President-elect Richard Nixon since the election . . . and (though still publicly unknown) since LBJ had caught Nixon with "smoking gun" evidence of Nixon's interference with the Vietnam peace talks.

Just days before this White House meeting, LBJ once again let Nixon know he had the goods on him. On a newly released tape of a November 8 phone call, Johnson told Nixon that some Nixon supporters were continuing to urge South Vietnam to stay away from the bargaining table until Nixon took over on January 20.

> **Nixon:** I know who they're talking about too. Is it [Senator] John Tower?
>
> **Johnson:** Well, he's one of several. Mrs. [Anna] Chennault is very much in there.
>
> **Nixon:** Well, she's very close to John.

What Nixon was undoubtedly referring to when he tossed loyal Republican John Tower [no friend of LBJ anyway] under the bus as a possible traitor was that Tower — then unmarried — was dating the widowed Anna Chennault. Pillow talk by Tower, Nixon seemed to be suggesting, could have been responsible for Anna's possible knowledge of the dirty GOP dealings on Vietnam.

135

The president-elect was obviously trying to shift suspicions away from Chennault, his true back-channel emissary to South Vietnam's president, Nguyen Van Thieu. An authoritative former Tower associate acknowledges the senator's intimacy with Chennault during this period but insists on never having heard Tower express any knowledge of her Nixon-initiated success in keeping Saigon from the peace talks. Chennault had proved her worth to the new president as a trusted expert at guanxi—a Chinese term Westerners interpret as involving "bribery, political fixing and general corruption."[1]

President Johnson concluded the Vietnam segment of the November 8 phone conversation by stressing to Nixon: "You tell your President [Thieu] that he'd better get his people to that [peace] conference and get them there quick. And what he does there is a matter for his judgment, but he oughtn't refuse to go to a room and meet."

Nixon responded, "Okay. We'll work on it."[2]

I chatted with Bob Moore, a radio reporter for Metromedia, as we tended to our respective tape recorders at the November 11 White House stakeout. Bob broke up the crowd when, pretending to be broadcasting live, he dramatically voiced, in his deepest, most dulcet tones: "And I confidently predict that we will soon learn the details of President-elect Nixon's secret plan to end the Vietnam war."

The line was particularly funny because no one, not even most Republicans, ever believed Nixon had any kind of magic formula to quickly "end the war and win the peace," as the candidate had implied at nearly every 1968 campaign stop. The secret plan had become a top joke among most politicians and political reporters and late night comedians.

But to give Nixon some credit, he never actually said he had "a secret plan" to end the war. Because he refused to define at least an outline of his plan, however, Nixon had become saddled in the public mind as having actually said he had "a secret plan." For Nixon opponents, his unexplained alleged blueprint for Vietnam peace bore all the markings of Nixon's lifelong personal devotion to deception and trickery. From the outset, though, Nixon was at least consistent in his standard campaign alibi for not disclosing even a hint about his plan that would supposedly lead to a quick peace breakthrough.

I was fortunate to have caught up with Nixon on that very issue quite early in 1968. It was in an emptying motel parking lot after a Nixon rally in snowy New Hampshire, the first primary in the nation. No Secret Service agents were assigned to candidates in those days, and only his "bag carrier," the young, affable, and handsome Dwight Chapin, accompanied the former vice president.

To my surprise, on that winter day in that parking lot, the usually unapproachable Nixon was approachable — maybe there really was a "new Nixon." The candidate answered about ten minutes' worth of questions patiently, articulately, and reasonably. On his Vietnam peace plan, he was prepared with a deft reason for declining to discuss it: he would not do or say anything that might undercut the Johnson administration's peace efforts. That, more or less, remained his line for the entire campaign.

But now, on November 11, Richard Nixon — the hawk in peacenik's clothing — was meeting as president-elect with the hawkish Pres. Lyndon Johnson. LBJ was still actively working for peace, of course — but those prospects looked quite bleak (thanks in large measure to Nixon's clandestine anti-peace machinations.) Saigon was still boycotting the talks, and Johnson was just a lame duck until Nixon took office in January.

Bob Moore and I pondered what these two political giants would discuss about the number-one issue of the day. Would Nixon reveal at least some of his Vietnam plan — and if so, might it find support with LBJ? Or would Nixon back the policies of the outgoing administration? Perhaps Nixon would offer to fly to Saigon or Paris on a mission for peace. (This was a story I had broken a few days earlier, based on "reliable sources" in the Nixon camp. The sources turned out to be right, but President Johnson never took Nixon up on what Nixon himself feared would be seen by LBJ as grandstanding.) Such was some of the voluminous speculation circulating among reporters gathered for the post-election Johnson-Nixon talks.

As a chilly night fell on the White House, those who were covering the event were rewarded with actual news. With President Johnson at his side, Nixon announced he was endorsing LBJ's Vietnam policies: "If progress is to be made on matters like Vietnam . . . it can be made only if the parties on the other side realize that the current administration is setting forth policies that will be carried forth by the next administration."[3]

Turning on Co-conspirators

Following Nixon's inauguration and his abrupt double-cross of his co-conspirators, no one could have been more furious than Madame Chennault and President Thieu. After all, Nixon had promised them South Vietnam would get a better deal if Thieu helped Nixon's candidacy by staying away from the peace talks. Chennault and Thieu felt duped and betrayed.

Nixon soon sent "strong word" to Thieu to attend the talks. Described as "flabbergasted" by Nixon's new Vietnam line, Anna asked John Mitchell, "what makes you change your mind all of a sudden?" His response: "Anna, you're no newcomer to politics. This, whether you like it or not, is politics."[4]

Many years later, Mrs. Chennault let off steam about being manipulated by Nixon: "To end the war was my only demand, but after [Nixon] became president, he decided to continue the war. Politicians are never honest."[5]

Nixon, indeed, filled his presidential inner circle with the same scheming politicos who had assisted in the sabotage. John Mitchell, Nixon's go-between with Chennault, was appointed attorney general of the United States, and Henry Kissinger was upgraded from mole to national security advisor.

Curiously, it was Nixon himself who later outed Kissinger as a mole in his 1978 memoirs, *RN*. The ex-president cited Kissinger's Paris espionage as proof of his ability to keep his lips sealed: "One factor that had most convinced me of Kissinger's credibility was the length to which he went to protect his secrecy."

Why did Nixon, of all people, blow the whistle on Kissinger's double-dealings in Paris? (Nixon conveniently neglected to expose his own use of Kissinger's intel to scuttle 1968 peace efforts.) One possibility is that the two men were hardly speaking by that time, and Nixon might have wanted to get in a free dig.

The former president, for example, might have still been smarting over Kissinger's widely publicized 1975 description of Nixon as "odd," "artificial," and "unpleasant." As Pres. Gerald Ford's secretary of state, Kissinger had uttered those words about his old boss while talking into what turned out to be an open mic at a ceremonial dinner in Ottawa.

So despite Nixon's admiration for Kissinger's ability to keep secrets in 1968, there was never any love lost between the two men once they became partners—and rivals—for power in the White House. As star Watergate reporters Bob Woodward and Carl Bernstein observed in *The Final Days*, "Kissinger really didn't like the President. Nixon had made him the most admired man in the country, yet [Kissinger] could not bring himself to feel affection for this patron."

Nixon might also have thrown Kissinger under the 1968 bus in his memoirs because he was the obvious source of an unflattering story about Nixon when the two men met in the Lincoln Sitting Room during one of Nixon's final nights in office. At Nixon's request, both men fell to their knees and held hands while Nixon tearfully prayed to God for help, peace, love, and rest. And the president—who sobbed hysterically at times—swore Kissinger to secrecy about his behavior. "Henry," he slurred in a subsequent phone call, "please don't ever tell anybody that I cried and that I was not strong."[6]

When a detailed account of this strange event appeared in 1976 in Woodward and Bernstein's *The Final Days*, Nixon could not have been pleased.

The first journalist to reveal Kissinger's 1968 espionage was Seymour Hersh. "It is certain," Hersh declared in his 1983 book, *The Price of Power*, "that the Nixon campaign, alerted by Kissinger to the impending success of the peace talks, was able to get a series of messages to the Thieu government (in Saigon) making it clear that a Nixon presidency would have different views on the peace negotiations." Kissinger denounced Hersh's book as a pack of "slimy lies" but did not specifically deny being Nixon's mole in Paris.[7]

Hersh struck back in a 2002 TV interview: "Do I think [Kissinger] saw what he did as a betrayal of the peace process, or the move by Johnson to start the bombing halt? I really think this guy doesn't see it that way. He saw it as a means to an end—which is why he's such a good apparatchik. He then was getting that job [as Nixon's national security advisor]."[8]

Chennault did visit President Nixon at the White House a number of times. On her first visit, the president took her aside to thank her for her key role in his election victory. As noted earlier, she responded that she had "paid dearly for it" — alluding to news stories about her suspected role in stalling the peace negotiations. Nixon answered, "Yes, I appreciate that. I know that you are a good soldier."[9]

Chennault conferred with Nixon on April 13, 1971, the same day the veteran anticommunist president received the ambassador from what was then known to most Americans as "Red China." Nixon's chief of staff, Bob Haldeman, wondered if this could possibly be coincidence. He said those meetings "should make the press sit up and wonder what we're up to, and could be kind of intriguing."[10]

As Haldeman knew, the Dragon Lady was deliberately kept out of Nixon's ultra-selective China policy loop, meaning that she (like most of the world) was unaware that the president had, for some time, been eagerly seeking eventual renewed relations with Mainland China. This policy was anathema to the rabid anticommunist Chennault and her China Lobby constituents. On July 25, 1971, Nixon announced that he would be going to Peking the following year, and Anna Chennault had another reason to feel that politicians are never honest.

Nixon's about-face on China was related to his dealings with Vietnam. The president was counting on a "triangulation" gambit that played China against the Soviet Union in an effort to get Hanoi to make concessions at peace negotiations.

The flawed concept was ridiculed by Chinese premier Chou En-lai when Nixon visited China in February of 1972: "The most pressing question now is Indochina. The [U.S.] Democratic Party tried to put you [Nixon] on the spot on this question by alleging that you came to China to settle Vietnam. Of course this is not possible. We are not in a position to settle it in talks."

Chou ended his blunt lecture to the American president with a few wise words: "You went in there by accident. Why not give this up? Be bold."[11]

During Nixon's China trip, the Vietnam War was still going poorly. And there was little hope for a negotiated peace. The fact remains that in 1968 Richard Nixon and Henry Kissinger feared the political consequences of a pre-election breakthrough for peace in Vietnam and conspired to sabotage the ability of the Johnson administration to end the war. History, however, has illustrated the incredibly deceitful nature of these promises.

President Nixon did not capitalize on the impressive framework of peace negotiations built by the outgoing Johnson administration. Dramatic bombing halts had proved successful in bringing the North Vietnamese to the table at the peace talks in Paris, yet it was the United States' own ally Nixon had convinced to sit out the talks.

In hindsight, President Thieu and Anna Chennault knew they had been played by a scheming Nixon, who immediately turned after the election to supporting the peace proposal on the table in an attempt to pressure the South Vietnamese into accepting the deal he had urged them to reject. Unsurprisingly, when the South Vietnamese scoffed at the double-crossing, Nixon was perfectly content with allowing the war to resume in its bloody capacities.

Yet the most disturbing aspect of President Nixon's sabotage of peace efforts in 1968 for political gain are not in his willingness to let the war drag on; it lies, rather, in his decision to expand the conflict dramatically. In just his second month in office, the freshly sworn-in Nixon added to his impressive string of deceptions of the American people. This time Nixon made the extraordinary decision to begin a brutal series of carpet bombings in the neutral country of Cambodia. Congress, the news media, and the American public had no idea that their "peace with honor" candidate was now elevating the prolonged war to its most extreme heights.

Nixon and Cambodia

In March of 1968, Nixon began this four-year illegal bombing campaign of Vietnam's neighbor. At one point, even as those bombs were falling, the president assured the nation in a televised address that we were strictly observing Cambodia's neutrality.

Bob Haldeman recorded Nixon's decision to bomb Cambodia in his diary entry on March 17, 1969, writing, "Historic day. K's [Kissinger's] 'Operation Breakfast' finally came off at 2:00 our time. K really excited. As is P [the president]."[12]

Nixon's secret expansion of the war, codenamed "Operation Menu," went on incessantly for years. In an attempt to protect themselves politically and legally, Nixon and Kissinger made the decision to inform five members of Congress of the secret bombings, yet this was done months after the attacks had already begun. Undoubtedly the president had exceeded his authority by carrying out an extensive year-long war against a country the American people and the United States Congress never wished to attack. Given the fact that it was an entirely secret war, there was no public debate on the matter, let alone a congressional declaration of war.

Kissinger has since attempted to defend the decision to bomb neutral Cambodia with a string of falsities. In an interview with historian William Shawcross, Kissinger went on a rant blasting those Americans upset over the revelation that they had been in a war for over a year they never knew about. As he explained, "People usually refer to the bombing of Cambodia as if it had been unprovoked, secretive U.S. action. The fact is that we were bombing North Vietnamese troops that had invaded Cambodia, that were killing many Americans from these sanctuaries, and we were doing it with the acquiescence of the Cambodian government, which never once protested against it, and which, indeed, encouraged us to do it."[13]

Obviously Kissinger's assertion that the bombings were not "secretive U.S. action" flies in the face of the complete shock that hit the American people and Congress when they finally found out years later that they had actually occurred. Even the pilots initially dropping the bombs were told they were conducting missions in South Vietnam, only to be diverted in the air to targets actually across the border in Cambodia.[14]

Furthermore, Cambodian ruler Prince Norodom Sihanouk publicly denounced the bombings in his country. Sihanouk had allegedly expressed previously a willingness to allow minimal U.S. involvement in the country to eliminate some North Vietnamese bases, but only under the condition that such actions did not target Cambodian civilians caught in the crossfire. The Nixon carpet bombing could hardly have been more indiscriminate in its killing and therefore drew the ire of Cambodians. Surely it cannot be said that the Cambodian government was a willing target of tens of thousands of U.S. bombs.

In April 1970, Nixon took US involvement a step further and illegally invaded Cambodia, couching the offense in the rhetoric of an "incursion." He assured the nation that American and South Vietnamese troops were attacking only North Vietnamese enemy forces: "This is not an invasion of Cambodia," he maintained. "The areas in which these attacks will be launched are completely occupied and controlled by North Vietnamese forces. Our purpose is not to occupy the areas. Once enemy forces are driven out of these sanctuaries and their military supplies are destroyed, we will withdraw."[15]

Public opposition to the president's move was fast and widespread. In the words of Vietnam expert William Duiker, "now unrest resurfaced on college campuses throughout the country . . . Congress grew more reluctant to Nixon's policies in Indochina and eventually forced the administration to agree to withdraw all U.S. forces from Cambodia by the end of July."[16]

In the immediate aftermath of the invasion, the president gave young peace activists even more reason to protest. After a briefing at the Pentagon, the chief executive publicly asserted his low opinion of the anti-war youth: "You see these bums, you know, blowing up the campuses. Listen, the boys that are on college campuses today are the luckiest people in the world, going to the greatest universities, and here they are, burning up the books, storming around about this issue . . . you name it. Get rid of the war and there will be another one."[17]

Nixon was in an equally pugnacious mood when he raged at his Pentagon briefers: "I want to take out all those sanctuaries. Make whatever plans are necessary, and then just do it. Let's go blow the hell out of them! Knock them all out so that they can't be used against us again. Ever."[18]

Nixon's secret bombing of Cambodia continued until August 1973, when Congress exposed and put an end to it. In the interim, more than three million tons of bombs rained down on that nation, killing an estimated half-million peasants. The $1.5 billion air operation was as futile as the 1970 ground operation (which never found COSVN, a highly mobile enemy communications center, the intended main target of U.S. and South Vietnamese troops).

When the Cambodian operation was launched, Nixon was drinking heavily and watching the movie *Patton* at Camp David with his constant companion Bebe Rebozo. Slurring his words,

Nixon told Kissinger in one of his many boozy phone calls that night, "Wait a minute, Bebe has something to say to you."

"The President wants you to know if this doesn't work, Henry," said Rebozo, "it's your ass."[19]

Beyond its immediate devastating impact, the bombing of Cambodia had profound long-term implications, leading to widespread political instability. Racked by confusion and turmoil in 1975, Cambodia witnessed the rise to power of Pol Pot, a communist political and military organization that oversaw a reign of terror and atrocious human rights violations, and their Khmer Rouge movement.

The cost of the entire Indochina military misadventure has been quoted at 58,151 American deaths and more than 300,000 casualties. Untold millions of North and South Vietnamese, as well as Cambodians and Laotians, were killed or injured. And the cost to the United States Treasury was $670 billion.

Nixon continued the crime of his original 1968 sabotage by breaking the promises Thieu and the South Vietnamese relied on to end the bloody conflict. Instead, he only added to the carnage that Johnson could have ended that October.

On the Verge of Catastrophe

While the Vietnam War will be remembered for the staggering losses suffered on all sides of the conflict, we have only learned recently that they nearly went down in history as just the tip of the iceberg. In one of the most alarming moments in presidential history, a heavily intoxicated President Nixon ordered what would have been the only nuclear strike outside of the two bombs dropped by the United States against Japan in World War II. The revelation was jaw-dropping.

To his immense credit, Henry Kissinger ignored that order from the commander in chief, which was overheard by Kissinger aide David Young. Young told a colleague "of the time he was on the phone [listening] when Nixon and Kissinger were talking. Nixon was drunk, and he said, 'Henry, we've got to nuke them.'"[20]

Remarkably, this was not the only time Nixon directly ordered a nuclear attack that would have been carried out but not for the courageous decision by his aides not to follow them. In a similar incident, the CIA's top Vietnam expert, George Carver, reportedly said the president "became incensed and ordered a tactical nuclear strike" when North Korea shot down a U.S. spy plane in 1969. "The Joint Chiefs were alerted," according to Carver, "and asked to recommend targets, but Kissinger got on the phone to them. They agreed to do nothing until Nixon sobered up in the morning."[21]

Nixon's nuculear inclininations were not exclusive to his drunken episodes, however. In 1972, with the Nixon administration considering a tactical bombing of North Vietnamese dams and dikes along the Red River designed to cause countless deaths throughout the region, Nixon made clear his desire to hit them even harder.

> **Nixon:** I still think we ought to take the dikes out now. Will that drown people?
> **Kissinger:** About two hundred thousand people.
> **Nixon:** No, no, no, I'd rather use the nuculear bomb.[22]

An assuredly stunned Kissinger told the president, "That, I think, would just be too much." Nixon was no doubt puzzled by his national security advisor's hesitation at such unimaginable destruction. "The nuclear bomb," he asked his soon-to-be secretary of state, "does that bother you? . . . I just want you to think big, Henry, for Christsakes."[23]

The pattern of terrifying presidential orders went beyond the threat of nuclear annihilation. President Nixon's final defense secretary, James Schlesinger, should also be credited with doing the right thing when the commander in chief was depressed, drinking heavily, and on the verge of having to resign under the pressures of Watergate.

After learning that the joint chiefs of staff had been asked by Nixon "whether in a crunch there was support to keep him in power," Schlesinger instructed the chiefs not to obey any military orders coming from the White House.[24]

Schlesinger feared that Nixon might try to hang on to power through his crony, Gen. Robert Cushman—who was then commandant of the U.S. Marine Corps and a member of the joint chiefs. As Schlesinger later reflected, "[Cushman] might have acquiesced to a request from the White House for action. The last thing I wanted was to have the Marines ordered to the White House and then have to bring in the army to confront the Marines. It would have been a bloody mess."[25]

Author and journalist Christopher Hitchens says the episode resembled that of a "banana republic" or a "rogue state." In the Nixon era, the United States had a ruthless, paranoid, and unstable leader who did not hesitate to break the laws of his own country in order to violate the neutrality, menace the territorial integrity, or destabilize the internal affairs of other nations.[26]

After Nixon was safely out of the White House, the *Washington Post* disclosed that "Schlesinger requested a tight watch in the military chain of command to ensure that no extraordinary orders went out from the White House during the period of uncertainty [and] that no commanders of any forces should carry out orders which came from the White House, or elsewhere, outside the normal military channels."[27]

In 2000, Schlesinger defended his move, declaring: "I am proud of my role in protecting the chain of command. You could say it was synonymous with protecting the Constitution."[28]

One would be hard-pressed to look back at some of the horrors created by Nixon the politician—the clandestine sabotage of peace efforts in Vietnam, the total escalation of the war, and the public-trust-shattering Watergate saga—and contend that the country got off easy. Yet these recent revelations indicate just that.

Chapter 10

1968 All Over Again

The treasonous actions of the Nixon camp in the 1968 election cropped up in a fascinating twist of irony four years later when the president squared off against George McGovern in the 1972 presidential contest.

This time around, Nixon was the incumbent and Vietnam had become his mess, no longer Johnson's. As can be observed repeatedly throughout Nixon's political career, his willingness to toss principle to the wind in favor of personal success dominated his campaign tactics. While in 1968 that involved Nixon and Kissinger conspiring to prolong the war through clearly illegal backchannels, in 1972 the pair was concentrating on the positive impact a negotiating success would have on Nixon's reelection campaign.

In 1968, Republican presidential candidate Nixon wrongly believed President Johnson halted the bombing of North Vietnam to help Vice President Humphrey's political prospects. Just before the 1972 election, Kissinger had declared that "peace is at hand" (even though it wasn't)—which many observers thought was an effort to boost Nixon in the polls.

The contrasts, similarities, and ironies between the two campaigns do not stop there: In 1968, President Johnson could not drag South Vietnam's President Thieu to the bargaining table because he was hoping for a better deal from the prospective Nixon administration. In 1972, President Nixon also had a major problem with Thieu—who refused to sign a peace agreement Kissinger had negotiated with the North Vietnamese.

Furthermore, there was a pre-election bombing halt in 1968 and a significant post-election escalation of the bombing in 1972. Both moves were designed to entice North Vietnam into meaningful talks.

So let us take a more thorough look at how Nixon and Kissinger handled the war in 1972—as a political issue at home, a diplomatic process in Paris and Saigon, and as a military tactic in Vietnam. Thanks to newly available transcripts of tapes dealing with Nixon's foreign policy decisions, a more complete picture of that period is now emerging.

Nixon, Kissinger, and Thieu: Round 2

On August 2, 1972, Oval Office tapes recorded a conversation between the president and his national security advisor. Just back from productive talks with the North Vietnamese in Paris, Kissinger was optimistic about peace prospects:

> **Nixon:** The advantage, Henry, of trying to settle now, even if you're ten points ahead [in the polls] . . . you assure a hell of a landslide. And you might win the House and get increased strength in the Senate.
> **Kissinger:** And you'd have . . .
> **Nixon:** You'd have a mandate in the country.
> **Kissinger:** And you have the goddamned nightmare off your back, I mean . . .
> **Nixon:** Yeah.
> **Kissinger:** It's . . .
> **Nixon:** It's very important. Because you know it is a nightmare being there.[1]

Later in this same conversation, the two men discussed using the coming presidential election as leverage against North Vietnam in Paris:

> **Kissinger:** After November 7, if you get—there's no question you'll get reelected . . .
> **Nixon:** If we win . . . after November 7, school's out.
> **Kissinger:** That's right . . .
> **Nixon:** No foolin' around, because you say . . .
> **Kissinger:** We can't go through another two years . . .
> **Nixon:** [Unclear] we're going to take out the heart of, the heart of the installations in Hanoi.
> **Kissinger:** Right.

Nixon: We're going to take out the whole dock area, [Soviet] ships or no ships. Tell them, "Clear out of there." We'll stay away from the Chinese border. And, frankly, Henry, we may have to take the dikes out, not for the purpose of killing people.

Kissinger: Mr. President . . .

Nixon: Warn the people, tell them to get the hell out of there.

Kissinger: It's the dry season. I would take the dikes out.

Nixon: Sure.[2]

The Nixon team was undoubtedly motivated by the same political aims they once incorrectly accused the Johnson administration of acting on.

President Nixon's struggles with South Vietnam president Nguyen Van Thieu proved to be just as difficult as President Johnson's had been. After their first meeting, in Guam, Nixon told House and Senate leaders that Thieu "is the most impressive South Vietnamese leader I've met. That isn't saying a great deal."[3]

After Thieu rejected a new Nixon-endorsed peace plan in late September 1972, U.S. foreign policy honcho Henry Kissinger called both the North and South Vietnamese negotiators "insolent," but he saved his worst wrath for the communists. They were "just tawdry little shits," he asserted, according to Nixon.[4]

Finally, fed up with Thieu's intransigence, Nixon wrote him a not-so-subtle threat—delivered by hand by Amb. Ellsworth Bunker in late September 1972. Nixon alluded to the assassination of Thieu's predecessor, Pres. Ngo Dinh Diem, by his own officers in a U.S.-approved coup, instructing: "I would urge you to take every measure to avoid the development of an atmosphere which could lead to events similar to those we abhorred in 1963 . . ."[5]

In another verbal stab at Thieu, this one discovered on a recently released White House tape, Nixon tells Kissinger he would do anything to get the South Vietnamese president to accede to U.S. demands, even "cut off his head if necessary."[6]

On October 6, 1972, Nixon and Kissinger candidly addressed their problems with Thieu. In a newly released tape of that Oval Office discussion, Kissinger reported that Thieu was so upset with the current U.S. negotiating position, he believed "somewhere down the road he'll [Thieu] have no choice but to commit suicide. And he's probably right." A little later, Kissinger added: "And I also think Thieu is right, that our terms will eventually destroy him . . . given their weakness, their disunity, it will happen."[7]

Kissinger raged on against the Thieu regime: "They've lied to us again. They've substituted planes that they told us were better, that [NSC deputy Alexander] Haig [who had just returned from a fact-finding trip to Saigon] has found out aren't really so good. We're dealing with a sick military establishment, on top of everything else."

Nixon concurred, telling Kissinger: "Well, if they're that collapsible, maybe they just have to be collapsed . . . we've got to remember we cannot—we cannot keep this child sucking at the tit when the child is four years old."[8]

The month before the 1972 presidential election quickly developed a brimming optimism within the Nixon camp that they would be able to end the war before the election and waltz into a second term.

On October 11, Kissinger and North Vietnam's Le Duc Tho concluded meetings in Paris on a working draft of new Communist proposals. Kissinger flew back to Washington confident that he had just personally negotiated the end to one of the most vilified wars in American history. By all accounts the entire administration believed they had successfully pulled off a most impressive pre-election maneuver.

That night, the president met with Kissinger, Chief of Staff Bob Haldeman, and Deputy Assistant to the President for National Security Affairs Alexander Haig. Kissinger opened the meeting with a beaming smile, "Well, you've got three for three, Mr. President,"[9] referring to Nixon's opening up China, repairing diplomatic relations with the Soviet Union, and now apparently ending the Vietnam War. Kissinger went on to inform the president that the deal was far better than they had ever anticipated.

Nixon tried his best to temper his joy, asking Kissinger repeatedly about whether he thought Thieu would accept the terms hammered out with the North Vietnamese—and whether this truly was a done deal. Kissinger assured him that Thieu would be happy to accept any plan that kept him in power. Haig, who had gone to Paris with Kissinger, was less certain. Haldeman noted in his diary later that Haig "thought we were screwing Thieu . . . he is concerned whether we can sell Thieu on it."[10]

Haig's foresight would prove exceptionally accurate, as Thieu would continue to throw a serious wrench in the ambitious plans of Nixon's White House. Yet the optimists ruled the night. A celebratory Nixon ended the meeting, ordering up steaks from the White House mess and a bottle of the best wine in the house—a Lafite-Rothschild.[11]

Later that night, Nixon's chief of staff penned in his diary that "overall, it boils down to a super-historic night if it all holds together, and Henry [Kissinger] is now convinced it will. He thinks that he's really got the deal. So we'll see."[12]

The plan was then to start working on Thieu. Kissinger was soon off to Saigon to outline the agreement to the South Vietnamese president and voice Nixon's desire for a signing ceremony in Paris on October 31. However, the trip would prove to be much less fruitful than all had hoped for.

What exactly were the reasons for Thieu's reluctance to agree to the terms Nixon so strongly tried to force upon him? For starters, at the heart of all disagreement was what would be done with the approximately thirty thousand communist political prisoners being held by the South Vietnamese.

At his talks with Le Duc Tho in Paris, Kissinger effectively sidestepped the issue, telling the North Vietnamese, "We have looked for a formula in which we did not have to settle this issue now, but at the same time, retain the possibility of using our maximum influence to bring about a favorable result with our ally after a settlement is arranged."[13]

Tho and Kissinger elaborated on this soft promise that the U.S. would use its "maximum influence," and each side left the talks confident in the prospects of peace. After returning home and celebrating with Nixon, Kissinger was now off to Saigon to get Thieu to put his signature on the deal.

One could hardly imagine a worse meeting than the tense two-hour sit-down between Kissinger and Thieu in Saigon on October 19. Right off the bat, Thieu kept a "seething" Kissinger waiting for more than fifteen minutes, sensing that the Nixon administration that had so underhandedly betrayed him in the past was on the verge of selling out the South Vietnamese once again.

Thieu was right. Kissinger and the Nixon team were up to their old tricks. The president's emissary presented the main points of the agreement to Thieu, who scoffed at the notion of releasing some thirty thousand enemies of his nation while his strongest ally in the world removed itself from the conflict. And then when the South Vietnamese president naturally asked for a copy of the proposal agreed upon to review, Kissinger handed him a version in English that omitted much of the new, highly accelerated timetable based on Nixon's desired signing date of October 31. When Thieu demanded a copy in Vietnamese—which is obviously how the North Vietnamese would have been presented with the document as well—Kissinger apologized and claimed he forgot to bring it to the meeting.[14]

The South Vietnamese delegation was outraged, as one of Thieu's aides shouted at Kissinger: "We cannot negotiate the fate of our country in a foreign language!" Following this belligerent response, Kissinger gave Thieu a stern warning from President Nixon: "I believe that we have no reasonable alternative but to accept this agreement. It represents major movement by the other side, and it is my firm conviction that its implementation will leave you and your people with the ability to defend yourselves and decide the political destiny of South Vietnam."[15] By the end of the meeting, after Kissinger had left, Thieu expressed his frustration frankly: "I wanted to punch Kissinger in the mouth."[16]

Many in the Nixon administration simply could not believe that Thieu had the nerve to hold out on them and scoffed at Thieu's notion that he could get something better after the election. As Nixon's chief of staff so bluntly put it:

> Henry's convinced that he's got it settled, that it will work out and that we can talk Thieu into it. I would think he could, because the settlement he's got is the best Thieu is ever going to get and, unlike '68, when Thieu screwed Johnson, he had Nixon as an alternative. Now he has McGovern as an alternative, which would be a disaster for him, even worse than the worst possible thing that Nixon could do to him.[17]

On October 20, Gen. William Westmoreland explained to Nixon that Thieu was being so ornery because a U.S.-imposed settlement could prove fatal to Thieu's political future. Describing the South Vietnamese leader as an "extremely suspicious man who was devious, capable of sharp turns, and had a conspiratorial outlook that had enabled him to survive through many difficult years," Westmoreland went on to say it was "essential that the United States work patiently with Thieu and recognize the difficulty that relinquishment of his territory would pose."[18]

Thieu however, remained unconvinced. And as the election ticked ever-closer, President Nixon began to panic in regards to what to do about his South Vietnamese counterpart.

At a subsequent meeting with Thieu in Saigon, Kissinger read a telegram from Nixon putting further pressure on the South Vietnamese leader. The president threatened a cut off of American aid to Saigon: "Were you to find the agreement to be unacceptable at this point and the other side were to reveal the extraordinary limits to which it has gone in meeting demands put on them, it is my judgment that your decision would have the most serious effects upon my ability to continue to provide support for you and for the government of South Vietnam."[19]

Just as they had in 1968, Nixon and his team had pulled out all the stops, though this time Thieu would not buy into the group that had turned its back on him. Thieu did not budge — telling Kissinger, "I will not sign and I would like you to convey my position to Mr. Nixon."[20]

Thus, Kissinger returned from the talks in Saigon in a much less optimistic mood, and the Nixon team was left scrambling to try to produce the October Surprise they wanted to spring on McGovern. It appeared at this point that there would be no agreement to end the war before the election. Still, Nixon and his pals were undaunted, as they had a commanding lead in the polls.

Kissinger Takes Center Stage

However, things dramatically changed with a phone call from a frantic Henry Kissinger to Bob Haldeman at three o'clock in the morning on October 26.

It was just five days before the agreement was supposed to have been completed with that quintessential photo-op in Paris. But since Thieu had stopped all momentum of a potential deal in its tracks, the North Vietnamese had done something drastic in an attempt to force the other side to cooperate.

An irate Kissinger explained to Haldeman that the North Vietnamese had just leaked the details of the potential peace proposal to the media. As Haldeman later recollected of the phone call, "K[issinger] had been having considerable difficulty getting Thieu to accept the agreement, and the North Vietnamese had broadcast the plan to put pressure on Thieu and the U.S."[21]

The issue—the potential end of the war—immediately escalated from a major national news story to *the* world news story. Nixon was livid at the news, which came just weeks before the election that he seemed to have in the bag, and took it as an incredibly unwelcome wild card. He yelled at his aides, "Only great events can change things in the campaign now, and Vietnam is the only great event happening." Again, Nixon and his team attempted to hide the fact that they were behaving with the same political chicanery they routinely accused opponents of using. The president warned that above all they had to make sure it did not appear as if they were "playing politics with Vietnam."[22]

At a meeting later that day, Nixon made his deepest motivation unmistakably clear: to maintain the power he had so unscrupulously grasped rather than honor any commitment to admirable principles. Meanwhile, the peace talks remained a front-page issue and a lead story for the media. When presented with the question of whether to institute a bombing halt on the North Vietnamese or to maintain pressure to get them to cave, Nixon ordered his aides to conduct a poll.

The leak by the North Vietnamese government put the negotiations in a precarious situation. Some in Nixon's camp feared that they would be on the losing side this time around, just as Johnson and Humphrey were run out of the White House in 1968 by the same war.

As he often did, evangelist Billy Graham visited the White House on October 27, just ten days prior to the election. Unsurprisingly, the visit was all about politics and the minister's take on what Nixon ought to be doing to stay in the White House. He expressed a similarly dire concern for the situation with Vietnam. Haldeman noted that Graham "feels that if North Vietnam blows the peace deal it will be a real problem."[23]

Despite Thieu's hard line, Kissinger held an October 26 press conference in the White House briefing room. For Kissinger, it was a rare appearance before television cameras. Nixon and his aides thought Kissinger's German-accented, monotone voice would turn off viewers if he were regularly exposed to the medium.

At that session, Kissinger provided reporters with a run-for-the-telephone moment. He declared: "We have now heard from both Vietnams, and it is obvious that a war that has been raging for ten years is drawing to a conclusion . . . We believe peace is at hand. What remains to be done can be settled in one more negotiating session with the North Vietnamese negotiators—lasting, I would think, no more than three of four days."[24]

Though his national security advisor's declaration would certainly help him on Election Day, Nixon was worried that Kissinger had overstated the case for an imminent accord. Tape recorders in the Old Executive Office Building were rolling when Nixon told Bob Haldeman that Henry's statement would make it harder for U.S. negotiators to get concessions from Hanoi: "Now that sets up a hell of a hurdle. I wouldn't have said that."[25] Nixon viewed the press conference as Kissinger's attempt to equate solely himself with any potential peace settlement in Vietnam, thereby outshining Nixon on the issue. (As it happened, Kissinger and Le Duc Tho were awarded one of the most controversial Nobel Peace Prizes in history for their efforts to end the Vietnam War.) Bob Haldeman recalled: "We [Haldeman and Nixon] got into some discussions about Henry's attitude, along the same lines that Haig had expressed to me. . . . He shares the P[resident]'s view that Henry is strongly motivated in all this by a desire for personally being the one to finally bring about the final peace settlement."[26]

Nixon's own reelection team expressed similar concerns in the days winding down to the election. On October 24, exactly two weeks before votes would be cast, Nixon sat down with a few of his top political strategists for a regularly scheduled campaign meeting. Former Texas governor John Connally, who had been seated next to President Kennedy that fateful day in Dallas in 1963 and had since been nominated by President Nixon to serve as secretary of the treasury, dominated the meeting. He vocalized a concern that many had on their minds: "It's important that it appears that the President is in charge, that it's not Kissinger who is running this."[27]

In response to Kissinger's press conference, Nixon quickly and publicly tempered expectations for an early agreement. On the very night of Kissinger's announcement, during a campaign appearance in Huntington, West Virginia, the chief executive told an airport rally, "There has been a significant breakthrough [but] there are still differences to be worked out." Undoubtedly Nixon was frustrated at Kissinger's decision to speak confidently on the subject of the war, which forced the president to moderate the public's reaction.

From this point on, Nixon sought to direct more of the negotiations himself instead of using Kissinger as his proxy. The president's motivation for this decision was likely twofold: First, Nixon feared Kissinger would steal his limelight. Second, the prospects for ending the war now seemed strained at best, and Nixon believed that he needed to meet personally with Thieu to wrap up negotiations and effect a peace agreement once and for all. Kissinger strongly disagreed with this second point, of course, advising that Nixon merely send a "Presidential letter so they'll work on that basis."[28]

Kissinger's behavior in this matter followed a pattern that was also reflected in his involvement with the 1968 election: he pursued his own self-interests, regardless of past loyalty. Remember that Kissinger had been Nixon's mole in the 1968 peace talks; yet he nonetheless flirted with the notion of switching to the Humphrey camp when Humphrey picked up late momentum in the polls. Now, four years later, Kissinger would manipulate those around him to get ahead, regardless of the cost. If the war was going to end, it would be Kissinger — not Nixon — who would take the credit and enjoy the subsequent praise. But if the conflict in Vietnam dragged on, it would be the president — not the publicly optimistic and hardworking national security advisor — who would shoulder the blame. (Surely bitter about the entire situation, Nixon eventually added Kissinger to the list of individuals he illegally wiretapped.)

Kissinger's "peace is at hand" proclamation outraged Democratic presidential nominee George McGovern. He called it "a cruel political deception," adding: "There has been no major breakthrough for peace . . . instead there has been a fatal breakdown on the central issues and now this chance for an agreement is gone."[29] Election Day came and went, and the Vietnam War continued to rage on.

Nixon's Reelection

In the November 7 election, Nixon trounced McGovern, who won only Massachusetts and the District of Columbia in the Electoral College. Never mind that the peace talks had failed; Nixon had gotten the last reelection he would ever need. A celebrating Nixon probably enjoyed his White House dinner that night a little too much—a dental bridge came loose during the meal and the president lost a tooth. The incident put a damper on Nixon's plans, as the next morning he had to delay a trip to his Key Biscayne retreat a few hours to go to the dentist.

When Nixon called his chief of staff the night of the election to talk about the results, Haldeman recalled, "As he called me from the Residence, I worked in my office, I could hear his 'Victory at Sea' record playing loudly in the background."[30]

For his part, Sen. George McGovern was flabbergasted at the election results. "If anyone had told me [in 1968] that the war would be raging four years later, with the architects of that war victorious in 49 of 50 states, I would have said he was crazy," he admitted.[31]

When Nixon's 1968 campaign rival, Hubert Humphrey, telephoned the White House to congratulate the president, Nixon initially did not take his call. Around midnight, he decided to return it. Nixon shared with the Minnesota senator his optimistic take on the chances for a Vietnam settlement:

> **Nixon:** Hubert. How are you?
> **Humphrey:** Well, fine, and I wanted to call up just to congratulate you on this historic victory.
> **Nixon:** Well, thank you very much.
> **Humphrey:** You really racked 'em up.
> **Nixon:** You've been a very statesmanlike man. As I always, just speaking as friends, people ask me very privately to compare this with '68, and I said, "Well, the difference is that when Senator Humphrey and I were campaigning and we had this terrible issue of Vietnam, we both put the country first." And I said, "This time, we had a problem where one fellow [Senator McGovern] said any goddamn thing that came into his head."
> **Humphrey:** Yeah.
> **Nixon:** For your private information, you should know that for three days, I had the whole thing [the agreement] in my pocket.

Humphrey: Yes.

Nixon: [laughs] As you probably guessed.

Humphrey: Yes. I had a talk with Henry [Kissinger] a couple days ago.

Nixon: Right.

Humphrey: They asked me whether or not we could have got a settlement like this in '69, and I said no.

Nixon: Well, you made a great statement. I asked Henry to call you. I think you should know that . . .

Humphrey: Thank you.

Nixon: . . . within ten days you will see, it's all fallen into place.[32]

In this chat, Humphrey could have well countered Nixon's claim that they both "put the country first" in 1968. But he was too polite to rain on the president's victory parade by citing Nixon's 1968 betrayal of his country's search for peace in Indochina. The president, in turn, was himself putting a Kissinger-like spin on peace prospects. For Thieu was still not onboard. In fact, soon after the election, North Vietnam negotiators had second thoughts about the agreement.

Out of Vietnam

Let down by their failure to end the war by the election and riled up by Nixon's victory, the president and Kissinger were soon reconsidering intensifying the bombing in Vietnam as a way to push the negotiations back on track. The critical decision to do so was made at a lengthy Oval Office meeting among Nixon, Kissinger, and Alexander Haig on December 14. During that long brainstorming session, Nixon suggested that the bombing be cloaked with a false reason—a buildup of communist troops, perhaps.

Kissinger initially recommended that intensified B-52 raids be carried out over a six-month period. Haig even brought along the estimated cost of a six-month bombing campaign: $3 billion. This meeting resulted in what immediately became known as the "Christmas Bombing." At one point, Kissinger seemed to be almost begging the commander in chief to act:

Kissinger: Mr. President, if you don't do this . . .
Nixon: [laughs]
Kissinger: . . . you'll be . . .
Nixon: I'll do it.
Kissinger: . . . then you'd really be impotent, and you'll be caught between the liberals and the conservatives. And, besides, we'll be totally finished by February. They'll just be chopping the salami.[33]

Nixon and Kissinger eventually got Thieu to go along with a peace accord in early 1973. Just before the treaty was signed, Kissinger advised Nixon against announcing that this was a "lasting peace or guaranteed peace because this thing is almost certain to blow up sooner or later."[34]

On January 23, 1973, President Nixon neglected the Kissinger-nixed superlatives, but he did state in a nationwide address that a peace agreement had been initialed in Paris "to end the war and bring peace with honor in Vietnam and Southeast Asia." What he also left out was that—in order to get our stubborn ally to sign off on the deal—Nixon had pledged Thieu $1 billion in military equipment, an amount that would provide for South Vietnam to become the fourth-largest air force in the world, according to a later PBS investigation. Nixon also assured Thieu the United States would re-enter the war if North Vietnam broke the treaty.[35]

Nixon's promises were empty, as they usually were to the South Vietnamese. With his war powers now greatly reduced and anti-war sentiment on the rise at home, the president had become a scandal-diminished chief executive whose own party leaders would soon force from the White House in disgrace.

By 1975, the North-tilting 1973 treaty—which left 140,000 North Vietnamese troops *inside* South Vietnam—collapsed (as Nixon and Kissinger had privately and cynically predicted). The consequences of the communist takeover included America's first lost war and the end of Thieu's regime. The South Vietnamese leader would have been much better off had he *not* listened to Richard Nixon and gone to Paris to negotiate on Pres. Lyndon Johnson's 1968 proposals.

Nguyen Van Thieu, the last president of South Vietnam, was cornered with plenty of time to ponder the gruesome slaying of his predecessor, Ngo Dinh Diem, in a 1963 CIA-backed coup. During this coup, Diem and his brother Ngo Dinh Nhu escaped the presidential palace in a limo with a suitcase filled with $1 million U.S. dollars and 88 pounds of two-pound gold ingots.[36] Apparently the looting was the norm for corrupt South Vietnamese presidents. But brothers Diem and Nhu eventually surrendered; and as they were being transported to military headquarters, both were assassinated, shot at point-blank range with a semi-automatic firearm. Their bodies were then sprayed with bullets and repeatedly stabbed with knives.

One of the first White House tasks of E. Howard Hunt, later to become Nixon's spymaster, was to fabricate State Department documents that would make it look as though President Kennedy had approved the 1963 Diem assassination. But the intended source to publicize this faked material, *Life* magazine, was not fooled. Hunt had to rely on a razor blade and a Xerox machine to create his unconvincing counterfeit concoction of JFK era cables. The "exclusive" story was spiked.

Nixon himself, however, had gotten into the act of sliming JFK for Diem's murder. At a September 16, 1971, news conference, he was asked about Sen. Henry Jackson's comment that the president possessed great leverage in Vietnam because of the massive U.S. aid program. The answer was completely unanticipated. Nixon had JFK and Diem on his mind: "If what the senator is suggesting is that the United States should use its leverage now to overthrow Thieu, I would remind all concerned that the way we got into Vietnam was through the overthrowing of Diem, and the complicity in the murder of Diem."

Nixon biographer J. Anthony Lukas says Nixon's answer puzzled White House and State Department officials who say they do not know where the President got such information. "They say there is nothing to support it in the briefing book prepared for that press conference, nor in any position paper or research document they know of."

When the impending overrun by communist troops loomed over Saigon in 1975, the CIA's Frank Snepp was dispatched to pick up Thieu so he could be taken out of the country on a secret flight: "He was dressed in a gray sharkskin suit. His hair was slicked, his face oiled. But he was drunk. He had been drinking heavily. His aides, as we invited him to get into the limousine, came running out of the bushes with suitcases. And, as they shoved them into the back of my car, you could hear the clink of metal upon metal. He was moving the last of his personal fortune out of the country — millions and millions of dollars in gold bullion, I'm told."[37] Thieu wound up living quietly in an affluent Boston suburb, where, in 2001, he died at age seventy-six. In its obituary of the former South Vietnamese president, the *New York Times* observed that Thieu's government was based on personal loyalty from his generals and provincial chiefs: "It was an old-fashioned, Confucian system, often greased by corruption, that had great difficulty competing against the better organized and motivated communists, despite the support of 500,000 American troops [at the height of the war] and billions of dollars in aid."[38]

What the *Times* did not mention was that U.S. troops had left behind a military gold mine for the South Vietnamese when they pulled out in 1973: $5 billion dollars' worth of top-of-the-line equipment — including hundreds of tanks; 500 fighter-bombers; 625

Presidents Nixon and Thieu make a joint statement at Midway Island, June 8, 1969, that 25,000 American troops would be withdrawn from Vietnam by the end of August 1969 (Courtesy National Archives and Records Administration)

helicopters; plus an arms supply that could equip a 700,000-man army. But that didn't stop advancing communist forces from facing only feeble resistance as they routed the ill-disciplined and starving South Vietnamese foot soldiers they encountered during their 1975 push south.

President Richard Nixon's ultimate Vietnam strategy—U.S. troop withdrawals and intensified B-52 bombings—was doomed. As Adm. Elmo Zumwalt later opined: "There were at least two words no one can use to characterize the outcome of the two-faced policy. One is 'peace.' The other is 'honor.'"[39]

Nixon conspired to keep the Vietnam War going in 1968 and was unable to end it for a political boost in 1972. As a result of his playing politics with the war, 11,780 American soldiers died in 1969, the year Nixon took office and inherited a war he prevented his successor—and the American people—from ending.

President Nixon escalated the war, and a total of 21,195 Americans died in combat during his presidency alone.[40] During his years in the White House, more than three times as many soldiers died in Vietnam than have died in the wars in Iraq and Afghanistan combined; this loss of life during the Vietnam War was potentially avoidable had Johnson been given a fighting chance to end it in 1968.[41]

Chapter 11
Covering Up the Crime

Richard Nixon employed his presidential powers not only to escalate and expand the Vietnam War but also to find and bury any evidence of his criminal derailment of previous Democratic efforts to bring a negotiated end to the conflict. After months of hounding the CIA, Nixon was unable to obtain any of its files on his 1968 sabotage. When he learned that the full files on his "treason" might be housed at a liberal Washington think tank, the Brookings Institution, he was excited—and determined to steal them.

On June 17, 1971, Nixon met in the Oval Office with Henry Kissinger, Bob Haldeman, and John Ehrlichman to discuss the files he so desperately desired to discover and destroy:

Haldeman: The bombing halt stuff is all in that same file or in some of the same hands . . . [Haldeman thought LBJ's 1968 bombing halt decision was a political move to help Humphrey win the election— which it was not—and that such information could be used to blackmail the ex-president into supporting Nixon's Vietnam policies.]

Nixon: Do we have it? I've asked for it. You said you didn't have it.

Haldeman: We can't find it.

Kissinger: We have nothing here, Mr. President.

Nixon: Well, damnit, I asked for that because I need it. [Nixon needed the file for his political survival—to determine whether the NSA, CIA, and FBI had directly implicated him in the sabotage.]

Haldeman: We have a basic history in constructing our own, but there is a file on it.

Nixon: Where?

Haldeman: [Presidential aide Tom Charles] Huston swears to God there's a file on it and it's at Brookings [the left-leaning DC think tank about a mile from the White House].

Nixon: . . . Bob? Bob? Now do you remember Huston's plan [for White House-sponsored break-ins as part of domestic counter-intelligence operations]? Implement it.

> **Kissinger:** . . . Now Brookings has no right to have classified documents.
> **Nixon:** Now I want it implemented . . . Goddamnit, get in and get those files. Blow the safe and get it.
> **Haldeman:** They may very well have cleaned them by now, but this thing, you need to . . .
> **Kissinger:** I wouldn't be surprised if Brookings had the files.[1]

Of course, Kissinger was just as anxious as Nixon to obtain the files, for they might well expose his tawdry role in the sabotage when he served as candidate Nixon's informant inside LBJ's delegation to the 1968 Paris peace negotiations.

To Nixon, as he later conceded, Brookings seemed like the reasonable repository for LBJ's Vietnam files: "It was the government-in-exile for the liberal Kennedy-type Democrats who hoped to be back in power. And the Brookings Institution had plans—after the Pentagon Papers came out—to put out a further study with regard to the war in 1969 and 1970."[2]

What Nixon did not know was that the material covered in the Pentagon Papers only considered events through mid-1968, months before the height of his own sabotage efforts, the LBJ bombing halt, and the start of the Nixon presidency.

On July 30, 1971, Nixon held an Oval Office session with Haldeman, Kissinger, John Mitchell, Ron Ziegler, and Melvin Laird at which he ordered that his chief White House spy—E. Howard Hunt—be directed to burglarize the Brookings Institution:

> **Nixon:** They [Brookings] have a lot of material . . . I want Brookings. I want them just to break in and take it out. Do you understand?
> **Haldeman:** Yeah. But you have to have somebody to do it.
> **Nixon:** That's what I'm talking about. Don't discuss it here. You talk to [E. Howard] Hunt. I want the break in. Hell, they do that. You're to break into the place, rifle the files, and bring them in.
> **Haldeman:** I don't have any problem with breaking in. It's a Defense Department approved security . . .
> **Nixon:** Just go in and take it. Go in around 8:00 or 9:00 o'clock.
> **Haldeman:** Make an inspection of the safe.
> **Nixon:** That's right. You go in to inspect the safe. I mean *clean it up*."[3]

The president wasn't taking any chances his orders might be

ignored. After all, he needed those files to avoid impeachment and a possible prison sentence. His White House dirty-tricks specialist, Charles Colson, was also tasked to confiscate the Vietnam files: "I was in the president's office one night and the president turned to me and he said: 'You get a hold of John Ehrlichman and you tell him to get a hold of the Pentagon, and get a hold of the FBI — and do whatever is necessary. I want those documents back from Brookings.'"[4]

In the end, Ehrlichman, Colson, Hunt, and G. Gordon Liddy were among Nixon's chief operators in the Brookings burglary conspiracy.

To further his plot to gain the Vietnam files, Nixon secretly set up the Special Investigations Unit within the White House. Known as "the Plumbers" — as its ostensible aim was to find and plug leaks — the unit was also authorized to break the law in order to protect national security. FBI chief J. Edgar Hoover had earlier nixed such a plan as illegal, but Nixon didn't see it that way. He seemed to believe in the divine rights of presidents: as noted earlier, he later infamously declared, "When the President does it, that means it's not illegal."[5] So the Plumbers were off and running — running wild, it seems, with a harebrained scheme "masterminded" by Liddy, who was considered the loosest of cannons even by many of the president's top aides.

The scheme called for the firebombing of Brookings by Hunt-recruited Cuban exiles from Miami (who would later break into DNC headquarters at the Watergate). The exiles would arrive at Brookings in an old fire truck, repainted with the markings and insignia of the DC Fire Department. After firebombing the building, the fake fire crew would rush into Brookings, break into the vaults, make off with the Vietnam files, drive the truck a few blocks, and transfer the incriminating files and themselves to a waiting van — then safely speed away in the ensuing confusion.

First, however, at Ehrlichman's direction, ex-New York City detective Tony Ulasewicz "cased the joint." Placed on the White House payroll by Ehrlichman as an all-purpose spy, Ulasewicz pretended to be a tourist at Brookings: "I reported by phone . . . that it certainly was a great looking establishment, all marble halls, [but] well-guarded."[6]

When Nixon's White House lawyer John Dean got wind of the Brookings plan, he had a far more sensible take on the projected operation. Dean convinced Ehrlichman that if anyone died in the firebombing, it would be a capital crime that might be traced back to the White House. Ehrlichman later acknowledged shutting down the bizarre idea and confirmed that Nixon knew of it in advance.[7]

Had Dean not prevailed, had the firebombing and break-in actually occurred, had it involved a death, and had it been botched as badly as the 1972 Watergate burglary, then murder and domestic terrorism might well have been added to Nixon's record of impeachable offenses.

However, the Brookings break-in plan had an even greater drawback: the Vietnam files were not there. President Johnson had taken all of the CIA, FBI, and NSA documents with him in January 1969 when he left the White House and retired to his Texas ranch.

The Pentagon Papers

At the same time Nixon suspected Brookings might well possess his "treasonous" secrets, another Vietnam disclosure heightened his natural paranoia about the very same concern: On June 13, 1971, the *New York Times* published the first installment of what could appropriately be dubbed a journalistic bombshell on a timer, entitled "Vietnam Archive: Pentagon Study Traces Three Decades of Growing US Involvement." The material would soon become widely known as the Pentagon Papers.

The information published came from a leaked copy of a study commissioned by Secretary of Defense Robert McNamara—without the knowledge of President Johnson—in 1967. It was intended to be "an encyclopedic record of the Vietnam War" for reference by future administrations. The study comprised forty-seven volumes, including three thousand pages of historical studies and four thousand pages of government documents. Only fifteen copies were printed, and the tome was labeled "Top Secret-Sensitive," denoting potentially embarrassing content.[8]

In charge of the study was John McNaughton, assistant secretary of defense for international security affairs. One of the other men who worked on the study was Daniel Ellsberg, a Harvard PhD in economics and a familiar face to many in Washington. After serving in the Marine Corps, Ellsberg worked for the RAND Corporation before spending a year as McNaughton's special assistant. Ellsberg was responsible for reviewing all incoming information on Vietnam. Following his tenure in this position, Ellsberg spent some time in Vietnam as a foreign service officer and then was recruited by Henry Kissinger to work directly on the Pentagon Papers as a consultant to National Security staff.

In 1969, having returned to RAND the year before, Ellsberg requested copies of the study on which he had assisted; at the urging of Morton Halperin (a friend of Ellsberg's who similarly had deep reservations about many key foreign policy decisions and was originally suspected by the Nixon administration of being "Deep throat"), Leslie Gelb, one of the officials who had worked on the Vietnam study, supplied Ellsberg with the file. During his time in and studying Vietnam, Ellsberg's views had become staunchly opposed to the war, and now that he held "7,000 pages of documentary evidence of lying by four Presidents and their Administrations over 23 years to conceal plans and actions of mass murder," he was determined to "get it out somehow."[9]

Ellsberg recruited a friend and colleague, Anthony J. Russo Jr., to help with the effort, and on the night of October 1, the two went to work copying the study, page by page, on a machine owned by a friend of Russo's. Multiple copies were made of the papers, which Ellsberg smuggled by briefcase, volume by volume, out of RAND each night and returned the following morning.

Quietly, the soon-to-be-whistleblower offered the explosive documents first to Washington officials including Sens. J. William Fulbright and George McGovern, under the theory that their privilege as members of Congress would entitle them to immunity if they read the documents into the record. He was repeatedly turned down. But in February 1971, Ellsberg finally found a taker: Neil Sheehan, a reporter for the *New York Times*.

In March, Ellsberg provided Sheehan with forty-three of the volumes, withholding only the four volumes that covered the period between 1964-1968, desiring to avoid accusations that his leaks had damaged the ongoing peace process. Years later, Ellsberg recalled: "I omitted them because I thought that Nixon would use the release as an excuse for breaking off negotiations with North Vietnam. I frankly didn't want to give him that excuse."[10]

Sheehan approached his editors, who consulted their lawyers. They were warned against publication by outside attorneys, but the *Times'* in-house counsel, James Goodale, argued in favor of publication based on the First Amendment. The editorial board gave the green light, and the first installment screamed across the front page of the Sunday edition in black-and-white glory.[11]

Rather than publish all seven thousand pages, which would be an impossible task (and profoundly tedious to readers and editors alike), the *Times* planned to print 134 of the study documents along with introductions and summaries written by the newspaper's staff. Still, the initial publication was lackluster, described by *Time* magazine as "six pages of deliberately low-key prose and column after gray column of official cables, memorandums, and position papers. The mass of material seemed to repel readers and even other newsmen. Nearly a day went by before the networks and wire services took note."[12]

Initially, even Nixon seemed unconcerned, as the Pentagon Papers covered the Vietnam War only through most of the Johnson presidency. The Republican president believed most of the blame would fall on the Democrats who had unleashed full-scale war.

Henry Kissinger, however, vehemently warned Nixon that action must be taken to control and rectify "this wholesale theft and unauthorized disclosure." As Kissinger would write later in his memoirs, "The massive hemorrhage of state secrets was bound to raise doubts about our reliability in the minds of other governments, friend or foe, and indeed about the stability of our political system."[13] And, of course, Kissinger had to protect himself — it was his own underling who had leaked the study. Even more potentially damaging, though, was the prospect that his role as Nixon's spy at the 1968 Paris negotiation might be found in the Vietnam files.

Inevitably, the news spread and the public awakened to the delicious developing scandal. And so unfolded the events of the greatest whistle-blowing event of the twentieth century.

Almost immediately, the Nixon Justice Department intervened

to stop publication of the Pentagon Papers. Other news sources that attempted to publish the documents found themselves hindered by similar restraining orders.

Ellsberg returned to the idea of publishing the documents through a member of Congress. This time, Democratic senator Mike Gravel of Alaska accepted the mantle. Using Ben Bagdikian, editor of the *Washington Post,* as a go-between to transfer the documents, they made the switch in the dark of night outside the Mayflower Hotel in downtown Washington, with Gravel speeding away as soon as the briefcase was placed in his trunk.

On June 29, Gravel attempted to read the Pentagon Papers into the Senate record as part of a filibuster of Nixon's request to renew the draft. Parliamentary procedure precluded Gravel from doing so. Instead, he resorted to calling a late-night hearing of the Public Buildings and Grounds Subcommittee (on which he sat), presented a carefully constructed argument for relevancy, and read aloud from the papers for three hours. His point made and physically exhausted, Gravel submitted the entirety of the report to be published in the official *Congressional Record.*

The next day, June 30, the United States Supreme Court ruled in *New York Times Co. v. United States,* now a landmark case in First Amendment jurisprudence. Though each of the nine justices wrote his own opinion and disagreement on substantive issues was laced throughout, the essence of the 6-3 ruling was that the government did not meet the burden of proof required for prior restraint of publication. The *New York Times* and other news outlets could and would continue publication of the Pentagon Papers. The same day, Daniel Ellsberg was indicted by the U.S. Attorney for two counts of theft and espionage.

The Pentagon Papers were not so much surprising as irrefutably conclusive — confirming much of the worst that many in America and the international community had long suspected. The *Washington Post* editorialized: "The story that unfolds is not new in its essence — the calculated misleading of the public, the purposeful manipulation of public opinion, the stunning discrepancies between public pronouncements and private plans — we had bits and pieces of all that before. But not in such incredibly damning form, not with such irrefutable documentation."[14]

To start with, the United States had actually been involved in Southeast Asia since the Truman administration, which provided military aid to France as the latter nation waged a colonial war against the Viet Minh. The documents also contained evidence that the Kennedy administration, contrary to public proclamations of shock as events had unfolded, was in fact directly involved in the November 1963 coup against South Vietnamese president Ngo Dinh Diem. A cable from late August of that year put Amb. Henry Cabot Lodge on record with the words, "We are launched on a course from which there is no respectable turning back: the overthrow of the Diem government."[15] Not the first or last coup orchestrated by American forces, but certainly an explosive one.

It also became apparent that Johnson had inveigled the country into continued war by quietly escalating operations under cover. A September 1964 memo by McNaughton suggested that U.S. action "should be likely at some point to provoke a military response [and] the provoked response should be likely to provide good grounds for us to escalate if we wished" — all while ensuring that such action not be "distorted to the U.S. public."[16]

Furthermore, the entire purpose of the war — ostensibly to prevent the hypothetical domino effect from turning Southeast Asia an alarming shade of communist red — came into question. Far from a goal of securing an "independent, non-Communist South Vietnam," as Johnson had claimed in 1964, a March 1965 "Plan for Action for Vietnam" written by McNaughton listed U.S. priorities as follows: "70 percent — To avoid a humiliating US defeat (to our reputation as a guarantor). 20 percent — To keep SVN (and the adjacent) territory from Chinese hands. 10 percent — To permit the people of SVN to enjoy a better, freer way of life. ALSO — To emerge from the crisis without unacceptable taint from methods used. NOT — To 'help a friend,' although it would be hard to stay in if asked out."[17]

"They Got Away With It"

Nixon, already in a perpetual state of stark paranoia even before this massive intelligence leak, became a man obsessed. Of utmost import to him was finding out what information on his own misdeeds had been recorded—and also ensuring any records or files were secure and safely out of the hands of any who might betray his secret.

The greatest threat of all was Lyndon Johnson, now retired in Texas but in frequent contact with Nixon (perhaps in a case of keeping one's friends close and enemies closer). Anything that was known about Nixon's sabotage was certainly known by Johnson; and he would also know (if not personally, then of) and have a level of control over anyone else that had knowledge. To make matters more volatile, Johnson was under heavy fire from all directions due to the information revealed in the Pentagon Papers—and Nixon couldn't be sure Johnson would not try to re-direct the public's venom toward him.

Nixon and his team still believed that Johnson's timing of the peace talks was directly related to desires to manipulate the election in Humphrey's favor and that Johnson had bugged their campaign plane. Furthermore, Nixon was coming to terms with the harsh reality that information, even the top secret type, can be terribly difficult to contain.

As noted, Nixon aide Tom Charles Huston suspected the Brookings Institution was in possession of a top-secret file on the 1968 bombing halt. Furthermore, Leslie Gelb was now at Brookings and vocally in opposition to the administration. In 1970, Huston had written a memo proposing a break-in to Brookings to retrieve this file. Though J. Edgar Hoover had rejected the idea, a year later and a year closer to election time, the proposal was resurfacing. That's when an unglued Nixon demanded: "Goddamnit, get in and get those files. Blow the safe and get it."

"But what good will it do you, the bombing halt file?" asked Kissinger.

"To blackmail him. Because he used the bombing halt for political purposes," Nixon explained.

"The bombing halt file would really kill Johnson," backed Haldeman.[18]

Thus, based on erroneous information about Johnson's misbehavior in the previous election, the Nixon team began plotting further criminal activity in order to both cover up Nixon's wrongdoing and to blackmail a former president of the United States.

It was at that same meeting that Henry Kissinger began a concerted character assault on Daniel Ellsberg. Kissinger accused the leaker of all manner of sin—from perverted sex acts to heavy drug use (which, the national security advisor posited, likely were the cause of Ellsberg's unfortunate deterioration into pacifism), and even concocted stories of his shooting peasants from a helicopter during his time in Vietnam.

In fact, it was Kissinger who hired Ellsberg as a consultant to the Security Council staff and who supported the younger man's quest to work on the Vietnam study. It was Kissinger alone—and not Nixon or the other aides—who was mentioned personally in the study itself. And it was Kissinger who stood to lose the most at Ellsberg's hand: his personal integrity, professional reputation, and political power all hung in the balance.

In maligning Ellsberg, Kissinger used exactly the tone and accusations that he knew would rile President Nixon—and he succeeded. Nixon, understanding from the start that the Pentagon Papers' release posed no major national security threat, decided to use the events to gain political capital with which to attack his much-hated Democratic and anti-war opponents.[19]

Supported by his inner circle, Nixon believed there was a full-blown conspiracy being waged against him by Ellsberg and other pro-peace members of the Democratic Party, perhaps assisted even by the communists (despite the fact that absolutely no evidence could be found supporting this).

So the Plumbers were founded and Nixon's order to break into Brookings was more than illegal, according to Terry Lenzner, a Senate Watergate Committee official. "It is the President ordering a felony to obtain information," he acknowledged. Lenzner opined that this, in itself, "would be an impeachable offense."[20]

Another of the early acts by the Plumbers was a Beverly Hills break-in to the office of Dr. Lewis J. Fielding, Daniel Ellsberg's psychoanalyst. Nixon hoped his men would retrieve Ellsberg's records or other blackmail-worthy material, but they came up empty handed.

Later the Plumbers would be responsible for the botched break-in at the Watergate complex, which led to the unraveling of Nixon's entire conspiracy-ridden presidency.

As the Nixon administration collapsed following the Watergate scandal, Walt Rostow wrote in a May 4, 1973, Memorandum for the Record for the LBJ Library:

> I am inclined to believe the Republican operation of 1968 relates in two ways to the Watergate affair of 1972.
>
> First, the election of 1968 proved to be close and there was some reason for those involved on the Republican side to believe their enterprise with the South Vietnamese and Thieu's recalcitrance may have sufficiently blunted the impact on U.S. politics of the total bombing halt and agreement to constitute the margins of victory.
>
> Second, they got away with it. Despite considerable commentary after the election, the matter was never investigated fully.
>
> Thus, as the same [Nixon] men faced the election of 1972, there was nothing in their previous experience with an operation of doubtful propriety (or even legality) to warn them off; and there were memories of how close an election could get and the possibility of pressing the limit — or beyond.[21]

In late December of 1971, Daniel Ellsberg faced further indictments, this time with Anthony Russo named as a co-defendant and co-conspirator. Ellsberg now faced five counts of theft and six counts of espionage for a total maximum sentence of 105 years; Russo faced one count of theft and two of espionage, with up to twenty-five years in prison.

In a twist of irony, it would be the Plumbers — acting on Nixon's orders — that saved the men from hard prison time. The break-in at Dr. Fielding's office failed to remain secret, prompting prosecutor Earl Silbert to dismiss all charges in May 1973 due to government overreach, informing Judge Byrne that, "On Sunday, April 15, 1973, I received information that on a date unspecified, Gordon Liddy and Howard Hunt burglarized the offices of a psychiatrist of Daniel Ellsberg to obtain the psychiatrist's filings."[22]

Ellsberg walked away a free man, his actions unsurpassed until the even greater intelligence leaks of Chelsea Manning and Edward Snowden swept the globe some four decades later.

In 2011, the U.S. government commemorated the fortieth anniversary of the Pentagon Papers leaks by finally declassifying the entire report, until then unpublished in full. The study can now be viewed online through the National Archives.

Chapter 12

"Nixon's the One"

The White House intelligence specialist who studied the question of whether the Johnson administration was playing politics with the peace negotiations in 1968 for President Nixon is now convinced that Nixon himself led the effort to keep Saigon from the 1968 Paris peace talks. The president ordered this top aide to dig up what he could on Johnson and Humphrey working together to swindle Nixon out of the election by propping up a peace negotiation right before the election. However, the aide walked away from the assignment with the exact opposite view, uncovering that it was actually Nixon who was playing politics with the war. Nixon loyalist Tom Charles Huston says, "I've concluded that there was no doubt that Nixon was—would have been—directly involved [because] it's not something that anybody would have undertaken on their own."[1]

Just who is this man President Nixon trusted so highly he chose him to dig around in the graveyard of Nixon's darkest secret? Young Tom Huston was a pro-war ultra-conservative who worked in the 1968 Nixon campaign while finishing up his service as an Army intelligence officer. At the Nixon White House, the twenty-nine-year-old was put in charge of a domestic security committee—where he pushed for a hard line against anti-war protestors and left-wingers. In one top-secret memo he wrote: "Perhaps lowered voices and peace in Vietnam will diffuse the tense situation we face, but I wouldn't want to rely on it exclusively."[2]

Huston went gung-ho in his new job—using a scrambler telephone he kept locked in a safe near his side to communicate with various intelligence agencies and police. This reportedly led at least one White House secretary to derisively refer to him as "X-5" behind his back.[3]

He quickly rose through the ranks, becoming one of Nixon's top young aides and gaining infamy in 1973 as the author of the eponymous "Huston Plan," which laid the foundation for the Watergate break-in. The plan was ordered by a power-hungry Nixon who wanted desperately to place federal intelligence gathering under White House control rather than the Federal Bureau of Investigation.

A secondary motivation for this order by the president involved Nixon's desire to enhance domestic surveillance on his political opponents and the "left-wing radicals" that were "tearing the country apart" in his view. According to Nixon's assuredly solid facts, "hundreds, perhaps thousands, of Americans — mostly under thirty — are determined to destroy our society." Huston was tasked with cooking up ways for the administration to better crack down on these dissenters, and his recommendations compiled in 1970 surely would have done just that.[4]

The forty-three page report initially called for some incredibly drastic and constitutionally repugnant practices to be implemented by the Nixon administration. The proposal was based around increased domestic electronic surveillance, illegal break-ins and mail openings, and the planting of more informants on college campuses. While some of the more extreme options — for example, detention camps — were initially struck from the original plan, it still remains one of the more shocking surveillance proposals in American history.

That being said, the Huston plan was never specifically implemented; intelligence guru J. Edgar Hoover refused to sign off on something so extreme, let alone anything that would remove the intelligence apparatus from the control of his beloved bureau of investigation. Despite Nixon's strong support for the recommendations Huston put forth, Hoover was able to stop the plan dead in its tracks.

The aging but still powerful Hoover told Atty. Gen. John Mitchell, his nominal superior, that he would not authorize actions he considered illegal without the president's signature. Clearly Hoover had the insight that many underlings of Nixon lacked: he would not do something illegal ordered by the president with only his own signature down on paper approving the plans. Nor would he share FBI information with other agencies. He also argued that times had changed and that, with more security guards and police now on the scene, secret intelligence agents were more likely to be caught. This, Hoover informed Mitchell, might lead to embarrassing disclosures of other instances of illegal government surveillance and arouse the passions of civil liberties groups and what Hoover called "the jackals of the press."[5] After his talk with Hoover, Mitchell informed the president that the Huston Plan was "inimical to the best interests of the country and certainly should not be something that the President of the United States should be approving."[6]

So J. Edgar Hoover had prevailed over Tom Charles Huston, the man he privately called "that snot-nosed kid" and "that hippie intellectual." Most important, Hoover had defeated a plan the president had endorsed. Nixon would soon be plotting to replace Hoover with a more compliant FBI chief, but this would turn out to be something else the president was unable to pull off.

However, history has proven that parts of the plan clearly made it into the Nixon playbook. Most notably, the creation of the Plumbers unit was straight out of the Huston Plan, the group eventually being caught for breaking into the Democratic Headquarters at the Watergate hotel.

When the Huston Plan was made public in the summer of 1973, Senate Watergate Committee chairman Sam Ervin said it reflected a "Gestapo mentality."[7] It certainly appeared at the time to be the basis for many of the "White House Horrors" (so described by Atty. Gen. John Mitchell) that shook the nation and ousted a sitting president for the first time in American history.

Intelligence Relating to a 1968 October Surprise

While the Huston Plan has garnered significant attention over the years, obviously due to its relevance in the affair that actually produced the demise of Nixon, it is one of Huston's other intelligence projects that is of vital interest to our inquiry of the 1968 election.

The aforementioned stunning comments made by Huston condemning his own boss, President Nixon, for committing what could be defined as treason came in declassified interviews released by the National Archives in 2014. The 1971 report he prepared on Johnson for Nixon, though, remains classified. Several portions of these Huston interviews have been redacted for reasons of national security. It was not known until their release that such a report was ever made for Nixon.[8]

As mentioned earlier, a consistently "paranoid" Nixon, as many of his aides would later describe him, believed that President Johnson was conspiring with his vice president, Humphrey, to give him an incredible October Surprise. According to Nixon's suspicions, the bombing halt Johnson instituted in the months before the election was a desperate attempt to end the war and gain momentum for Humphrey in the polls. It wasn't. Rather, Johnson was more concerned with genuinely ending the war that by all accounts took years off his life in stress as he paced the halls of the White House. Johnson saw a genuine opportunity to end the war, as he believed the North Vietnamese were on the verge of agreeing to sit down for talks. His suspicions were correct, and the bombing halt helped bring them to the table.

We know of Nixon's duplicitous nature through conversations he had with both Johnson and Humphrey leading up to the election, conversations that Huston very well may have dug up during his investigation of the matter.

On October 16, 1968, with the election just a few weeks away, the president called for a conference call just before noon as he often did with all three major presidential candidates: Nixon, Humphrey, and George Wallace of the American Independent Party.

Johnson: This is in absolute confidence because any statement or any speeches or any comments at this time referring to the substance of these matters will be injurious to your country. I don't think there's any question about that.

First I want to say this: That our position, the government position, today is exactly what it was the last time all three of you were briefed. That position namely is this: We are anxious to stop the bombing [of the North Vietnamese] and would be willing to stop the bombing if they would sit down with us with the Government of [South] Vietnam present and have productive discussions. . . .

Now, very frankly, we would hope that we could have a minimum of discussion in the newspapers about these conferences, because we're not going to get peace with public speeches, and we're not going to get peace through the newspapers . . .

I know you don't want to play politics with your country. I'm trying to tell you what my judgment is about how not to play politics with it. And I know all of you want peace at the earliest possible moment. And I would just express the hope that you be awfully sure what you're talking about before you get into the intricacies of these negotiations. Over. Now, I'll be glad to have any comment any of you want to make or answer any questions.

Humphrey: No comment, Mr. President. Thank you very much.

Nixon: Yep. Well, as you know, my– this is consistent with what my position has been all along. I've made it very clear that I will make no statement that would undercut the negotiations. So we'll just stay right on there and hope that this thing works out.[9]

Nixon was obviously lying through his teeth as the man who was personally orchestrating the entire scheme that was designed precisely to undercut the negotiations.

At a particular moment in that conference call, Johnson seemed to let on that he knew exactly what Nixon was up to. In an incredibly astute analogy of the peace talks, Johnson somewhat vaguely spelled out the entire Nixon sabotage operation over the phone with the three candidates.

> **Johnson:** If I've got a house to sell, and I put a rock bottom price of $40,000 on it, and the prospective purchaser says, "Well, that's a little high, but let me see." And he goes–starts to leave to talk to his wife about it, and [First Lady] Lady Bird [Johnson] whispers that, "I would let you have it for $35,000" . . . Well, he's not likely to sign up.
> **Nixon:** Yeah.[10]

Undoubtedly frustrated after initially suspecting and eventually getting the goods on Nixon for back channeling with the South Vietnamese, Johnson judiciously hinted at Nixon that he was on to him.

One can only imagine how angry Johnson was when he learned of the extent of the Nixon sabotage. Famous in the Senate for his unparalleled ability to get things done and strong-arm the other side into a deal, in this case Johnson never really had a chance in what he surely viewed as the defining battle of his legacy. The war utterly consumed him in his final days in the Oval Office, and he threw everything he had at this last attempt to end the stain on his career of service that was the Vietnam War. Yet not even the master wheeler-and-dealer could outmaneuver Thieu while he was being undermined by his own countryman.

Once Nixon took office, he immediately had a new assignment for his intelligence teams. In early 1969, according to Huston, the president ordered Henry Kissinger, his national security advisor (and his double agent at the 1968 Paris peace talks), to find out as much as he could about President Johnson's bombing halt decision. Presumably, the new president was also anxious to discover exactly how much Johnson knew about his own backstage success in sinking the Paris negotiations. Surely after conversations such as the previously referenced conference call, Nixon had to suspect that Johnson very well knew about the entire scope of the sabotage.

Kissinger's National Security Council staff put together a report that was not to the president's full satisfaction; Huston recalls that the NSC study did not go into detail on the role politics may have played in LBJ's decision to halt the bombing. Huston says the NSC eventually submitted a "God-awful boring memo . . . and [the President] was not happy with it." So, in September 1969, Huston was assigned the job of finding out whether there was any evidence that, in his words, "would suggest that the timing of [LBJ's] decision may have been politically motivated."

Going deeply into the politics behind the bombing halt, Huston says he ran smack into "what Johnson was looking at." According to the Nixon aide, "What Johnson was looking at was this perception that the Nixon campaign was doing whatever it could to sabotage his efforts to achieve a bombing halt."

Huston eventually found out so much about what the 1968 Nixon campaign was doing that he filed a separate report to the president dealing with "the Chennault Affair." His report was submitted to the president in early 1971. Yet Huston rather freely reveals much of what that report apparently contains in his own recently released interviews. In them, Huston criticizes the CIA and NSA for not cooperating with his study: "As you might expect, NSA claimed they knew nothing about it. Of course that was nonsense, because I had other information that I knew what some of their activity had been. And the CIA, I mean, for heaven's sake, 'we wouldn't know anything at all about that,' says Dick Helms, which was nonsense too."

But Huston does praise the FBI—especially "Nixon's man" there, William Sullivan—for apparently turning over copies of all the information the bureau had, including surveillance logs on Anna Chennault. "[Mrs.] Chennault was physically monitored. . . . Her movements were monitored," Huston states. "There was electronic surveillance of . . . both the South Vietnamese Embassy and the chancery. So they were picking up any communications, plus there was physical surveillance so that anyone going in or out of the embassy was identified and reported immediately to the White House."

Huston says he learned that President Johnson "was following [the Chennault Affair] directly. . . . I mean this was going right to the top all along." He said Deke DeLoach, "Johnson's man at the FBI," would "directly" and "immediately" report to the president "anything that came up that he thought that Johnson would want to know."

What does Nixon's intelligence specialist think of President Johnson's use of government intelligence agencies to spy on domestic political opponents? Huston asserts that "Johnson had a legitimate reason to be concerned about any efforts that were being made to interfere with his diplomatic efforts. He was the president of the United States. He was trying to negotiate an end to a war, and to effectively do it, he needed to know whether somebody was trying to thwart what he was trying to do."

Huston's Conclusions

The 1971 Huston report found no "smoking gun" evidence that Nixon was directly involved in the Chennault Affair. But Nixon's own investigator did determine that "clearly [John] Mitchell was directly involved." And Huston stressed: "It's inconceivable to me that John Mitchell would be running around, you know, passing messages to the South Vietnamese government, et cetera, on his own initiative."

The situation certainly reeks of the Watergate saga, where Nixon used a similar defense by claiming that drastic intelligence operations were never actually ordered by him, just his loyal underlings acting on their own reckless accord. At some point, the notion becomes too absurd, as even Huston admits that there is no chance the president was not signing off on these incredibly brash operations.

Huston's remarks are important to the "treason" story for several reasons: They mark the first time a Nixon aide has confirmed, in any detail, the Nixon campaign's pressure on Saigon to boycott the Paris negotiations. Huston also disclosed, for the first time, that President Nixon received a report (minus any direct input from the CIA or the NSA) on LBJ's investigation of the Chennault Affair. And, perhaps most important, it's the first time any Nixon aide has expressed the belief that the GOP candidate himself was supervising the Dragon Lady's anti-peace activities.

Certainly the potential link to the Watergate saga is strengthened by Huston's testimony. By definitively illustrating that Nixon knew Johnson had the goods on him for the sabotage, an explanation for Watergate being at least partially motivated by a fear of Larry O'Brien outing him during the 1972 election is more than plausible. After all, O'Brien was a top advisor during the Johnson administration and, as mentioned earlier, was one of the few who Nixon knew was fully informed of the sabotage. Is it a coincidence that his office was the target of two break-ins, the second of which led to the Plumbers being arrested as the first domino in the scandal that brought down the Nixon White House?

What does Huston think of the Nixon campaign's interference in the Vietnam peace talks? While not defending those activities, Huston argues that they didn't make any difference in the outcome of the 1968 election. He explains that "President [Nguyen Van] Thieu doesn't need Nixon's people to tell him this is not a good deal, from his perspective." (Opponents of this contention might reply that even if Nixon's subversion of the peace talks made no political difference, it was certainly still against the law.) Furthermore, as mentioned earlier, Johnson had an incredible track record for getting negotiations done, and on terms incredibly favorable for his party. The president became known for the "Johnson Treatment," his own brand of negotiating in which he would use his domineering size and scream, cry, insult, plead, and threaten until he got his way. Few presidents have been as admired as Johnson for their powers of persuasion.

Contrary to what FBI director J. Edgar Hoover once told Nixon, Huston says he found no evidence that Nixon's 1968 campaign plane was bugged. In Huston's view, after the election there was an "implicit understanding" between Johnson and Nixon not to bring up the possible bugging of Nixon's plane or the Chennault Affair. He reasons that the "two very politically sophisticated people" said to each other, "Hey, look. This thing is over, neither one of us are going to gain anything by stirring this pot, and let's leave it alone."

Did Huston's separate study of the bombing halt lead him to think President Johnson's move was aimed at helping Hubert Humphrey?

> No, it didn't. I mean I don't think any decision that Lyndon Johnson made, just like there was any decision Richard Nixon ever made, that didn't have a political calculation with it. But I think that Johnson really believed and was convinced that this was the opportunity, and might be the only opportunity he was going to get . . .[11]

At the same time Tom Huston was investigating the Chennault Affair and the bombing halt decision for the president, Nixon was again seeking alternate ways to obtain such information. But, in early 1971, CIA chief Richard Helms rejected Nixon-initiated appeals for those files from both Henry Kissinger and domestic affairs advisor John Ehrlichman, according to newly released Nixon White House memos.[12]

As mentioned previously, on June 17, 1971, Nixon exploded during a meeting with Haldeman and Kissinger when he learned that both Kissinger and Huston thought LBJ's files might be at the left-leaning Brookings Institution in Washington. "Damn it! I asked for that [unintelligible]. I want it implemented on a thievery basis. Goddamn it, get in there and get those files. Blow the safe and get it."[13] On July 1, 1971, the president asked Haldeman, "Did they get the Brookings Institute [*sic*] raided yet? No? Get it done. I want it done. I want the Brookings Institute's safe cleaned out in a way that it makes somebody else responsible."[14] (Tom Huston says Nixon aides joked that Brookings was "the chancellery of the government-in-exile.")

As we now know, Nixon's directives were never carried out. Decades later, however, as previously mentioned, Senate Watergate Committee investigator Terry Lenzner pointed out that just ordering the Brookings break-in "would be an impeachable offense. It is the President ordering a felony to obtain information."[15]

Chapter 13
The Watergate Connection

The most intriguing consequence of the 1968 peace talks sabotage is the resulting web of secrecy and attempted blackmail, which—when unwound—point to a direct link between the interference of Richard Nixon in those critical negotiations and the Watergate scandal four years later.

Democrats who knew of Nixon's actions took Johnson's lead and maintained silence. But many factors between 1968 and 1972 made Nixon suspect that those zipped Democratic lips might ultimately come unsealed. Knowing Nixon's track record, the rule of law would be no object in attaining the information he needed to craft a strategy for covering up what would certainly have been the most sensational criminal scheme of his scandal-scarred career.

President Johnson's silence may have been motivated by a desire to maintain the illusion of clean government. In other words, he did not desire to reveal his questionable (but legal) use of NSA, CIA, and FBI surveillance. The NSA had intercepted and decoded South Vietnam's cable traffic. The CIA had carefully tracked South Vietnam's ambassador to Washington, Bui Diem, and installed a bug in the Saigon office of South Vietnamese president Nguyen Van Thieu. The FBI had wiretapped and staked out the South Vietnamese embassy in Washington and tailed Anna Chennault, Nixon's anti-peace go-between with President Thieu.

Had Johnson come clean, some civil libertarians and Republicans might well have blasted his use of government investigators and intelligence agents to probe domestic political developments. Indeed, Johnson's own secretary of state, Dean Rusk, warned, "I do not believe that any President can make use of interceptions and telephone taps in any way that would involve politics. The moment we pass over that divide, we are in a different kind of society."[1] (Nixon's use of such technology led to his downfall just a few years later.)

Other Johnson aides, however, strongly urged the Democrats to reveal Nixon's betrayal. Press assistant Tom Johnson later recalled: "I remain amazed that LBJ and Humphrey did not publicize the actions taken by the Nixon side in this ultra-sensitive matter. It is my belief that Nixon would not have been elected if the public had learned [of the sabotage]."[2]

Yet, while President Johnson's snooping uncovered a reprehensible scheme—a true national security breach—the president felt he was hamstrung to disclose it. Johnson addressed the reasons for his public silence in a private phone conversation at the time: "Now, I didn't expose it because I couldn't use those sources, and I didn't want to make it impossible for [Nixon] to govern. I think if I . . . had exposed this, brought it out, it would shock the country so, that he would have been seriously hurt. But that damn woman is still messing around causing trouble, Mrs. Chennault . . ."[3]

Thanks to FBI director J. Edgar Hoover's ingratiating exaggerations, Nixon came under the false impression early in his administration that Johnson had bugged Nixon's 1968 campaign plane. Thus, Nixon fretted, the Democrats might have tangible records of incriminating conversations directly linking him to his peace talk-wrecking co-conspirators.

If revealed, such communications could eliminate any plausible deniability on the part of the ringleader—who, otherwise, could blame the whole affair on unruly underlings. Hoover's claim was patently false, but Nixon saw no reason to doubt "my crony" (as he privately referred to the nation's top federal cop in his hip pocket).

In the waning days of the campaign, many of Humphrey's advisors implored him to release the tawdry evidence. As we have seen, the candidate's press secretary, Norman Sherman, was so eager to have the facts come out that he offered to disclose them himself—and then face the obvious personal consequences: being fired by Humphrey as an unauthorized leaker.

Yet Hubert Humphrey and his top staff, including Larry O'Brien and Norman Sherman, kept silent about the potential election-changer. Despite the fact that Humphrey "had sufficient evidence to consider going public," he decided to leave the sabotage issue alone because, in O'Brien's words, Humphrey "could hold his head high and not be accused of playing cheap politics at the end of a desperate effort to win an election."[4]

Nonetheless, as LBJ advisor and future high-ranking U. S. diplomat Richard Holbrooke later put it, the sabotage "set the pattern of [the Nixon team's] contempt for the law, which led ultimately to their downfall at the Watergate Hotel."[5]

On January 12, 1973, just before the start of his second term, President Nixon dispatched John Mitchell to meet with Larry O'Brien "and see what he could smoke out" about O'Brien's knowledge of the purported airplane bugs and the Nixon campaign's interference in the Paris negotiations.[6] Might Nixon have also hoped Mitchell would "smoke out" whether the Democrats might be willing to make a deal to continue to keep the matter quiet? Unfortunately, there is no known account of the outcome of the Mitchell-O'Brien talks.

At the same time, Nixon's top aide, Bob Haldeman, was told by a top FBI official, Deke DeLoach, that "bugging was requested on the planes, but was turned down, and all they did was check the phone calls, and put a tap on the Dragon Lady."[7] But Nixon was still not convinced.

So it is possible the president's motive for bugging Larry O'Brien's DNC offices in 1972 was to find out whether the Democrats would play the sabotage card on *him*—especially when you consider that this would not have been the first time Nixon attempted to get the incriminating Vietnam files.

Newly declassified documents reveal that, in March 1970, the president pressed CIA boss Richard Helms—through Henry Kissinger—for the agency's account of any possible connections among LBJ's bombing halt, the Paris talks, and the 1968 election. Helms said no dice.

In October 1970, Nixon ordered John Ehrlichman, his go-to guy on CIA matters, into action on getting the files from Helms. But he had no better luck that Kissinger. (Nixon eventually fired Helms after the CIA director refused to go along with the Watergate cover-up.)

In mid-1971, the president got unconfirmed word that the left-leaning Brookings Institution had documents showing (erroneously) that LBJ's pre-election bombing halt of North Vietnam was timed to help Vice President Humphrey at the polls, though the same documents would also certainly reveal Nixon's subversion of the 1968 electoral process. Top aide Bob Haldeman excitedly told Nixon that, to get the former president's support on Nixon's Vietnam policies, "You can blackmail Johnson on this stuff." So, as noted earlier, Nixon ordered that Brookings be broken into and the files stolen: "Blow the safe and get it!" he commanded.

Wiser heads at the Nixon White House ultimately prevailed, and the president's felonious demand to "rifle the files and bring them in" was never implemented. Yet the Watergate operation was carried out, albeit—as all are now aware—not quite as planned.

President Nixon reportedly blew up like Vesuvius when he heard about the June 17, 1972, arrests of his Watergate burglars. (He actually knew some of them through his Mafia-linked pal, Bebe Rebozo.) In a fit of rage he threw an ashtray against a wall. One can only imagine the string of expletives he fired off upon hearing the news that his "Plumbers" had been caught red-handed breaking into the headquarters of the Democratic Party.

Watergate and the Media

After he calmed down somewhat (perhaps with a few of his unprescribed anti-anxiety pills), the president employed his malleable young press secretary Ron Ziegler to utter the words that now live on as one of the biggest fibs (and jokes) in political history. There was hardly anything Ziegler ever said that Nixon didn't coach him to recite. In fact, Ziegler had a fantastic memory, and for those who knew him well, he would often delight us with his spiel from the days he was "Captain Ron" on an African jungle cruise ride at Disneyland. "I'm your skipper and your guide down the River of Adventure. . . . On the left, the natives on the bank. The natives have only one aim in life and that is to get a-head."

Nixon knew he couldn't offer a public reaction himself until the dust settled and more facts were known. In particular, he didn't want to make a statement on television, where his explanation might well come back to haunt him if things went south in what he knew was the biggest potential crisis of his scandal-packed life.

So when news of the Watergate break-in broke, Nixon rehearsed his spokesman on exactly what to tell the press. Ziegler, avoiding any cameras, pretended to calmly dismiss the importance of this event to those of us covering Nixon in Key Biscayne, Florida, where he was at the time. The president's puppet dismissed the crime as merely a "third-rate burglary attempt" even though "certain elements" would try "to stretch this beyond what it is." It would prove to be the first of a multi-year string of lies from the Nixon administration that would become the Watergate saga.

Nixon was also careful to make certain his own initial comments on Watergate would not be documented on film, which might later be used by his critics if his planned Watergate denials did not hold up. Shortly after returning from a weekend in Florida, he held an Oval Office press conference for radio only—no cameras. As he had instructed Ziegler to do earlier, Nixon lied when Watergate came up: "This kind of activity has no place whatever in our political process, or in our governmental process . . . the White House has had no involvement in this whatever in this particular incident."[8]

I knew Nixon and Ziegler were not being truthful. How? On Sunday, June 18, the *Washington Post* hit newsstands and porches. (The burglary had not taken place until the early morning of the 17, not in time for Saturday's editions). As he unfolded and read the paper, a young man in Washington placed a call to me in Key Biscayne and revealed that one of the burglars arrested at the DNC was not "Edward Martin," as identified under his photo in the *Post*. My informant was Tom Girard, a close friend who had worked with "Edward Martin" at, of all places, the Committee to Re-Elect the President (CREEP). Though he was a staunch Nixon supporter, Tom did appreciate the difference between right and wrong—and he wanted this news out—quoting him only as a "reliable source."

Indeed, as it turned out, the "Edward Martin" pictured in the newspaper was none other than James McCord, the former chief of security for the CIA—and the current chief of security for CREEP. Thanks to unsung Watergate hero Tom Girard, the first news of the story got out quickly over radio. (However, the diligence and dedication of Bob Woodward and Carl Bernstein made sure it stayed out there!) I kept my promise to Tom and did not reveal him as my source until he passed away in 2004.

Needless to say, my amiable relationship with Ron Ziegler took a nosedive after Watergate. There were no more leaks from Ziegler—who had called me into his office shortly after the break-in to claim that this very office had just been swept for possible Democratic-installed bugs. I just laughed to myself at the concept the president's press secretary was trying to sell me — that the Secret Service was not able to protect White House offices from political opponents' listening devices. I used the story but made certain to provide a line or two of conjecture about just how hard it would be to pull off such a feat.

For another minor example, there were no more joy rides for me in Ziegler's rented speedboat in Key Biscayne. (Early in the Nixon presidency, after I fell out of the full-throttled boat into polluted Biscayne Bay and wound up with Hepatitis, I can say truly that I was a pain in the butt to the president. That's because, like all who made that trip, Nixon had to pull down his shorts for a required gamma globulin shot. When I returned from my recuperation, Ziegler welcomed me at back at the White House by saying "Fulsom, your absence was sorely missed by all.")

Why Watergate?

For the next two years, Watergate produced both a national trauma and a serious constitutional crisis. The battle pitted Pres. Richard Nixon against Congress, a special prosecutor, the court system, and the press. This crisis — which saw the misuse of the CIA, the FBI, the Secret Service, and the IRS, among other government agencies — seriously tested the rule of law in this country. In the end, the constitutional system responded in the way the founders anticipated. That "the system worked" is now a cliché — but one that is accurate, and one that is probably the major lesson of Watergate.

So what was the now-infamous Watergate burglary all about? Over the years, a variety of theories have emerged, ranging from the absurd to the terrifying. None have been able to soundly explain such a seemingly desperate political act of espionage in what was so clearly a cake-walk reelection for Nixon. In fact, Nixon ended up carrying forty-nine states in one of the most lopsided presidential elections in American history. His 520 electoral votes were at the time second only to Pres. Franklin Delano Roosevelt's 1936 romping of Alf Landon. When all was said and done, George McGovern finished with only the support of Massachusetts and the District of Columbia, not even winning his home state of South Dakota.

Why, then, did the Nixon reelection campaign turn to such a

reckless act as a break-in of the Democratic National Headquarters? The apparent central purpose of the June 17, 1972, Watergate burglary was to repair a faulty bug on DNC chairman Larry O'Brien's phone. Surely Nixon was not merely fishing for an advantage in one of the most clear-cut elections in American history; there had to be more to it than that. Rather, Nixon figured O'Brien just might know some of Nixon's darkest secrets—at the center of which was Nixon's scuttling of the 1968 Paris peace talks, and possibly the hefty bribes he'd been taking over the years from the Mafia and billionaire business tycoon Howard Hughes. After all, O'Brien was the head of Humphrey's 1968 campaign and was present when the decision was made by the presidential candidate not to expose the potentially treasonous actions of his competitor. Without a doubt, Nixon could not quell the incessant fears that O'Brien would not be so hesitant to blow the whistle on the now-president's dirtiest tactics.

The supervisor of the Watergate burglaries, G. Gordon Liddy, has stated that he was ordered to photograph Larry O'Brien's "shit file" on Nixon. "The purpose of the second Watergate beak-in was to find out what O'Brien had of a derogatory nature about us, not for us to get something on him or the Democrats," Liddy wrote in his autobiography.[9]

At the time of Watergate, some Senate investigators concluded that Nixon was worried about the revelation of a secret $100,000 cash contribution to him from America's richest man, Howard Hughes. That's because O'Brien—who was on Hughes' payroll as a Washington lobbyist—might have had knowledge of that apparently illegal deal. Now that we know about Nixon's "treason," however, could that sinister 1968 deed have been the true overriding motive behind Watergate?

Investigative reporter Jack Anderson, one of the first to report on Nixon's meddling with the Paris peace talks, was among those who thought the Watergate burglars might have been looking for the Vietnam files. In his memoirs, Anderson called Nixon's anti-peace action in 1968 "the one that caused Nixon the most embarrassment."[10] Was it just a coincidence, then, that the Nixon White House targeted the intrepid reporter for assassination? Or was that murder plot—canceled at the last minute—connected to Nixon's fears that Anderson had access to the Vietnam files and would publish more stories about them?

The Watergate burglars were also looking for anything else they could find to discredit O'Brien or help Nixon defeat the Democrats that fall, as well as any potentially damning accusations coming from the Democrats. One of the five well-dressed intruders wearing blue surgical gloves carried a camera. Dozens of rolls of film were available to photograph any important documents they might stumble across during their visit to the Watergate complex.

This second Watergate operation was just getting underway when a night watchman by the name of Frank Wills found evidence of forced entry and called the police. The twenty-four-year-old had noticed that one of the locks on a door into the office building had been covered with duct tape. A nearby three-man team of casually clad, plainclothes DC cops—the so-called "Mod Squad" (because of their attire, long hair, and an eggbeater of an unmarked car)—soon snuck unseen into the DNC offices and arrested the lawbreakers at gunpoint.

The burglary was just one part of a clandestine Nixon re-election campaign plan that relied on illegal activities, including other break-ins and planned break-ins and a wide range of "dirty tricks." Like Nixon's sabotage of the 1968 peace talks, a pattern had been established that repeated itself: A paranoid politician believed that his opponents (or "enemies," as he called them) were concealing something or plotting against him—a notion that drove him to illegal tactics to uncover those secrets and seize an advantage.

Because of their impressive reportorial skills, and because they had a top FBI source (Mark Felt, "Deep Throat") willing to spill secrets, Bob Woodward and Carl Bernstein of the *Washington Post* broke the Watergate story wide open—with frequent page-one stories about various aspects of the scandal. After all was said and done and the president had left the White House in disgrace, the duo had published four hundred exclusives in all.

Yet, outside the Beltway, throughout the year 1972 the story made little news. CBS was the only TV network to run a special news program explaining the complex saga. Few listened when O'Brien himself, the most direct victim of the break-in, declared that the ordeal had "a clear line to the White House." On October 25, 1972, Democratic White House hopeful George McGovern devoted an entire televised speech to the issue, and he was not shy about blaming Nixon for Watergate: "The men who have collected millions in secret money, who have passed out special favors, who have ordered political sabotage, who have invaded our offices in the dead of night—all of these men work for Mr. Nixon. Most of them he hired himself. And their power comes from him alone. They act on his behalf, and they all accept his orders."[11]

Yet McGovern's speech got minimal public attention, and only murmurs of suspicion circulated that President Nixon himself could have been involved in this criminal enterprise. Most rumblings were dismissed as off-the-wall conspiracy theories. The Democrats never did leak information about Nixon's 1968 "treason." Whether they ever intended to may never be known for certain.

Political Consequences to the Nixon Administration

The president had always been a no-holds-barred political fighter. He wanted to win as big as possible in 1972. He wanted "four more years," as his fans had chanted during the campaign. He was not going to leave his future up to the democratic process, a strategy that had worked for him in nearly every election he had entered. But above all, he was not going to leave the future of his political career, and possibly his freedom, up to Larry O'Brien and his willingness to go public with what he knew about 1968.

That November, Nixon was re-elected in a landslide. At his inauguration, Nixon announced plans to dismantle his predecessor's landmark Great Society programs. Two days later, Lyndon Baines Johnson's heart gave out, and the lion passed away in his sleep. That very night, January 22, 1973, President Nixon announced an agreement to end the war.

Nixon was now free from the old threat posed by Lyndon Johnson. And Watergate, it seemed, was fading into the shadows of the past. Americans would move forward in a new era of rule by the Silent Majority, led by peacemaker Nixon. What Nixon did not count on was the political system working—for indeed Watergate was one instance in which it did.

Because of his Watergate crimes, Nixon would be forced out

of office long before the end of those "four more years" he had implored voters to grant him. His campaign was never really in doubt, making the true motives for Watergate, such a desperate yet seemingly unnecessary act of sabotage, all the more puzzling at the time. In fact, this logical disconnect even served as a defense to some of the public, as they could not understand why the president would order such a precarious operation. Only now with full knowledge of the true extent of Nixon's incredibly illegal series of actions, chiefly his potential "treason" just four years earlier, can the motives for the break-in truly be inferred.

Watergate was not a traditional espionage of campaign strategies for a tightly contested election in which either side, desperate for a leg-up, would make such an ethical lapse. Rather, it was merely a string in a long series of transgressions later dubbed by Nixon attorney general John Mitchell as "the White House horrors." Truly, they are more aptly referred to as being uniquely Nixon's, which certainly were present throughout his entire political career and not limited to his years as the nation's chief executive.

The reckless nature of the Watergate affair matched the incredible criminality required of Nixon and his cohorts in executing the break-in. Only by appreciating the severity of the information Nixon feared O'Brien could potentially release do the details of Watergate begin to add up. Nixon was undoubtedly paranoid; but with the unmatched legion of skeletons in his closet, his obsession with break-ins and other "dirty tricks" are unsurprising, even for him. O'Brien, being one of the only men who knew of both Nixon's potential treason as well as his insatiable appetite for bribes, was no coincidental target of the espionage.

Watergate was merely the proverbial straw that broke the camel's back for the Nixon administration. The final nail in Nixon's political coffin could have come years earlier had word leaked of his Plumbers' break-in of the office of Daniel Ellsberg's psychiatrist, a cock-eyed attempt to dig up dirt on the now-renowned leaker of the Pentagon Papers.

Or perhaps President Nixon could have been brought down if news of "Operation Gemstone" had leaked out. This convoluted plan crafted by Watergate mastermind G. Gordon Liddy called for planting prostitutes on major Democratic officials and the kidnapping of college students who protested the 1972 Republican Convention.

Then again, surely having fellow Watergate planner E. Howard Hunt falsify documents in hopes of developing a connection between former president John F. Kennedy and the assassination of South Vietnamese president Ngo Dinh Diem nearly a decade earlier would have been enough to end the administration of Nixon.

Finally, the saga that concluded with Nixon's demise could have begun the month before, when the Plumbers broke into the very same office at the Watergate complex to find out what O'Brien really had on the president. Had they not botched the initial attempt to access the headquarters, they would not have needed to return a few weeks later to replace a faulty bug, which drew the attention of security guard Frank Wills, the police, and eventually the entire nation.

As fate would have it, though, Watergate would be the lucky event that unraveled the most corrupt regime in American history. It had evolved from a modest, secretive operation that paled in comparison to the incredible schemes of Nixon and his closest men. However, it was Nixon's attempts to cover up this "third-rate burglary" that eventually sent him packing from the White House, rather than the break-in itself. The extensive steps taken by his administration to keep a lid on just how high the Watergate chain went involved an incredible number of illegal actions that flew in the face of the Constitution. Slowly, the best attempts to contain the matter began crumbling early the next year (1973) when one of the burglars—James McCord, of all people—started to talk.

Nixon knew he had to keep the burglars from turning on those higher up in the operation after they had been arrested. In an attempt to do so, he and his administration had been raising "hush money" for the burglars, though no amount could quell the fear instilled in them by the no-nonsense attitude of Judge John Sirica. Sirica, a law-and-order judge nicknamed "Maximum John" for his harsh sentences of offenders, presided over the trial that began in January of 1973. He sensed deeper involvement from those high in command within the Nixon reelection campaign and took the unconventional step of questioning witnesses in the trial himself, eager to put the hammer down on the burglars to entice them to talk. When James McCord was found guilty on eight counts of burglary, conspiracy, and wiretapping, it appeared that at least one of the intruders had decided no amount of money was worth facing a steep sentence from the infamous judge. McCord addressed a letter to Sirica detailing the involvement of the Nixon administration. The attention on Watergate quickly began to mount.

Their appetite whetted by the prospect of high-ranking government conspirators, the public's ears perked. Those two precocious reporters at the *Washington Post*, Bob Woodward and Carl Bernstein, fed this appetite with one of the most singularly important journalistic investigations in American history. Backed by their editor, Ben Bradlee, and the power of their newspaper's title and informed in large part by their deeply embedded, top-secret source, Deep Throat, the duo slowly untangled much of the complex web of secrecy within the Nixon White House.

Ironically, the president and his administration discovered Deep Throat's identity early on: Mark Felt, deputy director of the FBI (whom Nixon had passed over for promotion to director). But Felt's deep knowledge of the dark corners and hidden cobwebs of the Bureau made him an impossible target. Had his identity been revealed to the public, Felt could undoubtedly have exposed untold government secrets. Safe even from master-manipulator Nixon, his identity remained a much-speculated-on mystery until 2005, when an elderly Felt and his family finally announced his identity as arguably the most renowned secret source in American news history. (Woodward and Bernstein confirmed this news.)

Woodward, Bernstein, and their journalistic peers at newspapers across the country printed stories revealing secret campaign slush-funds full of dark money; financial payoffs to the Watergate burglars by the Committee to Re-Elect the President, aptly shortened to CREEP; White House interference into the Watergate investigation using the CIA, FBI, IRS, Justice Department, and Secret Service; and, at last, audio tapes supporting the claim that President Nixon had personally orchestrated the cover-up from day one.

It was never revealed, however, exactly what information the conspirators hoped to gain from their foray into Democratic territory.

As a result of both the determination of Judge Sirica and the efforts of Bob Woodward and Carl Bernstein, Sen. Ted Kennedy submitted Resolution 60 in February of 1973, calling for the formation of the Senate Committee on Presidential Campaign Activities (also known as the Watergate Committee), to get to the bottom of the complicated Watergate incident. After unanimous approval from his colleagues, the committee was established and granted a budget of $500,000 to investigate any and all illegal or unethical acts in the 1972 election.[12]

The Investigation

In the summer of 1973, the Watergate Committee opened public hearings that were watched by millions on television. All TV and radio networks carried the sessions live, and while some citizens complained about missing their favorite soap operas, the hearings became a kind of great public-affairs melodrama that was as riveting as any fictional serial. An incredible 85 percent[13] of households in the country tuned in at some point or another during the lengthy Senate investigation, and the matter quickly elevated from a possible partisan fishing expedition to a deep constitutional crisis admonished by all.

At the forefront of the committee was its chairman, the folksy Sen. Sam Ervin of North Carolina. Proper protocol was for the committee to be headed by the senator who proposed its formation, though Senator Kennedy, a prospective presidential candidate himself, declined to join the committee so as to avoid giving the appearance of partisanship. Ervin had once been a member of the North Carolina Supreme Court and had a strong respect for the law throughout his political career. In 1954 he had been appointed to fill the congressional vacancy left by the passing of Sen. Clyde Hoey, who had previously served as the fifty-ninth governor of North Carolina. In a twist of irony, the freshman Southern Democrat had actually been selected by none other than Vice Pres. Richard Nixon in 1954 to be a member of a similar committee tasked with investigating the abrasive anti-Communist hysteria manufactured by Sen. Joseph McCarthy.

One of the first of the many Constitutional crises uncovered by the committee emerged very early on in the investigation. Initially, under the guise of "executive privilege," Nixon refused to have his aides respond to subpoenas issued by the Watergate Committee. Long considered one of the top constitutional scholars in the Senate, Ervin would not relent, making the case that any privilege of the executive could not be extended to prevent a lawful investigation into alleged illegal actions pertaining to the validity of a presidential election. Merely a month into the investigation, a whopping 67 percent of Americans polled believed President Nixon was actively covering up information related to Watergate. As negative public opinion continued to mount, the president had no choice but to concede to the lawful subpoenas of his aides, allowing for the first on-the-record sworn testimony of key players in the Watergate scandal. These testimonies proved to be fatal for the Nixon White House.

So how did the Nixon-led cover-up of Watergate actually operate? As soon as news of the burglars' apprehension circulated, President Nixon placed one of his closest aides, White House Counsel John Dean, in charge of the day-to-day details of the scheme. There were two tracks to the cover-up: the aforementioned hush payments to the burglars and White House interference with official investigations.

John Dean provided some of the most critical testimony to the Senate's Watergate Committee, largely out of a very real fear that Nixon would attempt to use him as a scapegoat for the entire cover-up operation. As he had been tasked with handling the day-to-day aspects, Dean knew he was in an incredibly vulnerable position to be accused by Nixon of acting on his own volition and not under the orders of the president. His fears were seemingly confirmed when Nixon ordered him to write a detailed report of everything the administration had actually done in response to Watergate and then to sign the report for Nixon to review. To Dean, it was nothing short of asking for a confession to save the president's own skin.

Thus, the young and ambitious attorney made the calculated decision to come clean before the Senate Committee on Presidential Campaign Activities and to cooperate with the Special Prosecutor Archibald Cox, tasked by the attorney general with leading the independent investigation of the matter. Under oath,

Dean admitted that Nixon himself had approved the dual-pronged cover-up of Watergate. It was certainly dramatic testimony, though at best it seemed to create a "he-said, he-said" between a young and overambitious attorney who admitted he had participated in an obstruction of justice plot and the president of the United States. The special prosecutor knew he would need more to substantiate the charges that Nixon himself had sanctioned the plot.

Confirmation of the testimony from many of Nixon's aides came in the form of the now-infamous tapes of the Nixon White House. The prospect of a president having "bugged himself," a claim that surfaced during Dean's testimony, captivated the nation. He remarked that he believed Nixon may have been recording some of their cover-up conversations due to odd behavior within the Oval Office, and the committee immediately began asking potential witnesses whether Nixon did indeed have a secret taping system. John Dean later claimed incredible relief when Alexander Butterfield confirmed under oath that extensive recording systems were installed in various rooms within the White House, including the Oval Office—where many key meetings between Nixon and his aides took place in the days following Watergate.

After this major revelation, the scandal started revolving around whether the White House would make relevant Oval Office tapes available to Congress and the special prosecutor. Once again, Nixon claimed executive privilege in a vain attempt to escape confirmation of his personal guilt in the matter. Another Constitutional crisis was created.

The "Saturday Night Massacre" was the next major event in this historic battle. When Archibald Cox refused to give in to the president on the matter of the tapes and other issues, Nixon took the extraordinary step of having the special prosecutor fired. Atty. Gen. Elliot Richardson resigned in protest, leading the White House to announce that the office of special prosecutor would no longer exist. The public and congressional firestorm created by the massacre eventually persuaded Nixon to reconsider closing the office. Instead, he elected to replace Cox with Leon Jaworski. Nonetheless, the incredible move led the House Judiciary Committee to start impeachment proceedings.

If Nixon hoped that his new special prosecutor would be more lenient than Cox, he would soon be bitterly disappointed. Jaworski obtained a subpoena in April of 1974, once again demanding Nixon to turn over all relevant tapes and papers, prompting the president to finally release edited transcripts of more than forty conversations that had taken place in the White House.

Jaworski was by no means satisfied, and the legal battle quickly went up to the highest court in the land. Just four days after the Supreme Court began hearing oral arguments in the case *United States v. Nixon*, the president gave a very candid monologue to his national security advisor Henry Kissinger in the Oval Office:

> **Nixon:** As far as I'm concerned, so we'll have a Constitutional crisis. If we do, it'll be a Goddamn ding-dong battle and we might, if we lose, I'll burn the papers. 'Cause I got them. That's the point, 'cause I would never turn these papers over to a court. Never give them over to the Committee, you know that . . . I said, oh no, your counsel isn't gonna paw through my papers. I just used that word. He got the message.[14]

In July of 1974, the Supreme Court unanimously rejected Nixon's claim that his tapes were covered by "executive privilege." He had argued that the constitutionally sanctioned separation of powers (among the executive, legislative, and judicial branches) entitled him to withhold the tapes from the courts, the Congress, and the special prosecutor. The court balked at Nixon's view, which they referred to as an, "absolute, unqualified Presidential privilege of immunity from judicial process under all circumstances."[15] The impressive statement of the court appeared to signal the end for the deeply troubled president. He would resign the presidency only fifteen days later.

When Nixon finally surrendered key tapes, they exposed his leading role in the cover-up from the very beginning. And they demonstrated that John Dean had been telling the truth all along.

While the president refrained from following through on his promise to "burn the papers," there was a now infamous eighteen and a half minute gap in the recorded Oval Office conversation that occurred on June 20, 1972, just three days after the Watergate burglars were apprehended. The gap in the tapes provided endless fodder for conspiracy theorists as to what could have been discussed that day. It is probable that at least a portion of the conversation touched on

Nixon's desire to keep the FBI from digging too deep on the matter.

Chief of Staff H.R. Haldeman's diary on the date in question includes the following:

> "We got back into the Democratic break-in again. [The first known taped conversation regarding the break-in comes from after the June 20 meeting.] I told the President about it on the plane last night. . . . I had a long meeting with Ehrlichman and Mitchell. We added [Richard] Kleindienst for a little while and John Dean for quite a while. The conclusion was that we've got to hope the FBI doesn't go beyond what's necessary in developing evidence and that we can keep a lid on that, as well as keeping all the characters involved from getting carried away with any unnecessary testimony."[16]

Even today, the question of what was actually discussed during the erased portion of the recorded conversation remains. The "smoking gun" tape released that summer records Nixon ordering the CIA to tell the FBI not to investigate Watergate because it might uncover national security skeletons. The CIA cooperated at first but quickly separated itself from the cover-up track. CIA chief Richard Helms was eventually fired for disobeying these presidential orders.

Why would the Nixon team go through the trouble of erasing a taped conversation that covered the same actions they later discussed on tapes that they willingly submitted to the investigation? The situation suggests that there was something more incriminating, possibly on a separate but related subject, on those wiped recordings.

Perhaps the president touched on his Vietnam sabotage; it would have come up as he and Kissinger were both well aware that Johnson and O'Brien — the target of the Watergate burglary — had the goods on their sabotage. Did Nixon have the tape wiped because it mentioned the reasons for the break-in and described the potentially treasonous actions he and his soon-to-be national security advisor took in the 1968 election?

Just as damning evidence supports the theory that this deletion was intended to cover-up a different aspect of the Watergate affair: the initial hush money paid to the burglars to ensure their silence. In a conversation with his chief of staff, Bob Haldeman, just over a month after the break-in, an exasperated Nixon shouted, "Well . . . they have to be paid. That's all there is to that. They have to be paid."[17]

Nixon Faces Impeachment

By the summer of 1974, the House of Representatives was ready to vote to impeach Nixon—who, by then, had an approval rating only in the teens in public opinion polls. In the Senate, Nixon almost certainly had only eight to ten votes in his favor, against impeachment.

The House Judiciary Committee approved three articles of impeachment—charging Nixon with obstruction of justice, failure to uphold the law and contempt of Congress for refusing to turn over subpoenaed documents.

In a twist of irony for the ages, a beaten-down Nixon sat with his trusty one-time peace-talks spy Kissinger on July 12 and bemoaned the entire saga. Nixon described how he had already fired his two top aides, Haldeman and Ehrlichman, both on April 30 of 1973. Yet the scandal raged on.

> **Nixon:** I mean, I cut off two arms [Haldeman and Ehrlichman]. Who the hell else would've done such a thing—who ever has done that before? I cut off two arms and then they went after the body.
>
> **Kissinger:** Then you consider the meritorious things you have done for the country, the treasonable actions that these people condoned—
>
> **Nixon:** They are treason.
>
> **Kissinger:** Well, taking 10,000 government documents in the middle of the war [the Pentagon Papers], attacking the military, attack, having riots, attacking, I mean, on January 3rd, knowing I was going over for negotiations and [Senator Mike] Mansfield passed [legislation], that cut off funds [for] the war. That is immoral . . .
>
> **Nixon:** Well, don't you worry.
>
> **Kissinger:** Oh, I don't worry.
>
> **Nixon:** Keep, keep fighting.[18]

Both men, the masterminds of the scheme to illegally prolong the Vietnam War to win an election, settled on a perfect word to describe their phantom enemies: it was "treason," plain and simple.

Rather than face the certain humiliation of being the only president impeached and removed from office, Nixon resigned the presidency so he could keep the related perks—including lifetime

Nixon departs the White House, August 9, 1974 (Courtesy National Archives and Records Administration)

Secret Service protection, generous government retirement packages, transition expenses, free offices with a staff, and free limos and airplanes. Fighting it out in Congress looked like a lousy alternative to Nixon, for a conviction by the Senate would have denied him any of those special exit privileges granted to former presidents. And he would have become the only U.S. president ever convicted of impeachable crimes—an even more dishonorable fate than just being the only president to resign. Vice President Ford took the oath of office and became the thirty-eighth president of the United States.

A smart political schemer like Nixon probably would not have resigned unless he had a secret pre-resignation deal with Vice President Ford—a full and complete pardon for all of his illegal presidential activities. (Most of the Nixon and Ford aides who have weighed in on the subject believe there was such a deal.) More than anything, Nixon wanted to avoid testifying at trials (possibly even his own) and to escape any chance of incarceration. Toward the end, he self-pityingly told several aides, "Some of the best writing is done from prison."[19]

Nixon resigned from office August 9, 1974. He was the first and only president to quit the job. One month later, Pres. Gerald Ford pardoned his predecessor for all of his White House crimes.

One can only speculate what Nixon would have done had his burglars discovered the DNC headquarters fully informed and ready to go public with a national scandal—and, of course, managed not to get caught. As it stands, though, the incident history has painted as the greatest political scandal of the twentieth century was, perhaps, not what it appeared to be at the time. In fact, it may have been merely damage control for an affair deserving of such a title—Nixon's sabotage of the 1968 Vietnam peace talks.

Chapter 14

Nixon's War on the Left

On May 8, 1972, Pres. Richard Nixon announced that Haiphong Harbor had been mined and the carpet-bombing of North Vietnam resumed. A major port, Haiphong acted as a key military supply depot and had been repeatedly bombed from 1965 until 1968, when Pres. Lyndon Johnson curtailed it. Nixon's April 16, 1972, renewal of the bombing and the subsequent order to mine the harbor was the talk of the nation's capital.

To give itself a different angle for reporting on this highly controversial decision, the news department of local Washington television station WTTG decided to poll Washingtonians on their opinion. Ads were printed in a local newspaper with the request that readers clip out the ballot and mail it to the station.

Being on a fairly low rung on the newsroom totem pole, Bill McCloskey was assigned the task of opening the envelopes and tallying the results. As a stamp collector, the cub reporter—who went on to a long and distinguished career at the Associated Press— quickly noticed that many of the envelopes used commemorative stamps for postage as opposed to the regular issue eight-cent stamp of the day, which pictured Pres. Dwight Eisenhower. As the son of a printer, Bill also saw that many, if not most, of the envelopes were made of high-quality "rag bond" paper—not the kind of envelope most folks would have hanging around the house. "We suspected something was up," he says, "because all of these fancy envelopes with fancy stamps carried ballots favoring the President's action."[1] The final count showed 5,157 for the president's decision, 1,158 against.[2]

It wasn't until a year later that a Committee to Re-elect the President (CREEP) spokesman told *Washington Post* reporter Bob Woodward that, indeed, it was CREEP that was stuffing the ballot box. On the record, a CREEP spokesman told the paper, "We assumed the other side would do it also."[3]

Unbeknownst to McCloskey, CREEP and White House staffers set up an entire campaign apparatus that did nothing but mail out telegrams and letters and make phone calls *nationwide* on behalf of Nixon's action. On May 10, presidential press secretary Ron Ziegler announced that the reaction at the White House was running five or six to one in favor of Nixon. News photographers were ushered into the Oval Office to take pictures of the massive mound of telegrams and letters — many of them fake — that had been piled on Nixon's desk.

A History of Trickery

Dirty tricks, subterfuge, and sabotage were just business as usual for the Nixonites. The torpedoing of the Paris peace talks to win the 1968 election was perhaps the epitome of this sleazy political activity, but — where Nixon was concerned — it was hardly exceptional.

In 2014, for example, the *New York Post* broke a story that in 1969 Nixon "was the prime mover in another illegal action (aside from Watergate) that could have been grounds for impeachment." The newspaper said extensive research shows "Nixon initiated the campaign to sabotage the My Lai massacre trials so that no American solider involved in the killings would be convicted of war crimes."

In the massacre, which had been covered up by the military for more than a year, out-of-control U.S. soldiers slaughtered more than five hundred unarmed Vietnamese civilians, raping the women and murdering even infants. It was one of the darkest days in American military history — and undoubtedly the most shocking episode of the Vietnam War. Its disclosure prompted worldwide condemnation by peace and anti-war activists, galvanizing the left and providing further ammunition against what had now become "Nixon's War."

Nixon's sabotage worked, however, just as it had with the 1968 Paris peace talks. At the end of the My Lai trials, only one man was found guilty and sentenced to life in prison — Lt. William Calley. Nixon released Calley from the stockade after only three days and allowed him to live in his bachelor's quarters under house arrest while he appealed his conviction. Calley was eventually placed on parole in 1974 after serving one-third of a twice-reduced sentence.[4]

Justice for the My Lai villagers proved too elusive under Nixon's command.

White House tapes demonstrate that Nixon heartily cheered on dirty tricks against Democrat George McGovern during his 1972 reelection bid. During Oval Office conversations with aides, Nixon praised such tactics as disrupting McGovern's campaign rallies and unearthing information embarrassing to Democrats. One diabolical plan would have had McGovern literature spread throughout the Milwaukee apartment of Arthur Bremer, the man who shot and crippled presidential contender George Wallace. E. Howard Hunt was dispatched to Milwaukee, but the FBI had sealed off Bremer's apartment before he could get there and taint McGovern by association.

Decades later, when this trick was exposed on the White House tapes, *Newsweek*'s Meg Greenfield voiced her amazement: "The President of the United States did this—the man responsible for the federal agencies investigating this heinous criminal act. In effect, he authorized tampering with the evidence and jeopardizing the case in order to win a political, public relations point."[5]

The incriminating tapes plainly show Nixon as the chief overseer of day-to-day political combat with the Democrats, despite his public claim that he was too busy with the opening to China and détente with the Soviet Union to pay close attention to his reelection efforts.

On September 19, 1972, aide Chuck Colson bragged to Nixon that McGovern "had one hell of a bad day" because his campaign appearance had been disrupted by protestors secretly dispatched by the ruthless aide. Such tactics, Colson told the president, comprised "one aspect of your operation that's working very effectively." McGovern, he added, "is going to get it every place he goes." In the same discussion, Nixon defended efforts to infiltrate McGovern rallies and anti-war protests and foment confrontations embarrassing to the Democrats, whose unruliness he was eager to exploit. "I mean, after all," Nixon asserted, "if we weren't trying to put our people with the demonstrators, we'd be damn fools."[6]

Nixon spymaster E. Howard Hunt had an idea for embarrassing McGovern at the upcoming Democratic National Convention in Miami Beach. He authorized underlings to offer an extremely generous $700 per week to hire "hippies" to "throw rocks, break glass, defecate and urinate" outside McGovern's headquarters hotel. The plan was ultimately turned down because possible participants thought that for $700 a week Hunt and his cohorts "would want more for their money" than just those minor acts.[7]

One of Nixon's chief bullies against war protestors was an advance man named Ron Walker, who bragged about how he once handled sign-carrying anti-Nixon black women along a motorcade route the president was about to travel in New Jersey. "We simply went in and pulled them down. All the black ladies came falling to the floor . . . and the people were sitting, their signs were down and they were pulling splinters from their hands for a week. . . . I don't call that dirty tricks as much as, you know, guerrilla warfare."[8]

Presidential aide John Ehrlichman said Nixon's first solution to the anti-war demonstrators "was to order me to have the Secret Service rough up the hecklers." When the agency declined to engage in such roughhouse tactics, the aide remembered Nixon's next option: "He wanted me to create some kind of flying goon squad of our own to rough up the hecklers, take down their signs and silence them. He approved of strong-arm tactics."[9]

Nixon's all-out support for violence against opponents of the war was on full display on May 5, 1971, when he and his chief of staff, Bob Haldeman, discussed plans to disrupt a coming anti-war rally in Washington:

> **Haldeman:** And then they're going to stir up some of this Vietcong flag business, as—[presidential aide Chuck] Colson's going to do it through hardhats and legionnaires. What Colson's going to do on that, and what I suggested he do—and I think they can get away with this—do it with the Teamsters. Just ask them to dig up their eight thugs.
>
> **Nixon:** How?
>
> **Haldeman:** Just call what's-his-name? [Frank] Fitzsimmons [president of the Teamsters] is trying to play our game anyway. Is just tell Fitzsimmons [sic].
>
> **Nixon:** They've got guys who'll go in and knock their heads off.
>
> **Haldeman:** Sure. Murderers. Guys that really, you know, that's what they really do. Like the steelworkers have and—except we can't deal with the steelworkers at the moment.
>
> **Nixon:** No.
>
> **Haldeman:** We can deal with the Teamsters. And they, you know, it's the . . .
>
> **Nixon:** Yeah.

Haldeman: . . . regular strikebreaker-types and all that and they
. . . [tape whip] — types and just send them in and beat the shit out
of some of these people. And hope they really hurt 'em, you know
what I mean? Go in with some real — smash some noses. [tape whip]
some pretty good fights.[10]

As for Democratic politico and McGovern ally Larry O'Brien,
just mentioning his name around Richard Nixon was enough to
ignite the president's notorious rage. He "climbed the walls," as
aides described Nixon's irrational behavior at such moments.

Nixon vs. O'Brien

Why was Nixon so furious? It was not just O'Brien's mysterious
connection to billionaire Howard Hughes that galled and frustrated
the president. It was that O'Brien — a key political aide to Pres. John
Kennedy — was a passionate Kennedy loyalist; and Nixon feared a
1972 election run against another Kennedy brother, Massachusetts
senator Edward "Ted" Kennedy. Even more terrifying to Nixon,
O'Brien knew of Nixon's treasonous 1968 activities and could
possibly leak them. As Nixon spy G. Gordon Liddy later explained,
O'Brien kept files "of a derogatory nature about us . . ."[11]

O'Brien, it turned out, had no access to the "shit file" the Nixon
camp was hoping the Watergate burglars would uncover. Years
later, however, O'Brien saluted Hubert Humphrey for not bringing
up Nixon's sabotage as the campaign ended. "I think what came
across to me was [Humphrey's] concern about utilizing it — whether
it was justified, whether there was enough evidence so that he could
hold his head high and not be accused of playing cheap politics at
the end of a desperation effort to win an election."[12]

In Nixon's mind, however, O'Brien might at least know where
the incriminating sabotage files were located and might have just
talked about that fact over a tapped phone. That's why the burglars went back to the Watergate on June 17, 1972 — to repair the
faulty bug on O'Brien's phone and photograph as many documents
as possible. (The material gathered through the earlier break-in —
humdrum chatter on the wrong phone lines and photos of worth-
less documents — was, in the terms of the Nixonites, "a dry hole.")

Anxious about a possible teaming of O'Brien with an Edward

Kennedy candidacy, the president put the senator under 24-hour-a-day Secret Service surveillance in hopes of catching the renowned playboy "in the sack with one of his babes." When Nixon heard rumors in 1972 that another hated member of the Kennedy clan, Sargent Shriver, would be Sen. George McGovern's choice for vice president, he shouted to aides, "Kill him! Kill him!" The Nixonites soon started a false rumor that Shriver had slave-owning ancestors.[13]

Nixon's spies stalked and rumor-mongered about Larry O'Brien with more subtlety because Howard Hughes was one of President Nixon's most dependable and deepest-pocketed backers ever since Nixon's first run for Congress. Anything that might hurt O'Brien and/or his future boss Howard Hughes might end the lucrative Hughes-Nixon payoffs and paybacks. In return for presidential favors, Nixon's chief cash collector, Bebe Rebozo, kept a reputed "tin box" at his Key Biscayne bank for the millions of dollars in unrecorded cash "donations" from Hughes (and many others) to Nixon.

After Nixon took office, Rebozo accepted two separate payments of $50,000 from Hughes in apparent exchange for favorable rulings on several Hughes-owned businesses. Eventually, Watergate investigators began looking into this latest Hughes-Nixon entanglement. A previous $205,000 "loan," ostensibly to Richard's brother Donald for a failing franchise of "Nixonburger" eateries, helped sink Richard Nixon's candidacies for president in 1960 and governor in 1962. Years later, Hughes confided to a friend, Frank McCullough, that this account of a $205,000 "loan" for Donald was a false story. "It was for political purposes. It was for Dick, not his brother," Hughes revealed to McCullough, a veteran Los Angles reporter.[14]

In an astounding double-cross, shortly after Rebozo accepted the final payment in the $100,000 Hughes contribution, the cash collector joined a White House plot to link Hughes to Larry O'Brien and the Democrats. In a White House memo uncovered in 1973 by columnist Jack Anderson, Nixon chief of staff Bob Haldeman instructs Nixon counsel John Dean to lead this plot, even though it might be "embarrassing" to Hughes. Haldeman warned Dean, however, to "keep Bebe out of it at all costs."

Dated January 17, 1971, the memo urges Dean to start "an inquiry into the [financial] relationship between Larry O'Brien and Howard Hughes." Several days later, Dean reported his initial finding after speaking to the president's bosom buddy: "I discussed the matter with Bebe Rebozo who indicated that his information regarding [a retainer paid by Hughes to O'Brien] had come from Robert Maheu. . . . Bebe further indicated he felt he could acquire some documentation of this fact if given a little time and that he would proceed to get any information he could."[15]

Perhaps Rebozo hoped to get the "documentation" through a break-in at O'Brien's Democratic Party office at the Watergate. The burglars carried enough film during their second DNC raid—fifty rolls—to photograph as many as 1,800 pages documenting Nixon's crimes that the president wanted to burn or shred. Of course, the files were not at the DNC.

Even after the Watergate fiasco on June 17, 1972, Nixon's obsession with O'Brien never slackened. In a July 31, 1972, phone conversation with Bob Haldeman, Nixon urged his chief of staff to go "gung-ho" in digging up more dirt on the DNC chairman or determining just what Larry might have to use against Nixon and where it might be stored. The president barked, "I want every goddamn thing that there is on that son-of-a-bitch!"[16]

The thirty-seventh president was spooked enough to think the files that could do him the most danger could be anywhere. And he was certainly aware that, as a key advisor to Hubert Humphrey in 1968, O'Brien would be privy to the information those files contained. He was right; O'Brien did know. But Nixon was wrong in his assumption that O'Brien had the full goods on Nixon's sordid actions and that he knew where the "smoking gun" evidence was kept.

Like Nixon, O'Brien had no idea that LBJ had taken all the intelligence data with him when he left the White House. All the proof was now with the ex-president at his ranch in Texas. Not at Brookings. Not at Watergate. Not in the files of Daniel Ellsberg's psychiatrist. Not in the hands of Nixon's biggest political enemy, Edward Kennedy, or even with Kennedy confidante Larry O'Brien. And not in the possession of Nixon's most despised journalist, Jack Anderson.

Reporters Get Too Close

Or were they? Co-columnists Drew Pearson and Jack Anderson were among the first to publish some details of Nixon's interference with the 1968 peace talks, and they indicated they had many more Nixon-related Vietnam secrets to expose.

Nixon was so apoplectic about this prospect that his private illegal police force (contravening J. Edgar Hoover's firm veto of all of the Huston Plan illegalities) even got word that the future Watergate burglars (also known as the Plumbers) were expected to come up with potential plots to remove one of the most hurtful pebbles from Nixon's shiny wingtips.

The FBI boss wanted to keep "black bag" jobs and other nefarious activities to himself, but Hoover at least cooperated with Nixon, as did the CIA, in spying on Anderson. Jack's phones were tapped. (I talked to him once on his home phone. We both should have known better.) He was also being watched and trailed by Hoover's "G-men." Hoover despised Anderson with a purple passion, having privately called him a "jackal" with a mind that is "lower than the regurgitated filth of vultures."[17]

When Hoover sent agents to stake out Anderson's home, several of the reporter's nine children took the G-men's pictures and let the air out of their tires. Anderson also sent an underling to go through Hoover's garbage, but a huge cache of empty antacid tablet wrappers was the only intriguing find. (At least it established that the spymaster, or his roommate, Clyde Tolson, suffered from a major gastrointestinal issue.)

The president's own sleuths usually didn't mess around with such piddling pranks, especially when they wanted a prime enemy neutralized—meaning killed. The enemy this time was Jack Anderson, a longtime thorn in Nixon's side and the possible possessor of intelligence related to Nixon's 1968 anti-peace meddling. As Watergate ace Bob Woodward reported in the *Washington Post* on September 21, 1975, an unnamed White House aide gave Nixon's chief White House spy, E. Howard Hunt, "the order to kill Anderson."

One plan allegedly involved the use of a poison that could not be pinpointed during an autopsy. Anderson's house would be broken into and the lethal pill dropped into an aspirin jar in his medicine cabinet. Plumber G. Gordon Liddy termed the ploy "Aspirin Roulette." The plot, unruly in that the killers could not control for certain who would take the poison, would have also risked the lives of Anderson's brood—but innocent children were never the Plumbers' primary concern.

Woodward wrote that the assassination order came from a "senior government official in the White House" and that it was canceled at the last minute. Colson told Woodward he'd never heard of the aborted plan to murder the president's most despised reporter. But Howard Hunt said a frazzled-looking Colson dropped the idea after apparently seeing the president.

Jack Anderson was the nation's premier investigative reporter at the time. He had golden sources, was friendly with everyone, avuncular with his small staff, and—though I did not know him well—was very instructive to me. He pointed me down straight roads on several important stories, including the Senate censure of Thomas Dodd of Connecticut and reports of a fling between a possible communist spy and Pres. John F. Kennedy.

In the immediate aftermath of Watergate, on June 20, 1972, Nixon and Chuck Colson had the abominable Jack Anderson on their minds. They sought to minimize the seriousness of Watergate by comparing it to Anderson's award-winning story that the Nixon administration was tilting toward Pakistan in Pakistan's dispute with India. The story was totally accurate and led to loud complaining in the Oval Office:

> **Colson:** They gave Anderson a Pulitzer Prize. In other words, stealing documents [unintelligible] for [unintelligible].
> **Nixon:** Belonging to the government, top-secret shit . . . Did any of these people [who are criticizing the Watergate burglary] squeal about Anderson's actions then?[18]

In March 1972, Nixon Plumber G. Gordon Liddy, a bully who loved Nazi propaganda films and was brought up by a German nanny who played him Hitler's speeches on the radio, presided at a plot to knock off Anderson. The plotters assembled for a pricey luncheon at the posh Hay-Adams Hotel near the White House.

E. Howard Hunt was there, as was a CIA doctor named Edward Gunn. After abundant discussion there was a unanimous decision on how to kill their victim (though Liddy claims Dr. Gunn never knew the identity of the intended corpse).

Liddy peeled off a crisp $100 bill from a wad of CREEP intelligence funds for Dr. Gunn's consultative services, but none of the Anderson murder plans was consummated. Liddy finally volunteered to do the hit himself by "knifing [Anderson], slitting his throat. And staging it as a mugging that would look like a Washington street crime."

The "G-Man" went on to a post-prison job as a radio talk show host, and he actually appeared with Anderson on the same *Good Morning America* episode in 1980—telling his would-be victim: "Murder is a technical term. You call it murder because you think it is unjustified. I would say it was justifiable homicide given the truth of your situation."

Richard Nixon was never quizzed about the planned hit on Jack Anderson. But if he had been, and had he copped to the planned crime, he could have used one of his most famous lines from his million-dollar 1977 interview with David Frost: "If the president does it, that means it is not illegal." Gordon Liddy was unrepentant as recently as 2008, when he told Howard Stern—a rather shocked radio shock jock—"I was just doing my job."[19]

Anti-war poster boy Daniel Ellsberg is now convinced that he was also on Richard Nixon's hit list. In the summer of 1971, Ellsberg leaked the Pentagon Papers, the top-secret Defense Department study critical of the war and politically embarrassing not only to the Kennedy and Johnson administrations but also to the Nixon White House.

One misdeed Ellsberg did not report until August 11, 2010, was a bombshell. In an interview with the *Daily Beast*, he disclosed that the White House conspiracies against him included a murder plot: "On May 3, 1972, a dozen CIA assets from the Bay of Pigs, Cuban émigrés, were brought up from Miami [possibly the future Watergate burglars] with orders to 'incapacitate me totally.' I said to the [Watergate] prosecutor, 'What does that mean? Kill me?' He said it means to incapacitate you totally. But you have to understand these guys never use the word 'kill.'"[20]

Chapter 15

The X Envelope

It was purely due to government secrecy that Richard Nixon never saw justice for his actions surrounding the Vietnam peace sabotage. Had the public become aware of the drama behind the scenes, history would likely have been written quite differently. And in a government purportedly "by the people, for the people," it is up to the people to determine the nation's destiny.

A secret and paranoid person who had knowingly committed high crimes, Nixon was intent on keeping his dealings secret; ultimately, Johnson played right into his successor's hands by fulfilling that wish. Afraid of judgment for his own, lesser misdeeds, Johnson swallowed his anger and kept mute.

As the presidential baton passed from Lyndon Johnson to Richard Nixon, the elder statesman sought to secure the information he had on his successor: information so damning that he could not risk it falling into the wrong hands—or, indeed, any hands. President Johnson gathered together the cables, reports, transcripts, and news articles that comprised his knowledge of what he had dubbed Nixon's "treason." He filed them away and entrusted the volatile folder to the one man who had been by his side and privy to virtually every new development in the case: Walt Rostow, special assistant for national security affairs. Following Nixon's inauguration, his tenure at the White House up, Rostow moved to Texas and took a teaching position at the University of Texas at Austin, where the public affairs department would soon be named after Johnson himself.

Two days after President Nixon's second inauguration, during which he announced he would begin dismantling his predecessor's hard-won Great Society programs, Lyndon Johnson passed away. The very next night, Nixon announced he would finally end the Vietnam War.

With LBJ gone, Walt Rostow found himself the sole curator of a cache of top-secret, highly explosive documents, which he was to entrust to the LBJ Library. With the events of Watergate unfolding, Rostow had good reason to believe that the information contained in the file was at least tangentially related. On June 25, John Dean testified in hearings that the recently unraveling Watergate scandal was just one event in a years-long pattern of espionage by the White House — something of which Rostow was one of just a few people already well aware.

The day after Dean's testimony, Rostow penned a top-secret, handwritten note and attached it to the X Envelope. The note read: "To be opened by the Director, Lyndon Baines Johnson Library not earlier than fifty (50) years from this date June 26, 1973."[1] Rostow then typed out a memo to Harry Middleton, director of the LBJ Presidential Library and former Johnson speechwriter, labeling the document "Literally Eyes Only." He revealed:

> Sealed in the attached envelope is a file President Johnson asked me to hold personally because of its sensitive nature. In case of his death, the material was to be consigned to the LBJ Library under conditions I judged to be appropriate.
>
> The file concerns the activities of Mrs. Chennault and others before and immediately after the election of 1968. At the time President Johnson decided to handle the matter strictly as a question of national security; and, in retrospect, he felt that decision was correct.
>
> It is, therefore, my recommendation to you that this file should remain sealed for fifty years from the date of this memorandum.
>
> After fifty years the Director of the LBJ Library (or whomever may inherit his responsibilities, should the administrative structure of the National Archives change) may, alone, open this file. If he believes the material it contains might be opened for research, he should then consult the then responsible security officials of the Executive Branch to arrange formal clearance. If he believes the material it contains should not be opened for research, I would wish him empowered to re-close the file for another fifty years when the procedure outlined above should be repeated.[2]

Rostow addressed the package, labeled "Eyes Only," to Middleton, and in delivering the file shifted the burden of responsibility onto new shoulders.

~~Top Secret~~

To be opened by the Director,
Lyndon Baines Johnson
Library not earlier than
fifty (50) years from this
date June 26, 1973.

opened by rg 7/22/94
~~destructions~~ of HM/WNR

PRESERVATION COPY

REFERENCE FILE

COPY LBJ LIBRARY

Rostow's handwritten note on the top-secret X Envelope (Courtesy LBJ Presidential Library)

June 26, 1973

TO: Mr. Harry Middleton, Director, LBJ Library

Sealed in the attached envelope is a file President Johnson asked me to hold personally because of its sensitive nature. In case of his death, the material was to be consigned to the LBJ Library under conditions I judged to be appropriate.

The file concerns the activities of Mrs. Chennault and others before and immediately after the election of 1968. At the time President Johnson decided to handle the matter strictly as a question of national security; and, in retrospect, he felt that decision was correct.

It is, therefore, my recommendation to you that this file should remain sealed for fifty years from the date of this memorandum.

After fifty years the Director of the LBJ Library (or whomever may inherit his responsibilities, should the administrative structure of the National Archives change) may, alone, open this file. If he believes the material it contains might be opened for research, he should then consult the then responsible security officials of the Executive Branch to arrange formal clearance. If he believes the material it contains should not be opened for research, I would wish him empowered to re-close the file for another fifty years when the procedure outlined above should be repeated.

W W Rostow
W. W. Rostow

PRESERVATION COPY

REFERENCE FILE

COPY LBJ LIBRARY

Document 0 of the X Envelope, Rostow's typed memo to LBJ Library director Harry Middleton (Courtesy LBJ Presidential Library)

The X Envelope would be speculated upon for years. Ultimately, Director Middleton did not wait the half-century requested by Rostow prior to opening the envelope. With Rostow's consent, on July 22, 1994—three months to the day after Richard Nixon's death, likely a pertinent factor in Rostow's decision to bequeath early permission—the envelope was unsealed and archivists began reviewing materials.

Portions of the X Envelope still remain classified, but much of it has been declassified and is viewable by the public. The information therein makes up much of this book and can be reviewed in further depth in the appendix.

The file, as Rostow described it in a May 1973 memorandum for the record, contained "the information available to me and (I believe) the bulk of the information available to President Johnson on the activities of Mrs. Chennault and other Republicans just before the presidential election of 1968."[3] It revealed the actions of Madame Chennault, Ambassador Diem, and candidate Nixon and his staff, including John Mitchell; recorded for history Johnson's reaction, his exclamation that "this is treason"; and included Rostow's own speculation on the connection to Watergate.

Thus, like a time capsule, the X Envelope preserved the essence of a great, untold political scandal, one examined only partially by the media and otherwise left to fester, to erode the honor and integrity of the office of the presidency.

(Pop-culture sidenote: Though Nixon's "treason" was not yet revealed at the time, Chris Carter, creator of the longtime, popular TV series *The X-Files*, says his show was in large measure inspired by Nixon. "If there is a ghost animating the machinery of *The X-Files*, it is Richard Nixon, the icon of paranoia whose career virtually defined the golden age of American conspiracy theory," he said.[4])

One vital aspect of the story is that, for a brief moment in time, the scandal almost did not remain secret. Walt Rostow, Dean Rusk, and Clark Clifford discussed the option to go public with the information they possessed—information that undoubtedly could and would have impacted the decisions of perhaps millions of Americans in their voting behavior, both in the 1968 and 1972 elections. Had the American public been aware of Nixon's actions, the subsequent years could not have been the same. Even if the news had been released too late and Nixon still won the '68 election, his political capital would have been severely diminished; perhaps he would have been forced to end the war, or his resignation to avoid impeachment would have come a term earlier.

But instead, President Johnson's top advisors decided on the eve of the 1968 election that the public had no right to know of the events that had unfolded, and thus the entire story would be kept under wraps.

The Push for Transparency

It was journalists who ensured the story of Nixon's betrayal and arguable treason did not remain entirely secret, who fought for some modicum of transparency even as events unfolded. From Jack Anderson to Saville Davis and all of their colleagues who put ink to paper regarding this story, it was the members of the Fourth Estate who put two White House administrations on their toes and informed the American public to the best of their abilities.

During both the 1968 election season and the following summer, murmurs spread among the journalistic community that something was afoot. Several members of the press inquired with the White House, the Vietnamese Embassy, and others, their requests for information roundly rejected or avoided; several such transcripts were filed away in the X Envelope. What the journalists could confirm, they printed. But those in and out of government who knew the full story were remarkably tight-lipped, and very little information escaped uncontrolled.

Journalists thrive on sources of information, and without such sources, stories shrivel and die, never to go public. An informed electorate relies on not only journalists themselves but on their sources to supply information—and in an age of increasing government secrecy, sources become harder and harder to come by. They become labeled with terms such as "leaker" or "whistleblower," often targeted for prosecution by the government whose secrets they reveal.

The saying goes that sunshine is the best disinfectant. A transparent government is a clean government, while one shrouded in secrecy is a breeding ground for all manner of ills. And as of the early twenty-first century, the American government is getting more — not less — secretive. Pres. George W. Bush was a nightmare when it came to transparency, and President Obama, who vowed on his election eve to be different, has earned nicknames such as "the least transparent president in history" for his administration's failure to uphold its promise of openness.[5] Redaction and obfuscation are standard government procedure, and as a result decision-making by the public suffers from lack of information.

Recent explosions of information have occurred, much along the lines of Daniel Ellsberg's Pentagon Papers leak. Pvt. Chelsea Manning[6] leaked a tremendous cache of government documents in 2010 that confirmed many ills of the Iraq and Afghanistan wars and is now serving prison time under the Espionage Act. In 2013, national security contractor Edward Snowden set off a veritable atomic bomb of intelligence leaks as he teamed up first with London's the *Guardian* and later the *Washington Post* to reveal — for starters — the scope of the American intelligence community's surveillance and the utter deterioration of privacy in the twenty-first century. The reporting yielded a Pulitzer Prize for the two news outlets; their source, Edward Snowden, is wanted for prosecution in the United States and currently living under asylum in Russia.

The Manning and Snowden leaks give us a glimpse of the government's true behavior, powering the question of what dusty government files, what modern-day X Envelopes, might still remain closed — and what new ones are currently being filed away out of sight as we speak, never intended for public consumption.

For just one example, the National Security Agency continues to obfuscate the release of information relating to United States involvement in the 1962 arrest of Nelson Mandela, despite the passing of half a century and Mandela's release, election as South Africa's first black president, and death.[7] Countless other Freedom of Information Act (FOIA) requests have been similarly denied. On a separate topic, the CIA has recently been accused of manipulating information regarding its highly classified and highly illegal torture and rendition programs, about which the public was never supposed to know.

With official channels narrowing, the best sources of information for both journalists and the public become whistleblowers like Ellsberg, Manning, and Snowden. This means that, for the vision of a transparent and clean government, individual citizens must risk their freedoms — and even lives — to release knowledge that has been classified and closed. Aware of this fact, the Obama administration has vigorously prosecuted more whistleblowers than any president in history, with a disturbing tendency to classify those individuals in the same category as spies or terrorists. In a democracy, should the people not be aware of their government's actions?

Nixon's deeds reach far beyond a single diplomatic sabotage. His record spans blackmail, murder threats, instigating foreign coups, lying to the American public, and heavy drug use while holding the office of commander in chief. Likely he is not the only government official to commit such acts, but he was certainly one of the most flagrant, and seemingly one of the most careless.

Some modicum of secrecy surrounding high-level government officials' personal lives is to be expected and, in most instances, excused. But when the shroud covers all manner of ills, political and personal, both relatively insignificant and of global proportions, a question must be asked that will surely reverberate through administrations to come: where should the line be drawn? What, in the words of Lyndon Johnson's top advisors, is the "public right to know"?

Chapter 16
Was It Treason?

Upon discovering Nixon's back-door dealings with the South Vietnamese, President Johnson—furious and frustrated—exclaimed on the phone to Sen. Everett Dirksen, "This is treason!" Those words, though spat out in a heated moment, ring potentially true—certainly enough to merit further examination. Did the thirty-seventh president of the United States commit treason to obtain that office?

The definition of "treason" is spelled out in Article 3, section 3, of the United States Constitution: "Treason against the United States, shall consist only in levying war against them, or in adhering to their enemies, giving them aid and comfort. No person shall be convicted of treason unless on the testimony of two witnesses to the same overt act, or on confession in open court."[1]

In encouraging President Thieu to hold out on the peace talks, Richard Nixon prolonged a war in Southeast Asia in which the United States was heavily involved. Though South Vietnam, with whose officials Nixon was colluding, was not the enemy of the U.S. (the common enemy was rather communist North Vietnam), the overt extension of the war could viably implicate Nixon as a traitor.

Furthermore, though evidence does not suggest Nixon was colluding with the North Vietnamese (though, as noted, portions of the X Envelope remain a mystery and could be speculated on indefinitely), dragging out the war was favorable for the communist fighters. Rather than weakening North Vietnam's position, Nixon's actions empowered the Viet Cong in the long term; ultimately, the communists overran South Vietnam almost as soon as American boots had lifted off. Nixon's efforts, though perhaps indirectly, did clearly serve to aid the North.

The punishment for treason, according to 18 U.S. Code § 2381, is designated as follows: "Whoever, owing allegiance to the United

States, levies war against them or adheres to their enemies, giving them aid and comfort within the United States or elsewhere, is guilty of treason and shall suffer death, or shall be imprisoned not less than five years and fined under this title but not less than $10,000; and shall be incapable of holding any office under the United States."[2] Should Nixon have been tried in court for his actions, surely it would be determined that he owed allegiance to the United States and was thus beholden to this statute; were his actions then deemed traitorous, even if he had not been condemned to death, he would have been promptly precluded from ever holding elected (or appointed) office again—most certainly including the office of the president.

Though lacking the inherent, wrenching nature of a term like "treason," the 18 U.S. Code § 953 is also applicable to Nixon's actions. Also called the Logan Act, this law addresses private correspondence with foreign governments. The Act reads:

> Any citizen of the United States, wherever he may be, who, without authority of the United States, directly or indirectly commences or carries on any correspondence or intercourse with any foreign government or any officer or agent thereof, with intent to influence the measures or conduct of any foreign government or of any officer or agent thereof, in relation to any disputes or controversies with the United States, or to defeat the measures of the United States, shall be fined under this title or imprisoned not more than three years, or both.
>
> This section shall not abridge the right of a citizen to apply, himself or his agent, to any foreign government or the agents thereof for redress of any injury which he may have sustained from such government or any of its agents or subjects.[3]

Essentially, the Logan Act states that U.S. citizens may not exert sway over foreign governments in an attempt to influence their actions.

Importantly, during the time of the sabotage in 1968, Richard Nixon held no political office, elected or otherwise. He could not hide behind the cloak of government service or claim any level of diplomatic privilege. He was campaigning for an office that would give him credence to conduct foreign policy on the highest of levels;

but, until noon on January 20, 1969, he had none.

Yet Nixon was working his hardest to influence the South Vietnamese government, urging vehemently that they not sit down at the negotiating table as had been agreed upon with those who *did* have negotiating power. He had no authority of any U.S. officials (the tacit agreement by Henry Kissinger being virtually inconsequential, as Kissinger himself was betraying Johnson and may have been guilty of serving as an accessory), and Nixon's actions were not intended to redress any injury he himself had sustained by South Vietnam.

Thus, Nixon's behavior in clear violation of the Logan Act, it can be safely determined that he was in fact a criminal even before taking office, infamous for his false claim "I am not a crook." Had he been tried rather than elected, chances are he would have spent the turn of the 1970s not in the Oval Office but in prison.

Accusations

It is difficult to argue with two of the greatest constitutional experts and leading lawmakers of their time, Democrat Lyndon Johnson and Republican Everett Dirksen. They agreed that Republican presidential candidate Richard Nixon committed treason in 1968. And if treason means treachery against one's own government, it sure sounds like they were right.

Yet some constitutional scholars fear weighing in on that question in this case, mainly because the word "treason" is so frequently bandied about in today's ultra-heated political atmosphere that it has lost much of its meaning. An additional problem in deciding whether the law applies to this case is that no one has ever been tried for treason. Even if it were treason, all the major perpetrators have died — except for Henry Kissinger, Anna Chennault, and Richard Allen; putting these now-elderly players on trial at this point would be more than a tad too late, as well as ineffective at setting the proper precedent.

As we have seen, top LBJ intimates and advisors Abe Fortas and Clark Clifford told LBJ that "treason" had been committed. LBJ sent William Bundy to brief his vice president, "hoping *he* would blow the whistle on his opponent. Yet Humphrey balked, saying: 'It would have been difficult to explain how we knew about what [Chennault] had done.' . . . Johnson was furious with the vice president, believing it was 'the dumbest thing in the world not to do it.'"[4]

Another key LBJ adviser, Walt Rostow, never used the t-word himself, though it is clear he thought a serious violation of some human law had been carried out—a crime so hideous that Rostow decided it should not see the light of day for fifty years. Thanks to the X Envelope, we now know Walt Rostow's dire opinion. Back in 1968, on October 28, the president's national security advisor cabled LBJ about "the explosive possibilities of the information we now have [on the sabotage]" and warning him that "the materials are so explosive that they could gravely damage the country whether Mr. Nixon is elected or not."[5]

Then, on October 31, Rostow recommended that if Thieu kept refusing to go to Paris, Nixon should be summoned to the White House and shown some of the cards in LBJ's royal flush of intelligence data. "Give him the evidence," Rostow advised, "that the South Vietnamese are thinking they can turn down this deal until after the election."[6] (Obviously, nothing ever came of this idea.)

Many years later, Rostow observed: "I think there was an element of authentic shock [by LBJ] that [Nixon would] go so far as to try to suborn another government to do something that would help win the election. But it [Johnson's attitude] was tempered by the fact that he held a very low view of Nixon."[7]

On November 26, 1968, Pres. Lyndon Johnson complained to Nixon's friend Sen. George Smathers (D-Florida) that the president-elect was still meddling with the peace talks. Knowing his message would get back to Nixon, Johnson also clearly explained why he could *not* disclose Nixon's anti-peace activities: "Now, I didn't expose it because I couldn't use those [NSA, CIA and FBI] sources, and I didn't want to make it impossible for [Nixon] to govern. I think if I . . . had exposed this, brought it out, it would shock the country so, that he would have been seriously hurt."[8]

Nixon sent back word to Johnson through a third party that there was "not any truth at all in this allegation," but LBJ wanted to hear that directly from the GOP candidate. At this point, Nixon aide Bryce Harlow enters the picture as a middleman. He recalled telling Nixon, "You've got to talk with LBJ. Someone has told him that you're all over the South Vietnamese to keep them from doing something about peace and he's just about to believe it." Harlow is one of only a few Nixon aides to have ever discussed the Chennault episode. (Kissinger, for example, has never been asked to address the matter, to the author's knowledge and research.)

A class act and highly respected on both sides of the aisle on Capitol Hill (where he later served as President Nixon's chief congressional lobbyist), Harlow would not have been surprised if Nixon had been involved in such a scheme, and he vividly recalled his advice to the candidate:

> "If you don't let [LBJ] know quickly that it's not so, then he's going to dump [the sabotage story.] At least he says so. Ev [Dirksen] is just beside himself. He says that Lyndon Johnson is simply enraged and we ought to do something . . . you've got to do it." And so he did. [Nixon] called him. He got him on the phone and said there was absolutely no truth to it as far as he knew. I'm not convinced it was not true. It was too tempting a target . . .[9]

When Nixon's personal denial call came into the White House switchboard on November 8, 1968, President Johnson signaled his secretary to flip the "record" switch on his secret tape recorder. After a brief exchange of small talk, it was Nixon himself who brought up the war:

> **Nixon:** Now getting to the one, the key point: Is there anything I could do before [the two men were to next meet] on this business of South Vietnam? If you want me to do something, you know I'll do anything, because we're not going to let these people [his own people!] stop these peace things. If you think I can do something . . .
>
> **LBJ:** Dick, I told Dirksen last night I thought it'd be better to do it that way [presumably to get Nixon to stop his minions from blocking the peace talks] than to be calling on the trips. [Nixon had suggested making trips to Saigon or Paris to help the peace process.] I think this: These people are proceeding on the assumption that folks close to you tell them to do nothing until January 20.[10]

It's hard to pick out the biggest lie of Nixon's November 8

conversation with his predecessor, but it could be this somber pledge to LBJ: "Now let me say this, Mr. President, that there's nothing that I want more than to get these people to that table."[11]

"Yeah," the commander in chief responded sardonically. Of course, LBJ and his top advisors knew from a huge load of top-secret intelligence that Nixon was lying through his teeth. LBJ aide Joseph Califano would later describe President Johnson's disgust with Nixon, saying LBJ felt he was "a man so consumed with power that he would betray the country's national security interests, undermine its foreign policy, and endanger the lives of its young soldiers to win office."[12]

Copping to the Crimes

At an August 20, 1972, press conference near Nixon's San Clemente, California, estate, this author got a chance to ask the president about his inability to make good on his 1968 campaign pledge to end the war. My question came as a follow-up to Nixon's false press conference suggestion that LBJ's 1968 bombing halt was meant to help Vice President Humphrey. Nixon knew this wasn't true—because he and the other presidential contenders were getting regular updates from LBJ on the status of the Paris peace talks. Of course, the GOP candidate was also getting detailed top-secret notes and analyses on the 1968 talks from his spy in Paris, Henry Kissinger. So let's pick up the give-and-take with the previous question:

> **Q:** Is there a possibility that you would call off the bombing or slacken it even if there is no all-inclusive agreement on Indochina?
> **The President:** Absolutely not. I have noted some press speculation to the effect that, since the 1968 bombing halt seemed to have a rather dramatic effect on the election chances of Senator Humphrey—Vice President Humphrey, now a Senator—that people have suggested as a gimmick, or more or less an election-eve tactic, that we would call a bombing halt even though our prisoners of war are not accounted for. No progress has been made there, and even though the enemy continued its activities and was still stonewalling us in the negotiations, unless there is progress on the negotiating front which is substantial,

there will be no reduction of the bombing of North Vietnam and there will be no lifting of the mining.

Q: Mr. President, I would like to ask you about a 1968 statement you made and find out whether you still agree with it. It is: "Those who have had a chance for four years and could not produce peace should not be given another chance."

The President: I think the answer I gave to [a previous] question is as responsive as I can make it. We always, of course, set our goals high. We do our very best to reach those goals. I think there are those who have faulted this administration on its efforts to seek peace, but those who fault it, I would respectfully suggest, are ones that would have the United States seek peace at the cost of surrender, dishonor, and the destruction of the ability of the United States to conduct foreign policy in a responsible way. That I did not pledge in 1968. I do not pledge it now. We will seek peace. We will seek better relations with our adversaries — but we are going to keep the United States strong. We are going to resist the efforts of those who would cut our defense budget to make us second to any power in the world, and second, particularly, to the Soviet Union, and in order to do that, it means that we have to continue the responsible policy that we have carried out.[13]

Of course, in November 1972, just months after this press conference, Nixon won reelection by a landslide. He took forty-nine states while Democratic peace candidate George McGovern won only Massachusetts and the District of Columbia.

Neither Lyndon Johnson nor Richard Nixon nor Henry Kissinger nor Hubert Humphrey discussed Nixon's sabotage of the peace talks in their memoirs. Anna Chennault and Bui Diem have confirmed their roles in the plot, as has Richard Allen. Thieu never wrote or spoke publicly about his 1968 anti-peace deal with Nixon. John Mitchell never wrote an autobiography and never talked about the Chennault episode.

There is fresh evidence, however, that Mitchell seems to have had as few scruples as the rest of those involved on the Nixon side of the Chennault affair. In a recent book, Mitchell's biographer, James Rosen, acknowledges that Mitchell got away with a number of crimes, first among them "his illegal intervention in the 1968 Paris peace talks: when Nixon and Mitchell, with the aid of Anna Chennault, violated the laws of international diplomacy, directly contacting South Vietnamese officials to urge them not to be swayed by Lyndon Johnson's last-minute bombing halt."[14]

As a result of his leading role in President Nixon's Watergate scandal, Mitchell became the first former United States attorney general to serve time in prison. However, it was not known until recently that Mitchell was a serial liar, not unlike his former law partner, Richard Nixon. (Nixon surely knew of these skills, and this is a likely reason why the president asked FBI chief J. Edgar Hoover not to investigate Mitchell's background prior to his appointment.) Among the fictitious stories Mitchell told are the following, recounted in Rosen's biography: In an appearance on *The Dick Cavett Show*, Mitchell claimed to have once been a professional golfer. He wasn't. Similarly, he was never the pro hockey player for the New York Rangers his obituary asserted he was. Mitchell had neither commanded John F. Kennedy in the Navy, as his eulogy stated, nor been awarded the Navy's Silver Star for gallantry in combat. The future attorney general claimed he was twice wounded but, according to naval files, these reputed injuries were never verified, making it impossible for him to have been honored with two purple hearts.[15]

So did Nixon commit treason in 1968? I asked my old friend Sid Davis for his thoughts. During a long and distinguished career in Washington journalism, Sid was lucky enough to have covered Vice Pres. Richard Nixon (as a candidate for president in 1960) and Presidents John Kennedy and Lyndon Johnson. He later held high executive positions at NBC News and the Voice of America in Washington. Now in his early 90s, Sid doesn't use the term "treason" either, but he does take a very dark view of Nixon's actions:

> Watergate, it turns out, was not Richard Nixon's greatest crime. Although Watergate was an unprecedented, fundamental attack on our liberties. I am talking about the 20-thousand additional Americans soldiers who died in a prolonged war after Nixon became President. Those soldiers could have been spared had President Lyndon Johnson been allowed to hold peace talks in Paris in 1968 before he left office. . . .
>
> Even as President Johnson spoke to Nixon from the Oval Office, LBJ was sitting on wiretaps revealing phone calls, reportedly from Madame Anna Chennault to the South Vietnam Ambassador in

Washington urging him to tell the South Vietnamese to stay home, that Nixon would give them "a better deal." . . .

President Johnson is supposed to have urged Vice President Humphrey to go public with Nixon's alleged perfidy but Humphrey refused, believing the nation—already torn and in turmoil—could not endure such a scandal. . . .

Lyndon Johnson wanted nothing more than a face-to-face meeting with Ho Chi Minh, believing he would get a deal as he had with so many adversaries in Congress. He told me and two other reporters as much in a private session in the White House. "What does he want? We can do it."[16]

Astonished that the story of Nixon's sabotage has gotten such little play in the news media, Sid Davis is even more shocked at the American people for electing "such a man President, not once, but twice having known of his vicious political, sometimes racial tactics, of his successful character assassinations of opponents, of seeing 30 of his appointees go to jail in his behalf. Nixon died at age 81 in New York Hospital, April 23, 1994. So why this now about a dead President? People don't change because they are dead."[17]

While trying to determine whether Richard Nixon actually did commit treason in 1968 is an intriguing yet difficult question, one thing is certain: whatever you call it, it was entirely reprehensible conduct, and likely a violation of one or more laws, including the Logan Act.

In 2002, without knowing the full story of Nixon's anti-peace moves (and without entering the rather fruitless debate over just what constitutes "treason"), Christopher Hitchens knew enough to assert that the 1968 Republican candidate's "illegal and surreptitious conduct not only prolonged an awful war but also corrupted and subverted a crucial presidential election. The combination," he added, "must make it the most wicked action in American history."[18]

Chapter 17

Was Nixon Nuts?

Could Richard Nixon have pleaded insanity had he been tried for treason, breaking the Logan Act, or any of his other presidential illegalities? Perhaps by trying to answer this hypothetical question we might help start a realistic public conversation about how best to have kept a would-be Nixon from the presidency.

The question of whether Nixon had a few screws loose can actually be partially answered by taking a look at the Richard Nixon foreign policy playbook. Many Nixon supporters point to his foreign policy accomplishments—opening up China and reinstituting a civilized relationship with the Soviet Union—as the president's chief successes of his time in office. Yet few know that the basis of Nixon's foreign policy negotiations was really to exploit the fact that many people who knew him had no doubt he was mentally unstable.

Few have described this incredible foreign policy tactic better than Nixon himself, as he explained the self-named "Madman Theory" to a confused, and probably frightened, chief of staff H. R. Haldeman: "I want the North Vietnamese to believe I've reached the point where I might do anything to stop the war. We'll just slip the word to them that, 'for God's sake, you know Nixon is obsessed about communism. We can't restrain him when he's angry—and he has his hand on the nuclear button' and Ho Chi Minh himself will be in Paris in two days begging for peace."[1]

Nixon was a drama student in high school; it was where he learned to cry on the spot and produce a stream of tears on command. But perhaps this role was easier to slip into for the president than most others. In fact, one might say that it was a role Richard Nixon was born to play.

The strategy was used by many top Nixon aides in their negotiations with various communist countries, from Vietnam to the Soviet Union, and hinged partly on the notion of mutually assured destruction. The Nixon team wanted other nations to believe that the president was so bonkers, he would order a nuclear strike even on a power that possessed a nuclear stockpile of its own: the Soviet Union.

A dramatic critic might say that Nixon gave the performance of a lifetime. He apparently became lost in the role when he actually did order nuclear strikes, inebriated on the phone, and his aides had the good insight to disregard them.

One can imagine the theory being proposed either by those closest to Nixon or by the president himself. At the very least, it was inspired by strong suspicions that the president was not playing with a full deck. Though obviously unconventional, the Madman Theory was not altogether new. The political philosopher Machiavelli, who wrote about qualities a dictator may find most useful to rule with an iron fist, noted that it was "a very wise thing to simulate madness."

But how much of this was truly simulation? Was the thirty-seventh president of the United States truly mentally unstable? The question is legitimate, considering that Nixon's own psychotherapist, after Nixon's death, privately expressed concern over whether his most famous patient should have been allowed to hold high office. Dr. Arnold Hutschnecker described Nixon as "an emotionally deprived child" and noted that "Nixon's father was brutal and cruel. [He] brutalized the mother, and this is of enormous importance" to Nixon's mental stability.[2]

The question then remains: how could such a deeply troubled man swindle his way into the White House on a scheme as dastardly as Nixon's sabotage of the 1968 peace talks? Not much of the blame can be placed on an American public who simply was unable to sniff out Nixon's many lies. Perhaps the news media failed to properly report on some of Nixon's more glaring lapses on the campaign trail. It was a different time for political journalism in the United States, as the private affairs of politicians were considered off-limits in those days. Arguably, the changes in coverage towards a more no-holds-barred style of reporting has help prevent such troubled candidates as Nixon from ever reaching the White House again.

Yet, after observing the unhinged chief executive, some of those who knew Nixon best gained the impression that more safeguards were needed than an over-zealous news media. To them, a formal legal mechanism was required to ensure the mental stability of any future office holder of the presidency.

Publicly, Dr. Hutschnecker was a longtime advocate of a mental health evaluation for presidential candidates. Currently, no medical evaluations whatsoever are legally required of presidential hopefuls, though some have disclosed medical reports during elections, usually in response to nagging doubts in the news media. Sen. John McCain of Arizona, a presidential candidate in 2000 and 2008, faced repeated inquiries into his physical and mental health, eventually forcing him to respond. The senator served valiantly in Vietnam and was shot down flying a mission over Hanoi in 1967, captured by the North Vietnamese, and tortured until his release nearly six years later. Persistent doubts over his physical health due to war injuries and recent bouts with skin cancer led McCain to release all of his post-2000 medical records. However, despite probing questions regarding his mental health, McCain never did release his psychiatric records. Perhaps mandatory disclosure could have put an end to the speculation, or at least given voters accurate information regarding the legitimate question of a presidential candidate's ability to fulfill the monumental duties of the office.

On the other hand, several presidents have infamously withheld critical medical information from voters. Most notably, Woodrow Wilson hid a string of minor strokes from the American public leading up to his presidential bid, only to suffer a cataclysmic one in 1919 that paralyzed him. The final years of his presidency saw his wife, Edith, handling many of the executive affairs of the White House, only turning to her bedridden husband for advice on questions she deemed vital.

Dr. Hutschnecker's recommendation to require mental-health evaluations is undoubtedly a direct result of his first-hand glimpse into the deeply troubling Nixon "White House Horrors." Before many people knew he had treated Nixon, the doctor wrote an op-ed in the *New York Times* saying, "I cannot help [thinking] that if an American president had a staff psychiatrist, perhaps a case such as Watergate might not have had a chance to develop."[3]

A top psychiatrist who studied Nixon's life intensively for three years, Dr. David Abrahamsen, believed that Nixon was unfit for his position. In an interview with Abrahamsen, the author of *Nixon vs. Nixon*, Watergate good guy John Dean asked the doctor about his book's conclusion that Nixon had had a "character disturbance" since "early childhood." Nixon, the psychiatrist said, was "intrinsically unhappy, hostile, and therefore depressed" — a threat to himself and others. For good measure, Abrahamsen added that Nixon's "emotionally crippled state" prevented him from obeying and respecting the country's laws.

When Dean asked Abrahamsen if he thought Nixon was crazy, the doctor immediately answered, "Yes." To top this off, the psychiatrist expressed his belief that Nixon may have gotten off for being mentally unstable had he been tried for his Watergate crimes. Nixon was "not able emotionally to appreciate the wrongfulness of his act," asserted Abrahamsen, "so he would be declared insane."[4]

Evidence from Nixon's Acquaintances

In the nuclear age, one can think of no more horrifying scenario than an unbalanced or irrational chief executive of the United States commanding an arsenal of devastating atomic weapons. However, the prospect, without mandated mental evaluations of presidential candidates, is not as far-fetched as one might believe. A close examination of just how incredibly unstable the White House was under Nixon reveals compelling evidence for adding this new step to the process of how we go about evaluating our chief executives.

Those who knew him best thought Nixon might well be coming un-glued during his final months in Washington. White House chief of staff Alexander Haig directed Nixon's doctors to confiscate his drug supply. Secretary of Defense James Schlesinger ordered top brass *not* to obey any eleventh-hour military orders from the White House without his approval. When word of Schlesinger's unprecedented move later leaked, *New York Times* columnist William Shannon expressed relief: "The United States was lucky in August (when Nixon resigned without attempting a coup)" because, had conditions been slightly different, Nixon might have called up the military. "Next time," Shannon warned. ". . . the Secretary of Defense might be feeble and compliant."[5]

Secretary of State Henry Kissinger — who had been calling Nixon "Our Meatball President" for some time — regularly had to talk an irrational or drunk Nixon out of nuking North Vietnam or some other country. Edward Cox, Trisha Nixon's husband, watched with concern as his father-in-law prowled White House corridors late at night speaking to portraits of his dead predecessors. When this news finally leaked in 1976, *Saturday Night Live* mimicked its weirdness. Playing Nixon, Dan Aykroyd told Lincoln's portrait: "Well, Abe, you were lucky. They *shot* you." To Kennedy, he warned: "They're gonna find out about you, too. The president having sex — with *women* — within these very walls. That *never* happened when Dick Nixon was president."[6]

On his final full day at the White House, Nixon told his press secretary, Ron Ziegler, that he looked forward to writing — but that the writing might be done from prison; "Some of the best writing in history has been done in prison. Think of Lenin and Gandhi."[7] By resignation eve, Nixon was an emotional mess. Or a good actor. Or both.

The president's farewell to his Hill backers — "I'm sorry if you think I let you down" — was preceded by his final walk from the Executive Office Building to the Executive Mansion. Desiring peace and solitude — wanting to avoid running into any detested reporters — Nixon ordered that the press be locked inside their West Wing quarters during his stroll. The "lockdown" on the press area lasted about a half hour.

Lillian Brown, Nixon's TV makeup artist, remembers he was "a basket case" by the time he got to her just before his resignation address. The president had broken down in tears in her chair. She was able to calm him with her soothing voice and manner. Only a short time earlier, the president had likewise sobbed so hard at a White House meeting with his last-ditch supporters in Congress that he had to be led from the room by several of them. Having composed Nixon, for the most part, Brown applied her special pancake and antiperspirant combination that would keep the president's upper lip dry for up to 20 minutes. Nixon looked and sounded fine on TV — except for excess eyelash fluttering. His image on the tube, however, differed drastically from what those in the Oval Office had observed just minutes before the broadcast.

Sitting behind his desk for a microphone and lighting check, the thirty-seventh president suddenly blew a gasket because his still photographer, Ollie Atkins, was furiously clicking his lens and disturbing Nixon's concentration.

> **RN:** My friend Ollie always wants to take a lot of pictures of me. I'm afraid he'll catch me pickin' my nose. He wouldn't print that, would you, though, Oddie . . . ah, Ollie.?
> **OA:** No, sir.
> **RN:** You can take a long shot, but that's enough right now!

Just a few seconds later, an angrier Nixon lit into Atkins once again:

> **RN:** Okay. All right. Fine. Fine. I'm not going to make the other photographers mad by giving you so many. Now that's enough! Okay? Now, all Secret Service! Are there any Secret Service in the room?
> **Presidential aide Steve Bull:** Yes. Just one agent.
> **RN:** OUT! You don't have to stay do you?
> **Secret Service agent Dick Keiser:** Yes, sir.
> **RN:** You're required to?
> **Keiser:** Yes, sir.
> **RN:** I was just kidding you![8]

Some joke, eh? It seemed the president might be going bonkers just before appearing on live television and radio from coast to coast. But his off-camera behavior that night was nothing, psychologically speaking, compared to his near-meltdown in public the next morning, when he gave a televised farewell to the White House staff.

He praised his saintly mother (even though "no books will be written about her" — as they had been written about Rose Kennedy, he might have been thinking). Nixon's "old man" was "a great man because he did his job . . . to the hilt." Yet the departing president said nothing at all about the greatness of, or his love for, the family he had assembled, like mannequins, behind him.

They stood stiffly, near tears, as they saw a sweaty Nixon—

slurring his words now and again — falling apart before their eyes, and the nation's. Luckily the outgoing leader was able to stop before fully collapsing into in a heap of tearful self-pity, rambling memories, and curious advice to others. My favorite piece of advice was this beauty — described by historian Stanley Kutler as "autobiographical." Nixon asserted, "Those who hate you don't win unless you hate them, and then you destroy yourself."

A number of psychobiographers have also looked into Nixon's mental health. Historian David Greenberg notes that "collectively" they found "a man whose political behavior bubbled up from wellsprings deep in his character: aching insecurities, a furious drive for power, an insatiable hunger for love." Greenberg says those historians who probed Nixon's psyche linked Nixon's many character flaws to his earliest years:

> They traced those traits to formative childhood influences: his violent father, his controlling mother, the premature deaths of two of his brothers. And they suggested that Nixon suffered from peculiarities, if not deformations of character — rage competing with suppressed guilt, paranoia that bred secrecy and vindictiveness. A sense of injury. Almost uniformly, Nixon's psychobiographers saw him as a narcissist with a frail ego who lashed out when he felt wounded.[9]

At the height of the Watergate scandal, not long before Nixon's resignation, a half-dozen senators led by New York Republican Jacob Javits were so concerned about the president's emotional health that they consulted a psychiatrist. Dr. Bertram Brown reported back that "it wasn't clear what Nixon's mental status was. Whether he was going crazy, becoming psychotic, whether he would start a war . . . whether he would lose his cool." An unnamed Secret Service agent interviewed by reporter Ron Kessler had a similar take: "Towards the end Nixon got very paranoid. He didn't know what to believe or whom to trust. He did think people were lying to him. He thought at the end everyone was lying."[10] Nixon seems to fit the dictionary definition of a psychopath: "A person with an antisocial personality disorder, manifested in aggressive, perverted, criminal, or amoral behavior without empathy or remorse."[11]

An observant layman, onetime Nixon aide John Sears, recently opined that self-loathing was at the heart of Nixon's mean-spiritedness—and that the president's own lack of self-confidence led him to tear down others. "If you were out of his presence," Sears said, "and there was any way to pick you apart, he'd do it. That way he didn't feel so badly about himself. Of all the people who hated Nixon, Nixon had the lowest opinion of himself [of] anybody. It was always, 'Everybody's against me.'"[12]

A famous Washington psychiatrist, an expert who frequently analyzed foreign leaders for the CIA, weighs in on Nixon anonymously: "He was a psychopath . . . and, toward the end, definitely very, very paranoid."[13]

Nixon's Violence

A former Secret Service employee, speaking to historian Anthony Summers also on the condition of anonymity, observed a similar change in Nixon's behavior: "Nixon wasn't doing well under the stress and pressure and he became increasingly paranoid. It wore on his face. You could see it. He wasn't a classic alcoholic, but when he did drink on a few occasions he would drink to excess and become rather ugly. And there were two or three incidents in his career, one of which I was aware of, that he got a bit physical with his wife. The doctor would reveal that there was damage. Facial damage. That's all I can really go into."[14]

Investigative reporter Seymour Hersh has exposed three alleged Nixon wife-beating incidents—one of them reportedly sending Pat on a post-resignation ambulance ride to a hospital near San Clemente, California. Anthony Summers brings up several other incidents in which Nixon supposedly physically attacked Pat, including one after his loss to Gov. Pat Brown of California in 1962.

John Sears says he'd heard about that particular episode from two credible sources who indicated heavy blows were landed: "Nixon had hit her in 1962 and that she had threatened to leave him over it. . . . I'm not talking about a smack. He blackened her eye. . . . I had heard about that from Pat Hillings [a longtime Nixon friend] as well as from the family lawyer."[15]

Over the years, about a dozen aides had experienced Nixon's wrath in the form of violent outbursts. During his 1960 presidential campaign, for instance, Nixon became steamed over scheduling mistakes while he was touring Iowa by car. The vice president took out his anger on military aide Don Hughes. Bob Haldeman recalled that Nixon suddenly and "incredibly" began kicking the back of Hughes's car seat "with both feet. And he wouldn't stop. . . . The seat and the hapless Hughes jolted forward jaggedly as Nixon vented his rage. When the car stopped in a small town in the middle of nowhere, Hughes, white-faced, silently got out of the car and started walking straight ahead, down the road and out of town. He wanted to get as far away as he could from the Vice President."[16]

In 1960, another TV adviser, Everett Hart, absorbed a hard punch to the ribs from an irate Nixon during his presidential campaign against Sen. John F. Kennedy. Handicapped with a shriveled arm, and recovering from major cardiac surgery, Hart quit on the spot and never worked for Nixon again.[17]

In 1967, Nixon's target was Dwight Chapin, a young scheduling aide. "On one occasion [Nixon] was so enraged by some scheduling transgression that he threw Chapin against a wall, bruising his arm," according to Nixon biographer Jonathan Aitken.[18]

One of his final physical assaults on an aide took place in public in August 1973 as the president entered an arena in New Orleans. Nixon grabbed his press secretary, Ron Ziegler, by the shoulders, spun him around, and pushed him toward the reporters Nixon thought were following him too closely. This led columnist Nicholas von Hoffman to wonder whether Nixon was mentally ill: "Millions of us saw El Flippo on TV grab Ziegler by the arms, whirl him around and, with an expression on his face both frightening and frightful, shove him . . . Who can forget the picture of a President so out of control of himself that he expresses it by laying angry hands on a member of his staff in public?" Von Hoffman concluded that an "impression is gaining that Nixon is becoming dysfunctional, and the fear is growing that he may do something that we'll be sorry for."[19]

Letting Propriety Fall by the Wayside

Toward the end, the president was frequently "out of it." He would drink his troubles away almost every night. He was also taking Dilantin for anxiety (two pills a day) and one daily sleeping aid, Seconal—a dark red capsule known on the street as a "Red Devil" for its potency. (Nixon friend and televangelist Billy Graham blamed Nixon's downfall on those sleeping pills combined with what he termed "demons.")

Despite regularly mixing Seconal with the Dilantin and adding copious quantities of alcohol, President Nixon was still not able to get a good night's sleep. Unknown generally until now, he took daily afternoon naps on a cot in a small room just off the Oval Office—the same room later made famous as a trysting spot for Pres. Bill Clinton and White House intern Monica Lewinsky.[20]

Secretary of State Henry Kissinger dreaded those sleepless Nixon nights, particularly because they sometimes brought 3 a.m. phone calls from a boozy Nixon saying he and his friend Bebe Rebozo (a Mafia-linked Florida bachelor) wanted to bomb something to smithereens. When Al Haig got word of these calls he privately started calling Nixon "Our Drunken Friend."

Our thirty-seventh president had a life-long penchant for violent words as well as actions. He would blast the military over Vietnam, for example—once telling Kissinger that US pilots who were secretly bombing Cambodia were "just farting around doing nothing . . . running goddamn milk runs in order to get the Air Medal." His solution was to employ "armed helicopters, DC-3s, anything else that will destroy personnel that can fly. I want it done! Get them off their ass!"[21]

When he talked privately about the communists in Hanoi, Nixon would often use the language of a bully. Rejecting Kissinger's suggestions, which included conventional air attacks on power plants and docks, Nixon responded with the following:

> We want to decimate that goddamned place . . . North Vietnam is going to get reordered . . . It's about time. It's what should have been done years ago.

> The bastards have never been bombed like they're going to be this time!

> I'd rather use the nuclear bomb![22]

Much of such talk, of course, could be traced to booze — and not to a diagnosed mental illness. Yet alcoholism is now considered to be within the realm of psychiatric diseases. Using the *Diagnostic Statistical Manual IV*, a team of psychiatrists at Duke University Medical Center recently found that Nixon was, indeed, an alcoholic. One of that study's authors, Dr. Marvin Swartz, concluded: "The extensiveness of Richard Nixon's alcohol abuse was pretty remarkable and alarming, given the authority he had."[23]

So whether Nixon was a psychopath or just a drunk, there was something seriously wrong with "the strangest man" to occupy the Oval Office, as chief of staff Bob Haldeman described him.[24] And, over the long years of Nixon's political life, the American public deserved to have at least some facts about his mental condition and addiction before they went to the polls to vote for or against him.

Perhaps the country was let off easy with Watergate, though it was clearly the worst political scandal in American history. Were it not for the defiance on several occasions of some of Nixon's closest aides and political counterparts, the abuses of power perpetrated by Nixon could have easily included incalculable destruction greater than even the escalation and expansion of the Vietnam War.

Chapter 18

"Tricky Dick"

"All right, they still call me Tricky Dick," Richard Nixon conceded in 1967. "It's a brutal thing to fight." Nixon's nickname did indeed stick to him like flypaper. And only one year later— while promising that, if elected, "honesty will be the hallmark" of his presidency—he tricked his way into that office by what was arguably his most dishonorable move.

While this book has focused on Nixon's most heinous trick— the most damaging to his country, and what President Johnson called "treason"—it certainly wasn't one of his first or last. Nixon's penchant for underhandedness seems to fit a pattern that began in his childhood and continued with even greater gusto when Nixon assumed the presidency (after what now appears to have been an illegitimate victory in the 1968 election). So let's take an overview of some our thirty-seventh president's litany of tricks, capers, cons, cover-ups, illegalities, and subterfuges.

In January 1972, John Mitchell, the manager-to-be of Nixon's reelection campaign, gave the Watergate Plumbers preliminary approval to break into the Democratic Party's headquarters— proving that serial tricksters like Nixon can tumble into their own best-laid traps.

Nixon refused to take personal credit for the break-in at the Watergate, but the event led to a series of cover-up tricks that he conceived and executed: he made a generous offer of hush money to the ham-handed Watergate burglars; he ordered the secret manufacture and public presentation of fake transcripts of recordings from the Oval Office; he proposed to Congress that its most hard-of-hearing member, Sen. John Stennis, be charged with listening to the tapes to find incriminating evidence; he invented the "Rose Mary Stretch," which blamed eighteen-and-a-half minutes of silence in a key tape on his secretary's reaching for a phone in mid-transcription. And let us not forget his pre-impeachment resignation, which preserved his retirement perks, and his preemptive pardon, which kept him out of the slammer.

When Helen Gahagan Douglas branded her devious senatorial opponent "Tricky Dick" in 1950, she was merely giving a name to a pattern of behavior that had begun in Nixon's childhood, when he shed tears and acted, in his own words, "pretty convincing to avoid punishment." That pattern endured through his young manhood, when he was a pitch man at rigged carnival concessions; through law school, when he sneaked into the dean's office to peek at his grades; and through World War II, when adept bluffing (or marked cards?) won him big pots from fellow Navy officers at the poker table.

Nixon's natural aptitude for political trickery was no surprise, then, when he made his first run for elective office in 1946. In fact, a break-in helped him beat Congressman Jerry Voorhis, a Democrat from California. Voorhis's office was broken into and his campaign literature stolen. Men hired through theatrical agencies handed out the same material the next day, announcing: "We are Russians and we want you to vote for Mr. Voorhis."[1]

Over the years Nixon's tricks grew subtler and more intricate. For him, their final showcase was the privately funded $25 million Nixon library, which was built—under his personal direction—adjacent to the house in which Nixon claims to have been born in Yorba Linda, California. (His mother, Hannah, said Richard was born in a hospital.) The trick? First off, the sprawling ranch-style building was not a library at all. When it was opened in 1990, it had no books, only a glass-encased display of Nixon's autobiographies and ruminations on foreign policy.

But the absence of all other books wasn't as shocking as the way Nixon designed his "library" to keep the Watergate scandal from beating like a heart of darkness in an otherwise self-serving shrine. The focal point of the library's limited Watergate display, which was stashed away in a purposely darkened corridor, was the "smoking gun" tape that provided irrefutable evidence of Nixon's role in the scandal's cover-up. Irrefutable, that is, until Nixon started to tamper with it.

Nixon's job on the smoking gun tape makes Rose Mary Woods' eighteen-and-a-half-minute gap look like a third-rate erasure attempt. As a transcript of the tape scrolled by quickly on a video monitor, only selected portions of the text were highlighted for easy reading. Under the headphones, the library-goer heard only those portions, which, taken out of their highly incriminating context, could be reasonably construed as innocuous.

In actuality, this tape recorded Nixon approving a plan to use the CIA to obstruct the FBI's initial investigation into Watergate. But a library narrator asserted that what Nixon really said was: "The best thing to do is let the investigation proceed unhindered." There is nothing on the smoking gun tape that even remotely coincides with this flat-out falsehood. In reality, the real smoking gun tape features the president saying the CIA "should call the FBI in and say that we wish for the country, don't go any further into this case, period."[2]

Was it a crime to present a fraudulent display at a presidential library? If so, perhaps the Gerald Ford library could have granted some kind of executive clemency to the Richard Nixon library. In the end, however, that proved unnecessary. In 2011, several years after the National Archives took over management of the library, the whitewashed Watergate exhibit—including the fraudulent "let the investigation proceed unhindered" comment—was gone. In its place stood a brightened-up, enlarged, and truthful version of the scandal that brought down Nixon's presidency. At the ribbon-cutting, library director Tim Naftali—a professional historian— said the new gallery should bolster the confidence of the American people "that we have a government that is so transparent that it put on public display evidence of its own wrongdoing."[3]

As our president, Nixon's tricks ran the gamut from the mundane, such as cheating at golf and sending in trick plays to pro football teams, to the monumental, including the secret carpet bombing of Cambodia and the Watergate cover-up.

Nixon's Espionage

Aside from his 1968 treason trick, Nixon's darkest tricks are topped by his bald-faced denials of complicity in Watergate. But Nixon's love of spying is a close runner-up. A fascinating example of such espionage has surfaced in White House tapes released long after Nixon's 1994 death.

Bob Haldeman, the chief of staff in Nixon's White House, has observed that Nixon, like a shy or insecure predator, would attack a "problem or person by coming in at the side [rather than straight-on], often through subordinates, when the victim wasn't looking, and trying to strike his blow unseen."[4]

In the early days of 1973, when Nixon and Henry Kissinger should have been basking in *Time's* glorification of them as 1972's dual "men of the year," the paranoid president was spying on his equally paranoid national security adviser. Nixon was "coming in at the side" of Kissinger through Chuck Colson, his personal "hit man" and the chief of his "black" projects and dirty tricks.

In a new tape of a telephone chat between Nixon and Colson on January 5, 1973, Colson excitedly fingers Kissinger as the source of an unfavorable article by syndicated columnist Joseph Kraft. Nixon loathed Kraft, and Colson's discovery of a connection between Kissinger and Kraft was almost too much for Nixon to bear. "I'll be a son-of-a-bitch!" an astonished Nixon declares on tape. "That is unbelievable!"[5]

The President directed Colson to ask Kissinger outright whether he'd had any recent contacts with Kraft. "And if he lies on that," Nixon declares, "I want to know . . . It's very important that I know that."[6]

Nixon also ordered Colson to keep tabs on all of Kissinger's contacts with the press. Though the two men used the terms "monitoring," "checking," and "keeping a log" to describe how Colson became privy to certain of Kissinger's telephone calls, it's highly probable that these were just code words and that Kissinger's phone was being bugged.

After all, bugging was one of Nixon's habitual ploys. And what even Colson didn't know at the time was that Nixon was taping just about every office and telephone conversation he had in the White House — including their little conspiracy against Kissinger. (Kissinger, meanwhile, was recording all of his phone calls with Nixon.)

On occasions, Nixon had to dip into his bag of spying tricks for non-official purposes, according to Marty Venker, a former Secret Service agent. During a post-resignation visit to the Caribbean island of St. Martin, Venker says, Nixon couldn't keep himself from sneaking looks at "an unbelievably beautiful" woman in her late twenties who came out of her cabana topless whenever Nixon came to the beach.

"She would always place herself a discreet distance from Nixon, but close enough so he could still ogle her," according to Venker, who revealed what could be termed "the Crocodile Trick" in *Rolling Stone*. "He'd wade out into the ocean and lurk with that nose just covered by the water. Like a crocodile."

Venker says that the woman was, in fact, the lure in a "sex trap" that had been set up by an unidentified European steel magnate who wanted to make contact with Nixon. After spying on her from his watery lair, Nixon ultimately invited the woman to share a restaurant table with him and his pals Bebe Rebozo and Robert Abplanalp. Nixon later took her bait hook, line, and sinker as she coaxed her main admirer into joining her and the steel magnate for lunch aboard the businessman's yacht.[7]

A mutual interest in spying resulted in the unlikely alliance of Richard Nixon and Elvis Presley. They met after Presley had offered to become an undercover informer for Nixon on the nefarious activities of rock 'n' roll stars, hippies, and other anti-establishment types. In a letter to Nixon that preceded their meeting, Elvis said. "I have done an in-depth study on drug abuse and communist brain-washing techniques and am right in the middle of the whole thing, where I can do the most good."

The King showed up at the White House drugged and dressed in a violet suit and cape with a huge gold belt buckle. Over-sized amber sunglasses covered his eyes. When Nixon inquired about the garish get-up, the King responded: "Mr. President, you have your show and I have mine." At the meeting, Elvis bad-mouthed the Beatles for their "anti-American spirit."

Then Elvis asked for a Bureau of Narcotics badge—and Nixon complied. When the president handed the rock star the high-level law enforcement shield, the King was so overwhelmed he hugged the startled president. The badge allowed Elvis to achieve a longtime goal: to go anywhere he wanted with both drugs and guns.[8]

Nixon's Staged Dramatics

Crying ranks among Nixon's greatest tricks because he used it so often and so effectively to gain sympathy or escape from uncomfortable situations. Besides, of his myriad tricks, it's one of the few he actually admitted to performing.

Nixon confessed to trickery-by-tears during this exchange with television interviewer David Frost in 1977:

> **Nixon:** If I cry, I do it in the presence of others.
> **Frost:** But what about when you were alone with yourself? In a situation like that, didn't you ever break down?
> **Nixon:** No. That's not my way at all. You mean cry privately? No. I cry inside. But when I'm alone, I sit, I make notes. I think about it. No. My emotions are controlled.[9]

Albert Upton, Nixon's drama coach at Whittier College, takes credit for teaching young Dick to cry for a play called "Bird in Hand." According to Upton, "On the evenings of the performance, tears ran right out of eyes. It was beautifully done, those tears."

In 1952, when Upton saw a newspaper photo of vice presidential candidate Nixon crying on the shoulder of Sen. William Knowland, he bragged: "That's my boy! That's my actor!"[10]

Nixon's tears also ran the night Dwight Eisenhower told him that he could stay on the GOP ticket despite revelations by the *New York Post* that he'd raised a secret political slush fund from a wealthy California businessman. On an impromptu visit to Nixon's campaign plane, Ike capped his remarks of support for Nixon by declaring, "You're my boy!"

"Reporters in the central compartment watched in embarrassment as Nixon threw his hands to his face and again broke into tears," according to Nixon biographer Roger Morris.[11]

Ike and millions of other Republicans had been swayed by Nixon's defense of the secret fund in his nationally broadcast "Checkers" speech, but to many others who watched the schmaltzy address, Nixon came across as a royal phony. In his most unconvincing scene—just before he mentions the gift of the "little cocker spaniel dog" for whom the speech was immediately nicknamed—he raised one hand to his face for several seconds, as if to stifle tears.

To climax the Checkers story, Nixon asserted: "Regardless of what they say about it, we're going to keep him."

Columnist Walter Lippman was quick to brand Nixon's performance "the most demeaning experience my country has ever had to bear."[12]

In one of his many autobiographies, Nixon admits to stealing the idea for tossing Checkers into his speech from Pres. Franklin D. Roosevelt, who talked about "my little dog Fala" during a speech to help deflect criticism of some of his wartime policies. Nixon wrote that "reporters thought the Fala story was cute. They thought the Checkers story was corny. But the television viewers liked it, and that was all that mattered."[13]

While Nixon pretended to fight back tears in recounting the Checkers story, he cried in earnest shortly after the broadcast. Nixon thought—or pretended to think—he botched the whole performance because he ran out of time before he could announce where people could write to support him. He balled up his notes and threw them to the floor, then cried into the curtains at the rear of the set before he skulked off to the dressing room.

Watergate afforded Nixon an opportunity to shed plenty of tears in the presence of others. His domestic adviser, John Ehrlichman, said that Nixon "really began to cry" when he fired Ehrlichman over Watergate. Nixon cried again when he dumped Bob Haldeman[14]

After the two aides compared notes on their dismissals, they found that the president had told each of them the exact same thing: he was so upset by the prospect of having to let them go that he'd prayed the night before to never awake. Nixon also offered each man $200,000. The proposed shady payoffs—some might call it "hush money"—would have come from a secret slush fund kept by Nixon's gangster friend Bebe Rebozo. Both fired aides refused the offers.

Shortly before the midterm election of 1970, Pres. Richard Nixon pulled off a con so crafty it fooled even the Secret Service. He purposely incited a near-riot among young anti-war protestors by delaying his motorcade as he left a big, indoor, by-invitation-only Republican rally in San Jose, California. In contrast to the cheers inside, a large and rowdy crowd outside the event shouted vulgarities (which could be heard inside during Nixon's speech, distracting him several times). The perturbed president exited the city's convention center with the secret intent of stirring up trouble, or at least fake trouble.

On leaving the auditorium with the rest of the White House press corps, I spotted a buddy, Secret Service agent Joe Novak. In similar instances, Joe and I usually greeted each other, if only with a wave or a wink. This encounter was totally different: Joe wore a worried look and was preoccupied—speaking non-stop into his walkie-talkie on the secure Secret Service communication channel called "Charlie." I later learned that, on the San Jose trip, Joe was in charge of motorcade advances. No wonder he was so obviously concerned.

At about this same time, not far away, President Nixon climbed onto the trunk of his limousine and gave the demonstrators the "V" sign with both arms. "That's what they hate to see," he muttered, before hastily scrambling into his bulletproof car.

Nixon's gesture did, indeed, set off the peaceniks, as he had hoped and planned. The subsequent rock throwing and general turmoil that engulfed the motorcade and had truly frightened the Secret Service had granted Nixon the political payoff he had plotted all along.

Like the beleaguered Novak, all other agents on the scene believed this was not a staged event but rather a real danger to the leader of the free world. Their job, of course, was to take any potential threat seriously. Besides, the agents did not have access to Nixon's secret San Jose exit strategy, nor to Bob Haldeman's diary entry that confirmed that day's violence was contrived.

Haldeman, Nixon's chief of staff, was ecstatic: "San Jose turned into a real blockbuster. We wanted some confrontation . . . so we stalled departure a little so [the protestors] could zero in outside, and they sure did. Before getting in car, P stood up and gave the 'V' sign, which made them mad. They threw rocks, flags, candles, etc. as we drove out, after a terrifying wedge of cops opened up the road . . . Made a huge incident and we worked hard to crank it up . . ."[15]

Nixon himself cranked it up at the next campaign stop, in Phoenix. "The time has come," he righteously intoned, "for the great Silent Majority of Americans, of all ages and of every political persuasion, to stand up and be counted against appeasement of the rock-throwers and the obscenity-shouters."[16]

In a carefully choreographed echo, Vice Pres. Spiro Agnew chimed in from Bellville, Illinois: "When the President of the United States . . . is subject to rock and missile throwing, it is time to sweep that kind of garbage out of society."[17]

Neither man mentioned that the president had put his Secret Service detail, and others, in harm's way just to gain sympathy for himself and political profit for his party.

"A Funny Cheating Quality"

With the exception of bowling, Nixon wasn't known for his physical prowess in any sporting endeavor. To compensate, he apparently used his intellectual skills to trick the scorecard — especially in golf.

As president, Nixon took to the links one day in a foursome that included golf-great Sam Snead, who was an astonished but silent witness to one of Nixon's most brazen golfing deceptions. Many years later, Snead told the *Miami News* what he saw. On one hole, Nixon drove his ball so deeply into the rough that "no one could shoot out of it unless you had a bazooka." When Nixon thought no one was looking, he threw the ball back onto the fairway. "What could I say?" Snead lamented. "He was the president."[18]

On another golf outing, as cabinet officer George Shultz later disclosed, Nixon changed the initially agreed-upon individual handicaps after the first nine holes — a change that, in the end, allowed him and his partner to win.[19]

During a stint on the South Pacific island of New Caledonia during his Navy days, when he was known as "Dick the Card Sharp," adeptness (or cheating?) at poker enriched Nixon by about $10,000. He especially liked to boast that once, while holding a pair of deuces, he bet so boldly that he tricked a higher-ranking officer out of a $1,500 pot.[20] Nixon was so proud of the accomplishment that he displayed his winning hand inside a glass case in his Yorba Linda library. Trickster that he was, in an accompanying written commentary he implied that the displayed deuces were the actual, original cards that were used in the World War Two game. (Had he really preserved and saved them all that time?)

Former House Speaker Tip O'Neill has an entirely different memory of Nixon the poker player. In his memoirs, O'Neill said Nixon was "just miserable" at the game, that he talked too much, didn't follow the cards, and would "holler and complain" every time he lost a few bucks. O'Neill concluded that "any guy who hollers over a $40 poker pot has no business being President."[21]

Perhaps because he was frustrated by his ineptitude as a college football player, Nixon used the influence that comes with high national office to devise trick plays for pro football teams, especially for his beloved Washington Redskins. Why these teams employed his plays — especially after they proved to be flops — remains a mystery.

As vice president, in 1958, Nixon sold Redskins owner George Preston Marshall on the odd notion of inserting Gene Brito, an aging defensive end, into the offensive lineup so he could catch a pass. Brito, however, forgot to look and the ball struck him in the back. As president, Nixon sent a trick play to Redskins coach George Allen that unintentionally helped the San Francisco 49ers eliminate Washington from the playoffs in 1971. The trick end-around play produced an eight-yard loss. Washington's quarterback, Billy Kilmer, complained that Nixon was "really hurting us. He calls us all the time."[22]

President Nixon also had a channel to Miami Dolphins head coach Don Shula. He told Shula that the way to beat the Dallas Cowboys in Super Bowl VI was to send wide receiver Paul Warfield on simple down-and-in pass patterns. Shula tried Nixon's play four times, and the Cowboys foiled it each time. Miami lost the game 24-3.

The next year the Dolphins won the Super Bowl. According to *The Football Hall of Shame*, Shula "thanked half the world" after the big win. But he added: "I also want to thank the President for *not* sending in plays."[23]

While on a post-resignation trip to China with Nixon, John Lindsay of *Newsweek* overhead the former president disclose to a waitress why he ordered a shot of Scotch whiskey. He confided that he hated the taste of it and was therefore able to resist drinking too much. This is a rare example of Nixon deliberately tricking himself.

A self-styled wine buff, Nixon developed an affinity for a 1968 Chateau Margaux that sold for about $39 a bottle. In *The Final Days*,

Bob Woodward and Carl Bernstein revealed that when Nixon entertained large groups of congressmen aboard the *Sequoia*, he issued strict instructions to stewards aboard the presidential yacht: "His guests were to be served a rather good $6 wine; his glass was to be filled from a bottle of Chateau Margaux wrapped in a towel."[24]

Nixon's earliest recorded drinking trick goes back to the night of his first congressional election victory in 1946. He and other family members were at the home of Norman Chandler, the publisher of the *Los Angeles Times*. According to Mrs. Chandler, who was known as "Buff": "Nixon came out in the hall after everyone had ordered milk and said, 'Buff, could you get me a double bourbon? I don't want mother and father to see me take a drink.'" It was "a very small thing," Mrs. Chandler said in 1977. But "for a man that age, who'd just won an election . . . it showed a funny cheating quality that never changed through the years."[25]

What has made Nixon so appealing, in an ironically repellent sort of way, to the American public? Perhaps he represents for us what Carl Jung once described as the archetypal trickster: "a collective shadow figure, an epitome of all the inferior traits of character in individuals."[26] Or maybe our continuing fascination with Tricky Dick is much simpler than that. Before Nixon's death, Tom Shales, the *Washington Post*'s television critic, observed: "Nixon has become a wonderful, or horrible, sort of constant in an iffy world. He's as consistent as Muzak. He always gives us, and always has given us, a good show."[27]

Thanks to the declassification of Nixon's presidential tapes and documents, the Nixon Show went on for many years, even after his death. The material slowly emerged at irregular intervals until 2013. At times, as Tom Shales indicated, some of the revelations were unquestionably "horrible." Such is the case with the subject of this book — Richard Nixon's darkest and ultimately most-tragic trick.

Appendix

Contents of the X Envelope

The following is an index of the documents contained in the X Envelope, also called "South Vietnam and U.S. Policies." Most documents are numbered by hand in the upper-right-hand corner.

The documents from the folder break down into three groups: the first, originally fastened to the left side of the folder, date from October 1968 through November 12, 1969, and are numbered 1-38b. A portion of the first group has to do with Jack Gardiner, and the other portion deals with Anna Chennault. Loose documents within the folder date from October 1968 to May 1973 and are numbered 39-63. The third group, originally fastened to the right side of the folder, date from August through December 1968 and are numbered 64-114. Based on chronological order, some documents are missing due to the fact that portions of the X Envelope have yet to be declassified.

Processing Documents

0c. Memorandum for the record dated July 22, 1994, signed by Regina Greenwell. The memo states that "This package, labeled 'The X envelope,' was opened by me on this date, on the instructions of Harry Middleton, director of the Lyndon B. Johnson Library."

06. Hand-written, top secret note from Walt Rostow stating: "To be opened by the Director, Lyndon Baines Johnson Library not earlier than fifty (50) years from this date June 26, 1973."

0. "Literally eyes only" memo from Walt Rostow to LBJ Library director Harry Middleton dated June 26, 1973. The memo states:

Sealed in the attached envelope is a file President Johnson asked me to hold personally because of its sensitive nature. In case of his death, the material was to be consigned to the LBJ Library under conditions I judged to be appropriate.

The file concerns the activities of Mrs. Chennault and others before and immediately after the election of 1968. At the time President Johnson decided to handle the matter strictly as a question of national security; and, in retrospect, he felt that decision was correct.

It is, therefore, my recommendation to you that this file should remain sealed for fifty years from the date of this memorandum.

After fifty years the Director of the LBJ Library (or whomever may inherit his responsibilities, should the administrative structure of the National Archives change) may, alone, open this file. If he believes the material it contains might be opened for research, he should then consult the then responsible security officials of the Executive Branch to arrange formal clearance. If he believes the material it contains should not be opened for research, I would wish him empowered to re-close the file for another fifty years when the procedure outlined above should be repeated.

0a.   A scanned copy of the exterior of the X Envelope, addressed to Mr. Harry Middleton, Eyes Only.

First Group

1.   This document has only one word: "Gardiner."

2.   A November 20, 1968, memo from Walt Rostow to President Johnson stating: "At last we have a fix on Gardiner. He's a nut!"

2a.   An FBI report on John Pennington ("Jack") Gardiner, a former State Department employee, sent by request to the White House on November 20, 1968. Gardiner had sparked interest after meeting with a South Vietnamese official.

3.   A November 19, 1968 memo from the director of the FBI to the White House Situation Room reporting a meeting between Jack Gardiner and a Father Diego, who had ties to Vietnam.

The last sentence reads: "He [Father Diego] traveled in the United States and Europe with Ngo Dinh-Diem and went to Vietnam in nineteen fifty five where he remained until nineteen sixty four publishing papers and magazines."

4.   A handwritten memo dated November 19, 1968, attached to Document 3. Addressed to Mr. Rostow and signed by BKS (likely Bromley Smith, staff to the White House Situation Room), the memo comments on the Gardiner/Father Diego meeting: "There is little here of interest except the last sentence — not necessarily indicative."

4.   A memorandum for the record written by Walt Rostow on February 11, 1970, reporting a meeting with Tom Ottenad of the *St. Louis Post-Dispatch*. Ottenad desired information on Mrs. Chennault, which Rostow would not divulge. Instead, Rostow provided "an absolutely harmless account of events" relating to Vietnam.[1]

7.   A February 27, 1970, memo from Tom Johnson to LBJ. Tom Johnson had spoken to Bob Haldeman two days prior, and Johnson informed Haldeman that LBJ and his staff were refusing comment to Ottenad. Haldeman expressed his gratitude, saying "it looked as if the *Post-Dispatch* was trying to stir up more trouble on this matter and they sure did not need that."

4a.   November 19, 1968, memo from the director of the FBI to the White House Situation Room (attn: Bromley Smith) detailing further information on Jack Gardiner.

5.   November 18, 1968, memo from the director of the FBI to the White House Situation Room (attn: Bromley Smith) reporting that on that day Jack Gardiner had left a message for Truong Buu Diem at the Vietnamese Embassy.

6.   A November 18, 1968, "eyes only" memo from Walt Rostow to President Johnson stating: "In the light of this latest on Jack

Gardiner, I think we may have to level with Murphy—short of revealing our source—and get to the bottom of what Jack Gardiner is up to."

6a. November 19, 1968, memo from the director of the FBI to White House Situation Room (attn: Bromley Smith) detailing November 15 contact between Jack Gardiner and Father Diego.

7. November 18, 1968, memorandum for the president from Bromley Smith reporting on Jack Gardiner's activity with a South Vietnamese official and providing background information on Gardiner.[2]

7a. November 18, 1968, memo from the director of the FBI to the White House Situation Room (attn: Bromley Smith) reporting on Gardiner's contact with the Vietnamese Embassy.

7b. November 15, 1968, memo from the director of the FBI to the White House Situation Room (attn: Bromley Smith), further detailing Jack Gardiner's movements and contact with the Vietnamese Embassy.

8. November 16, 1968, memo from Walt Rostow to President Johnson stating:

It is unclear whether someone else—unauthorized—is getting into the Vietnam act, in this rather obscure report.
Nevertheless, because of certain references, I thought you ought to be aware of it.
We shall try quietly to get a fix on Gardiner.

8a. November 15, 1968, memo from the director of the FBI to the White House Situation Room (attn: Bromley Smith) detailing a meeting between Gardiner and Diem, during which "Gardiner indicated he might be able to do something for Diem's country [Vietnam]."

(Here in the file is an unnumbered page with the word "Chennault" alone.)

10. A *Washington Post* society article about Anna Chennault entitled "Next Perle Mesta?"

11. Tom Ottenad article entitled "Was Saigon's peace talk delay due to Republican promises?"

11a. An identical copy of the Document 11 Tom Ottenad article entitled "Was Saigon's peace talk delay due to Republican promises?"

12. A January 3, 1969, memo from Rostow to President Johnson informing on contact between Ambassador Bui Diem and the *St. Louis Post-Dispatch*.

12a. January 3, 1969, memo from the director of the FBI to the White House Situation Room (attn: Bromley Smith) detailing the conversation between Diem and Richard Dudman of the Washington, DC, bureau of the *St. Louis Post-Dispatch*. Diem denied contact with the Richard Nixon campaign prior to the election and circumvented questions about contact with Mrs. Chennault by stating that he could not recall exact dates.

13. January 3, 1969, memo from Rostow to President Johnson stating: "Herewith is the exact text of a telephone conversation this morning with Tom Ottenad of the St. Louis Post-Dispatch. As you will see, the Lady is about to surface."

13a. A January 3, 1969, transcript of the conversation between Ottenad and Rostow, who refused to comment on matters relating to Anna Chennault, Richard Nixon, and South Vietnam.

14. December 17, 1968, memo from Bromley Smith to President Johnson informing him that "The Lady continues her activities." Chennault had arranged an appointment between Diem and Senator Mundt and had accepted a message and gift for president-elect Nixon.

14a. December 17 report attached to Document 14 memo stating that Anna Chennault had arranged an appointment between Ambassador Diem and Sen. Karl Mundt of South Dakota.

14b. December 13 report attached to Document 14 memo stating that Anna Chennault would convey a message and gift from a Dr. Furk to president-elect Nixon.

15. December 10, 1968, "literally eyes only" memo from Rostow to President Johnson stating only: "The Lady is still operational."

15a. December 9, 1968, memo from the director of the FBI to the White House Situation Room (attn: Bromley Smith) detailing contact between Chennault and Nguyen Hoan, counselor at the Vietnamese Embassy.

16. November 27, 1968, memo from Bromley Smith to President Johnson detailing Chennault's contact with the Vietnamese Embassy to arrange an appointment with Ambassador Diem, who was out of town.

17. Copy of document 16.

17a. Undated memo from Bromley Smith to President Johnson stating only: "Here is further evidence of the continuing activity of the Lady with South Vietnamese embassy officials."

17b. Another copy of document 16.

18. Another copy of document 16.

19. November 26, 1968, memo from the director of the FBI to the White House Situation Room (attn: Bromley Smith) detailing further contact between Chennault and the Vietnamese embassy secretary attempting to set an appointment with Diem, who was still out of town.

20. November 12, 1968, "eyes only" memo from Rostow to President Johnson establishing that "These new times on

the gentleman in Albuquerque on November 2 suggest he had ample time to make the telephone calls to the Lady and Secretary Rusk while in Albuquerque, before departing for Texas," and including a timeline.

21. November 8, 1968, "literally eyes only" memo from Rostow to President Johnson stating: "I think it's time to blow the whistle on these folks."

21a. November 8, 1968, memo from the director of the FBI to the White House Situation Room (attn: Bromley Smith) detailing a message conveyed by Chennault from President Thieu to Ambassador Diem. The message, in part, was that "'they' are still planning things but are not letting people know too much because they want to be careful to avoid embarrassing 'you,' themselves, or the present U.S. government."

22. Copy of document 21a.

23. November 7, 1968, memo from the director of the FBI to the White House Situation Room (attn: Bromley Smith) reporting that the secretary at the Vietnamese Embassy contacted Chennault on that date to set an appointment with Diem, who was back in town. Chennault stated that she would be there after making a few important phone calls and asked that a message be relayed to Diem advising that she had been talking to "Florida."

24. November 7, 1968, memo from the director of the FBI to the White House Situation Room (attn: Bromley Smith) reporting that on that date Chennault had contacted Diem and advised him that she had made "contact already" and would contact the ambassador later.

25. November 6, 1968, memo from Walt Rostow to President Johnson reporting that on November 5, Chennault visited her voting precinct before traveling to New York City for the Nixon campaign's election party.

    The memo also reports that Diem said he is keeping his fingers crossed about the election. Should Humphrey win it would be difficult for the Vietnamese. Diem states that "in spite of his respect for Humphrey that he (Diem) had to side with those people who gave the Vietnamese the maximum of conditions [Nixon]."

25a. November 6, 1968, "literally eyes only" memo from Rostow to President Johnson accompanying Document 25 stating "Herewith two further reports."

25b. Memo accompanying Document 25 detailing Chennault's actions.

25c. Further details on Diem's statements from Document 25.

26. Copy of Document 25.

27. November 4, 1968, memo from Rostow to Johnson. Rostow met with Secretaries Rusk and Clifford, who agreed that Nixon was involved in the peace talk failure. The advisors agreed that information should not be voluntarily released, as there was no "public right to know," and national security was at stake.

Saville Davis, a reporter with the *Christian Science Monitor*, planned to publish a story saying Thieu, acting on his own, decided to hold out, but Davis was aware of the truth beyond that (that is, Nixon's involvement).

Also, a report on a visit by Chennault to the South Vietnamese Embassy and 1701 Pennsylvania Ave (identified in Document 28 as a Nixon office).

28. November 4, 1968, memo to the White House Situation Room (attn: Bromley Smith) detailing Anna Chennault's visits to 1701 Pennsylvania Ave (room 205, which was a Nixon office), the Vietnamese Embassy, the Chinese Embassy, and her own office.

29. November 4, 1968, memo from the director of the FBI to the

White House Situation Room (attn: Bromley Smith) informing of Anna Chennault's visit that day to the Vietnamese Embassy.

29-1. November 2, 1968, memo from the director of the FBI to the White House Situation Room (attn: Bromley Smith) detailing Chennault's contact with Diem on that day advising that she had received a message from "her boss," who had just called from New Mexico, that he wanted her to give to Diem. The message is to "hold on, we are gonna win" and "hold on, he understands all of it."

30. November 2, 1968, memo from Rostow to President Johnson informing him of the Chennault message from document 29-1, and advising that Chennault was planning to go to New York City, where she would await election results with Nixon. FBI surveillance was arranged for the trip.

31. November 3, 1968, memo from the director of the FBI to the White House Situation Room (attn: Bromley Smith), reporting that Chennault was in DC, not NYC, attending a movie with an unknown man.

32. November 2, 1968, memo from the director of the FBI to the White House Situation Room (attn: Bromley Smith) reporting on a *Washington Post* article about Chennault that stated she intended to watch the election results from New York City with Nixon himself. Arrangements were reportedly made for the FBI to follow her on the trip.

33. November 1, 1968, memo from the director of the FBI to the White House Situation Room (attn: Bromley Smith) advising that Chennault and Thomas Corcoran (an attorney) were observed leaving the Watergate East Apartments together before attending several parties and the theater.

34. November 1, 1968, memo from Rostow to President Johnson introducing the next two documents.

34a. October 31, 1968, memo from the director of the FBI to the

White House Situation Room (attn: Bromley Smith) reporting Chennault's attempted contact with Diem. Chennault was informed by an embassy employee that Diem was busy. She inquired if the ambassador intended to go to Vietnam, which the employee denied. Chennault left a message for Diem to contact her if he planned to leave town.

34b. A November 1, 1968, society article about Anna Chennault from the *Washington Post*. The article mentioned that she is one of a select group chosen to watch election returns with Nixon.

35. October 31, 1968, memo from Rostow to President Johnson: "The latest on the Lady."

35a. October 31, 1968, memo from the director of the FBI to the White House Situation Room (attn: Bromley Smith) informing that Chennault and Corcoran were about town again after Chennault's visit to the Vietnamese Embassy on October 30.

36. October 30, 1968, memo from the director of the FBI to the White House Situation Room (attn: Bromley Smith) confirming information earlier furnished by Bromley Smith. On October 30, Diem was contacted by an unidentified woman, possibly Chennault, whom he informs that something "is cooking." She asks if Thailand is going to be representative of both South Vietnam and the Viet Cong and he says "no, nothing of this sort yet." She says she will drop by to speak with him after luncheon for Mrs. Agnew that day.

37. October 30, 1968, report from Bromley Smith to Rostow informing that Chennault had visited the Vietnamese Embassy that afternoon for more than an hour.

38. November 8 note from LBJ stating only: "Put that with the other stuff on that woman."

38a. October 30, 1968 memo from Rostow to President Johnson introducing a memo from Deke DeLoach.

38b. Deke DeLoach's October 30, 1968, report about Chennault's conversation with Diem, during which he informs her that "something is cooking" but said he could not go into specifics over the phone. Conveys the same information provided in document 36.

Second Group

38-1. Processing note explaining that documents 1-38 were fastened to the left side of the original folder, and documents 39-63 were loose inside the folder.

39. May 14, 1973, memorandum for the record by Rostow as a guide to the file. "The attached file contains the information available to me and (I believe) the bulk of the information available to President Johnson on the activities of Mrs. Chennault and other Republicans just before the presidential election of 1968." Rostow delineates three periods of the story: October 17-29, October 29-November 5 (Election Day), and post-election.

Rostow outlines the events and closes with "personal reflections as of mid-May 1973":

I am inclined to believe the Republican operation in 1968 relates in two ways to the Watergate affair of 1972.

First, the election of 1968 proved to be close and there was some reason for those involved on the Republican side to believe their enterprise with the South Vietnamese and Thieu's recalcitrance may have sufficiently blunted the impact on U.S. politics of the total bombing halt and agreement to negotiate to constitute the margin of victory.

Second, they got away with it. Despite considerable press commentary after the election, the matter was never investigated fully.

Thus, as the same men faced the election of 1972, there was nothing in their previous experience with an operation of doubtful propriety (or, even, legality) to warn them off; and there were memories of how close an election could get and the possible utility of pressing to the limit—or beyond.

40. Log of calls made by Johnson from October 16-November 14. October 16 call to Humphrey, Wallace, and Nixon regarding Vietnam and peace negotiations. Calls to Dirksen spanning October 16-November 10. October 31 call to Humphrey, Nixon, and Wallace regarding the bombing halt. November 2 call to Dirksen about Nixon. November 3 call from Nixon in Los Angeles. November 8 call from Dirksen concerning his talk with Nixon about Vietnam. November 8 call from Nixon in Key Biscayne. November 11 lunch at the White House with Nixon and Mrs. Nixon. November 14 calls to Nixon.

41. Copy of document 27.

42. November 7, 1968, "eyes only" memo from Rostow to President Johnson stating: "Herewith a full chronological file of the special intelligence items you asked for. Key passages are marked."

43. Processing note: "Document #43 is a manila folder that was inside the labeled folder 'South Vietnam and U.S. Policies.' Documents #44-48 were inside this inner folder."

44. October 29, 1968, memo from Rostow to President Johnson introducing information from his brother, Eugene Rostow, and stating, "I asked him to go back to Alexander Sachs and see how much further detail he can get on the people involved and how close, in fact, they are to Nixon."

44a. October 29 memo from Eugene Rostow detailing the information he received from Alexander Sachs, who reported on a conversation between Wall Street bankers about Nixon trying to frustrate peace negotiations. Reportedly, Nixon was "letting Hanoi know that when he took office 'he could accept anything and blame it on his predecessor.'"

45. October 29 memo from Walt Rostow to Johnson introducing "a somewhat more detailed account from Gene [Eugene Rostow] about the conversation briefly reported to you this morning."

45a. October 29, 1968, memo from Eugene Rostow to Walt Rostow, providing greater detail on the reported conversation from the New York source (Alexander Sachs). The memo reads, in part:

The speaker said he thought the prospects for a bombing halt or a cease-fire were dim, because Nixon was playing the problem as he did the Fortas affair—to block. He was taking public positions intended to achieve that end. They would incite Saigon to be difficult, and Hanoi to wait.

Part of his strategy was an expectation that an offensive would break out soon, that we would have to spend a great deal more (and incur more casualties)—a fact which would adversely affect the stock market and the bond market. NVN offensive action was a definite element in their thinking about the future.

These difficulties would make it easier for Nixon to settle after January. Like Ike in 1953, he would be able to settle on terms which the President could not accept, blaming the deterioration of the situation between now and January or February on his predecessor.

46. November 4, 1968, memo that reads:

The object of the exercise was to nullify the political impact of the President's decision by making it dubious. They think that goal has been achieved. They think the political effect of the bombing halt has been reduced by 25%-33%.

The damage was done via Thieu in Saigon, through low level Americans.

They think the damage has been done.

Thieu, in their judgment, will continue on his present line until it becomes impossible.

Mitchell's strategy is for Nixon now to be a statesman. He can't do any more mischief politically at home, although his troops will continue to use the line here. He regards any further steps by him as counter-productive.

47. November 5 memo for the record stating that "Our contact with the man in New York" reports that Nixon was frightened on November 4 by the latest Harris poll and by Wallace speaking out against Nixon. "Therefore, on the question of the problem with Saigon, he did not stay with the statesman-like role but pressed publicly the failure of Saigon to come along as an anti-Democrat political issue." This was what was also happening on TV at the time.

48. Copy of 47.

49. November 2, 1972, memo from Rostow to Johnson: "The head of the South Vietnamese delegation arrived in Paris on December 8, 1968. On January 18, 1969, agreement was finally reached on the procedures for the Paris meetings. The first of the meetings was held on January 25, 1969."

50. November 2, 1972, note to Rostow informing him that Joe Volz of the *Washington Star* has phoned about "a major story about the Johnson administration."

50a. November 7, 1972, memo from Rostow to Johnson, informing that the *Washington Evening Star* has a story that runs as follows:

President Johnson put the FBI to work investigating the Nixon campaign in 1968. There are two versions of what the FBI did. One version alleges that President Johnson instructed the FBI to investigate Communist infiltration of the Nixon camp. The other version alleges that President Johnson instructed the FBI to investigate action by members of the Nixon camp to slow down the peace negotiations in Paris before the 1968 election.

After the election J. Edgar Hoover informed President Nixon of what he had been instructed to do by President Johnson. President Nixon is alleged to have been outraged. He stated that responsibility for investigating Communist infiltration of American political parties should be transferred to the CIA.

Mr. Collins went on to say that 4 of the men involved in the Watergate operation are believed to have had CIA connections. It is also reported that in 1969 the CIA, according to this account, investigated the possibility of Communist infiltration into the Democratic Party.

Rostow gave no comment on the story.

51. Copy of 42.

52. Copy of 49.

53. *Washingtonian* cover article on Anna Chennault entitled: "The Three Faces of Anna Chennault."

54. *Washington Evening Star* society article on Chennault entitled "Chennault Dinner Delights GOP Guests." January 15, 1969.

55. *Austin Statesman* article entitled "Did HHH's 'Fair Play' Cost Election?" July 9, 1969.

56. Copy of Document 55.

57. Copy of Document 11 (Tom Ottenad article).

58. Article on Anna Chennault from the Style section of an unidentified publication. January 15, 1969.

59. *Washington Evening Star* article about Chennault entitled: "White Reports Nixon Backer Tried to Block Peace Talks." July 9, 1969.

60. Article about Chennault entitled: "The woman who scared Nixon."

61. Letter to the Editor from Edmund Zawacki published in the *Washington Post* about Theodore White's book *The Making of a President 1968* and accusations therein.

62. *New York Times* article entitled: "Mrs. Chennault Denies Seeking Peace Talk Delay." July 23, 1969.

63. July 11, 1969, *Austin American* article entitled: "Humphrey Agrees With 'Sabotage' Charge."

(No document 64.)

Third Group

65. December 21, 1968, memo from the director of the FBI to the

White House Situation Room (attn: Bromley Smith) reporting that on that day, Diem was in touch with Vice President Ky in Paris. Ky had just appeared on *Face the Nation* and said the main cause of the war in Vietnam was the presence of North Vietnamese troops in the South, which required allied troops to be brought in, and that if "both kinds of foreign troops" were withdrawn, under international guarantee, then the internal problems of the South, including that of "the opposition," could be solved by the elected government. Also, he said, the NLF [National Liberation Front] could never be recognized as a legal entity, but "we" do recognize the "reality."

66. December 20, 1968, memo from the director of the FBI to the White House Situation Room (attn: Bromley Smith) reporting further contact between Diem and Ky. Diem told Ky, "They are very interested."

67. December 19, 1968, memo from the director of the FBI to the White House Situation Room (attn: Bromley Smith) reporting contact between Diem and Lawrence Spivak, moderator of the television program *Meet the Press*, discussing whether Vice President Ky would appear on *Meet the Press* or on *Face the Nation*.

68. A December 19, 1968, handwritten memo from "BKS" (Bromley Smith) to Walt Rostow introducing accompanying memos. "The information in these memos was incorporated in my summary memo — except for the paragraph about Kissinger's article being referred to as 'junk.'"

68a. December 19, 1968, memo from the director of the FBI to the White House Situation Room (attn: Bromley Smith) that accompanied the memo labeled document 68. On December 19, Diem told Ky he had an appointment to see Rusk and hoped to see "the other side" thereafter. Diem said he would try to be in Paris by Saturday morning. Ky discusses his "idea," not further explained, but Diem says he will not likely be able to bring it to the attention of Johnson, who was in the hospital. Ky wanted to know the reaction to his "plan" and wanted to announce it before he returned to Saigon. Ky reportedly made a statement at a reception calling an article written by Kissinger "junk."

68b. Another December 19 memo accompanying the memo labeled document 68. On December 18, Diem was in touch with an unknown man, possibly Ky. Diem said he explained to "them" that "we" had changed "means" and that there was no problem but on matters of "substance." As a result, ambiguities arose. Ky stated that at home there had been too much yielding already. Diem said he spoke with the "new people," to whom Ky wanted "my plan" explained.

69. A December 2, 1968, *U.S. News and World Report* article entitled "New Crisis for TFX 'Wonder Plane,'" about a $4 billion weapons program. On the second page is a blurb with a hand-drawn arrow pointing to it; the blurb states: "At least half a dozen Americans now in Saigon have been telling both Vietnamese officials and Americans that they are "Nixon contact men" — thereby aggravating an already messy negotiating situation involving the U.S. Embassy and top Vietnamese officials.

70. A handwritten, undated memo from "BKS" (Bromley Smith) to Walt Rostow stating "Sol W. Sanders is on staff of US News + World Report."

71. November 20, 1968, memo from Rostow to President Johnson introducing an attached document (71a): "Herewith Thieu holding forth expansively at dinner November 11-12."

71a. Thieu's remarks at a November 11 dinner. Thieu mentioned "betrayal" by the United States. Paragraph 4 is circled and states: "Thieu told his guests that during the U.S. election campaign he had sent two secret emissaries to the U.S. to contact Richard Nixon."

73. November 18, 1968, *Washington Evening Star* article entitled: "Nixon Holding Talks with Staff." A paragraph is circled and

states: "During the first 48 hours 'it [the bombing halt] gave a major shot in the arm to Mr. Humphrey and Democratic party workers,' he [Herbert Klein, a Nixon aide] said, but later, when it became apparent that the South Vietnamese were reluctant to go along with the plan, things 'started swinging back to us.'"

74. A November 17, 1968, *Washington Post* article by Drew Pearson and Jack Anderson entitled: "Washington-Saigon Feud: Details Leak Out of Backstage Fight Between U.S. and South Vietnam."

75. November 15, 1968, *Chicago Daily News* article by Georgie Anne Geyer entitled: "Saigon boast: 'We helped elect Nixon.'"

76. November 13, 1968, memo from Rostow to President Johnson introducing the accompanying document, labeled 76a, and stating "paragraph 15 (marked in red) will certainly interest you."

76a. November 13, 1968, cable accompanying Rostow's memo (document 76). The cable reports on a press conference by South Vietnamese Minister of Information Ton That Thien. Paragraph 15, marked, reads: "Asked whether Nixon had encouraged the GVN [Government of Vietnam] to delay agreement with the US, Thien replied that, while there may have been contacts between Nixon staffers and personnel of the SVN Embassy in Washington, a person of the caliber of Nixon would not do such a thing."

77. November 13, 1968, memo from Rostow to President Johnson stating: "Herewith the Vietnamese DCM in Washington reports in a straightforward way Nixon's and Clifford's statements."

78. November 12, 1968, memo from Rostow to President Johnson stating: "Herewith a cable from Thieu to Bui Diem (after Bui Diem left) indicating that, perhaps, Dirksen didn't complete the job and that Thieu retains an interest in the U.S. domestic political scene."

(No document 79 or 80 was present. Portions of the X Envelope have yet to be declassified.)

81. November 10, 1968, memo from the director of the FBI to the White House Situation Room (attn: Bromley Smith) discussing the travel plans of Bui Diem to the United States.

82. November 10, 1968, memo from Rostow to President Johnson stating: "Herewith a message of November 8 from Bui Diem to President Thieu's office indicating Nixon's apparent plans with respect to Vietnam as of that time."

83. November 9, 1968, memo from the director of the FBI to the White House Situation Room (attn: Bromley Smith) reporting that, on that day, Sen. Everett Dirksen contacted Diem to arrange an appointment to discuss a very urgent matter. The two set an appointment for 12 o'clock noon of that day.

84. November 9, 1968, memo from Rostow to President Johnson stating: "Herewith a conversation of yesterday between [name redacted] and a CIA official who has been in touch with him regularly. Dick Helms tells me he is a professional and accurate reporter."

84a. November 8, 1968, report on a breakfast meeting between "a reliable and trustworthy American" and Bui Diem on that date. Diem told the source that resuming negotiations would take some time, as relations between U.S. and South Vietnam needed to be repaired, and President Johnson would want to consult President-elect Nixon.

(No document 85.)

86. November 7, 1968, memo from Rostow to President Johnson accompanying document 86a and stating: "If you wish to get the story raw, read the last paragraph, marked."

86a. November 7, 1968, memo from the director of the FBI to the White House Situation Room (attn: Bromley Smith) reporting contact between an unidentified man and Major Bui Cong Minh, assistant armed forces attaché of South Vietnamese Embassy. The marked paragraph reads: "The unidentified man inquired as to how the peace talks were coming, and Major Minh expressed the opinion that the move by Saigon was to help presidential candidate Nixon, and that had Saigon gone to the conference table, presidential candidate Humphrey would probably have won."

(No document 87 or 88.)

89. November 6, 1968, memo from the director of the FBI to the White House Situation Room (attn: Bromley Smith) reporting that Mrs. Nguyen the Loc, second secretary, Embassy of Vietnam, contacted Mrs. Ross Adair (wife of Congressman Adaire of Indiana) to congratulate her on his reelection. Mrs. Adair expressed suspicion about votes not being properly counted.

90. November 4, 1968, memo from the director of the FBI to the White House Situation Room (attn: Bromley Smith) reporting the presence of an unidentified white male, later identified as Saville Davis of the *Christian Science Monitor*, at the Vietnamese Embassy on that date.

91. November 4, 1968, "eyes only" memo from Rostow to President Johnson reporting in detail on a conversation between Saville Davis and Bui Diem. On that date, Saville Davis requested appointment with Diem at "Embassy" to check a story received from a correspondent in Saigon. "Davis said that the dispatch from Saigon contains the elements of a major scandal which also involves the Vietnamese Ambassador and which will affect presidential candidate Richard Nixon if the Monitor publishes it. Time is of the essence inasmuch as Davis has a deadline to meet if he publishes it. He speculated that should the story be published, it will create a great deal of excitement." Davis was informed that Diem was busy, but went to the Embassy to wait for Diem to see him.

91a. November 4, 1968, unsigned note informing the unnamed recipient (possibly Rostow): "Saville Davis of the *Christian Science Monitor* is upstairs: 347-4953. He said they are holding out of the paper a sensational dispatch from Saigon (from their Saigon correspondent) the 1st para of which reads: 'purported political encouragement from the Richard Nixon camp was a significant factor in the last-minute decision of President Thieu's refusal to send a delegation to the Paris peace talks — at least until the American Presidential election is over.' He said he will await WWR's [Walt Rostow's] comments."

91b. Copy of document 91, but with handwriting in the margins reading "delivered to Pres at 1:23 pm."

92. November 4, 1968, memo from Rostow to President Johnson stating; "Herewith Bui Diem to Thieu on U.S. reaction to your speech."

93. November 3, 1968, memo reading:

Senator Smathers called [the White House] to report on a call he got from Nixon. Nixon said he understands the President is ready to blast him for allegedly collaborating with Tower and Chennault to slow the peace talks. Nixon says there is not any truth at all in this allegation. Nixon says there has been no contact at all.

Tonight on 'Meet the Press' Nixon will again back up the President and say he (Nixon) would rather get peace now than be President. Also tomorrow night, Nixon will say he will undertake any assignment the President has for him whether that be to go to Hanoi or Paris or whatever in order to get peace.

Nixon told Smathers he hoped the President would not make such a charge.

(No document 94.)

95. November 1, 1968, memo from the director of the FBI to the White House Situation Room (attn: Bromley Smith) reporting on a conversation in which Bui Diem discussed Vietnam with Spencer Davis of the Associated Press. Diem would not comment if he was going to Paris and requested that Davis not print anything until after Thieu spoke that night, and he agreed. Diem commented that as far as Washington was concerned, he thought the suspense was coming to an end. Davis remarked that he didn't notice any wild excitement but a lot of interest among average people, and he commented that there were hints that South Vietnam might not have its delegation there in time for the meetings.

97. Accompanies documents 97a and 97b and reads simply: "Take with us. LBJ:mr 11/1/68."

97a. November 1, 1968, memo from Rostow to President Johnson stating: "Here, again, from Thieu to the Koreans the wish to wait for Nixon."

97b. A partially redacted report on Thieu's October 28, 1968, speech. Thieu said that it appeared Nixon would be elected, and he believed it would be good to try to solve the important question of the political talks with the next president, no matter who was elected. The South Vietnamese public was aggravated at Humphrey's statement that "Vietnam does not have the right to reject a decision to halt the bombing." Rumors were spreading in U.S. that Thieu is unpredictable.

98. October 31, 1968, memo from the director of the FBI to the White House Situation Room (attn: Bromley Smith) reporting an October 30 visit to Vietnamese Embassy by a car belonging to a man named Charles Richard Mellor, who previously resided in Vietnam and was employed by a South Vietnamese company.

99. October 31, 1968, memo from the director of the FBI to the White House Situation Room (attn: Bromley Smith) reporting that on that day a man named Leon Davis was at Vietnamese Embassy in the company of a short, young oriental woman.

100. October 31, 1968, memo from Rostow to President Johnson accompanying two attached documents. "1. President Thieu's older brother told [several words redacted] that he believed that it would be better to deal with the next President, no matter who is elected, on issues pertaining to the peace conference. [Several words redacted] according to rumors, the U.S. did not expect President Thieu to take such a stubborn attitude." Also "2. South Vietnamese Foreign Minister Thanh told the Advisory Council on October 30 that Ambassador Bunker was not 'pressuring' President Thieu to accept an unconditional cessation of the bombing of North Vietnam."

101. A partially redacted 1968 memo (specific date redacted) from DIRNSA to the White House (attn: Mr. McCafferty) reporting on President Thieu's report of the Bundy-Bui Diem talk. "There is absolutely no change in the U.S. government's position as ?stated? in the U.S. three-point memorandum and in the draft joint announcement." "The elections have nothing whatsoever to do with the current developments. On this subject [redacted] there are signs that the coming elections and the rumors of an imminent bombing halt have made the situation here confused and tense." "As already [redacted] still in touch with the various political circles to try to find out what is going on, but without, however, making it too obvious because the situation is delicate and there is much danger of misunderstanding."

102. A partially redacted October 29, 1968, memo from DIRNSA to the White House (attn: Mr. Arthur McCafferty) reporting on Vice President Ky's opinions on the conduct of the bombing halt. "There cannot be an unconditional cessation of bombing of the north." "Although the U.S. wants a bombing halt in the interest of the number of votes for Vice President Humphrey, it is impossible without the concurrence of the Vietnamese [redacted] government, and there cannot be the ruination of [redacted] person for the sake of one person, vice president Humphrey." "If the U.S. unilaterally says to cease bombing of the North unconditionally, South Vietnam unilaterally should be able to carry out unrestricted bombing of the North." "South Vietnam will fight the communists until the end." "South Vietnam cannot recognize the NLF."

103. October 19, 1968, memo from the CIA to Walt Rostow and Dean Rusk, subject: "Presidential Views Concerning the Bombing Halt and the Paris Talks." Between 23 and 25 October, Thieu held discussions with government officials about bombing halt and Paris talks, emphasizing the need for Hanoi to be serious about the talks. Thieu was concerned North Vietnam was guaranteeing nothing in return for bombing halt, and that the U.S. government wished to do something "dramatic" in order to help Humphrey on 5 November.

The inclusion of the NLF at Paris would aid Humphrey, said Thieu, but the benefits were short-range. Thieu told Vice President Ky on 25 October that he was afraid the U.S. would force the GVN to deal with the NLF. Thieu also mentioned difficulty with Americans urging him not to speak to the press or make public statements and "noted that he was trying to convey the impression that he was a man of peace who would die, not for the world, but for the people of SVN."

(No document 104.)

105. A heavily redacted October 27, 1968, memo from DIRNSA to the White House (attn: Mr. Arthur McCafferty). A bracketed portion of the memo reads: "In accordance with [redacted] instructions, [redacted] continuing my conversations to try to gain a clear-cut attitude. [Redacted] the longer the situation continues, the more [redacted] favored, for the elections will take place in a week and President Johnson would probably have difficulties in forcing [redacted] hand. [Redacted] still in contact with the Nixon entourage which continues to be the favorite despite the uncertainty provoked by the news of an imminent bombing halt. [Redacted] informed that if Nixon should be elected, he would first send an unofficial person and would himself consider later going to Saigon before the inauguration."

106. A partially redacted October 26, 1968, CIA memo to Walt Rostow and Dean Rusk, subject: "President Thieu's Views Regarding the Issues Involved in Agreeing to a Bombing Halt." Portions of the memo read: "Thieu says he will never negotiate with the NLF as an equal." "Inherent in his concern about the status of participating delegations is Thieu's obvious desire to avoid appearing to be a 'U.S. lackey.'" "Thieu also sees a definite connection between the moves now underway and President Johnson's wish to see Vice President Humphrey elected."

(No document 107 or 108.)

109. October 29, 1968, memo from Rostow to President Johnson accompanying document 109a and stating: "Herewith a further [redacted] Thieu talking to the South Korean Ambassador in Seoul in quite a disturbing way on 18 October."

109a. A partially redacted October 19, 1968, memo from DIRNSA to the White House (attn: Mr. Arthur McCafferty) discussing Thieu's views on negotiations. President Thieu spoke to the South Korean ambassador about peace talks "in quite a disturbing way." "He said the U.S. can, of course, cease bombing, but is unable to block Vietnam (from bombing). Concerning the enforcement of the bombing halt, this will help candidate Humphrey and this is the purpose of it; but the situation which would occur as the result of a bombing halt, without the agreement of Vietnamese government, rather than being a disadvantage to candidate Humphrey, would be to the advantage of candidate Nixon. Accordingly, he said that the possibility of president Johnson enforcing a bombing halt without Vietnam's agreement appears to be weak; [redacted] just how effective can it be within the short time before the election, even though it is effectively enforced?"

110. October 18, 1968, memo from Rostow to President Johnson introducing document 110a, on Ky's views regarding negotiations.

110a. October 18, 1968, CIA memo to Walt Rostow and Dean Rusk, subject: "Reactions of the GVN and Vice President Ky Concerning the Proposed Bombing Halt." South Vietnam was unwilling to negotiate with the NLF, and it was necessary to extract concessions now before the bombing halts and leverage decreases. Ky was seeking to find a policy that would preserve "Vietnamese identity" without jeopardizing the GVN's vital ties to the U.S. or giving comfort to the DRV (Democratic Republic of Vietnam). Uncertain of Johnson's intentions, Ky believed it was time for him and Thieu to join hands in a true government of national reconciliation — that is, if Thieu was intent on genuine reconciliation. "Ky is considering what unilateral steps he might take if Thieu does not meet him halfway, but emphasized that he will do nothing to endanger changes for peace or strain relations with the GVN's allies. One possibility he is considering, if the U.S. stops the bombing without the GVN's agreement, is the issuance of a GVN statement reserving the right to bomb or take any other actions against North Vietnam which is deemed in the GVN national interest."

111. October 31, 1968, memo from the director of the FBI to the White House Situation Room (attn: Bromley Smith) reporting on a Normal Johnson of Evergreen Park, IL, who served in the Air Force in Vietnam and was injured prior to discharge.

112. August 29, 1968, State Department telegram to the American Embassy in Saigon urging public officials to take a position of "no comment" on the presidential campaign and suggest to South Vietnamese government that their officials do the same.

(No document 113.)

114. A completely redacted memo from Bromley Smith to President Johnson.

Notes

Cast of Characters

1. Phipps-Evans, Michelle. "Madam Chennault Celebrates 88 in Style." *Asian Fortune News*. N.p., 11 Jul. 2013. Web. 15 Mar. 2014. http://www.asianfortunenews.com/2013/07/madam-chennault-celebrates-88-in-style/.

2. From the Council for International Cooperation website. Accessed 15 Jun. 2014. http://cicwashington.com/.

3. Rosen, James. *The Strong Man: John Mitchell and the Secrets of Watergate*. New York: Doubleday, 2008. 14-16. Print.

4. Meyer, Lawrence. "John N. Mitchell, Principal in Watergate, Dies at 75." *The Washington Post* 10 Nov. 1988: A01. Web.

5. "Nguyen Van Thieu." *The Telegraph*. 1 Oct. 2001.

6. CIA official Frank Snepp in *Vietnam War Secrets*. Directed by Chris Noonan and John Duigan. 2007. DVD.

7. Butterfield, Fox. "Nguyen Van Thieu Is Dead at 76; Last President of South Vietnam." *The New York Times*. N.p., 1 Oct. 2001. Web.

8. Gamarekian, Barbara. "Bui Diem: A Voice From Vietnam Hoping to Be Heard." *The New York Times*. N.p., 25 Oct. 1987. Web.

9. Krebs, Albin. "Lawrence O'Brien, Democrat, Dies at 73." *The New York Times*. N.p., 28 Sept. 1990. Web.

Timeline of Events

1. Summers, Anthony and Robbyn Swan. *The Arrogance of Power: The Secret World of Richard Nixon*. New York: Viking, 2000. 166. Print.

2. Thompson, Robert. "North Vietnam Attack Urged by Nixon." *The Los Angeles Times* 19 Apr. 1964. Print.

3. Lukas, J. Anthony. *Nightmare: The Underside of the Nixon Years*.

Athens, OH: Ohio University Press, 1999. 283. Print.

4. This tape can be heard at the LBJ Library website: http://www.lbjlib.utexas.edu/johnson/archives.hom/dictabelt.hom/highlights/may68jan69.shtm.

5. Peters, Mike. *The Nixon Chronicles*. Dayton, OH: Lorenz, 1976. 153. Print.

6. This tape can be heard at the LBJ Library website: http://www.lbjlib.utexas.edu/johnson/archives.hom/dictabelt.hom/highlights/may68jan69.shtm.

7. LBJ conversation with Sen. Richard Russell, 20 Oct. 1968. http://www.lbjlib.utexas.edu/johnson/archives.hom/Dictabelt.hom/highlights/may68jan69.shtm.

8. Summers. *The Arrogance of Power*. 305.

9. Parry, Robert. "The Significance of Nixon's 'Treason.'" Consortiumnews.com. 9 Dec. 2008. https://consortiumnews.com/2008/120808.html.

10. Summers. *The Arrogance of Power*. 307.

11. Parry, Robert. *America's Stolen Narrative: From Washington and Madison to Nixon, Reagan and the Bushes to Obama*. Arlington, VA: Media Consortium, 2012. 49. Print.

12. Peters. *The Nixon Chronicles*. 157.

13. By then, more than three million tons of bombs had fallen on the neutral and defenseless country, causing the deaths of some half-million Cambodians. The cost of the bombings to U.S. taxpayers was later estimated at $1.5 billion.

14. Reeves, Richard. *President Nixon: Alone in the White House*. New York: Simon & Schuster, 2002. 105. Print.

15. Summers. *The Arrogance of Power*. 534.

16. Ibid., 306.

17. "Anna Chennault Works to Stop Vietnam War." *Shanghai Star*. 19 Sept. 2002. http://app1.chinadaily.com.cn/star/2002/0919/pr22-1.html.

Chapter 1

1. Muriel Dobbin, former White House Correspondent for the *Baltimore Sun*. Personal e-mail correspondence with the author. 14 Sept. 2012.

2. Updegrove, Mark K. *Indomitable Will: LBJ in the Presidency*. New York: Crown, 2012. 258. Print.

3. Folkenflik, David. "Walter Cronkite, The Nation's Narrator, Dies At 92." *NPR*. N.p., 17 July 2009. Web.

4. President Lyndon B. Johnson's Address to the Nation Announcing Steps To Limit the War in Vietnam and Reporting His Decision Not To Seek Reelection, LBJ Library Archives: http://www.lbjlib.utexas.edu/johnson/archives.hom/speeches.hom/680331.asp.

5. Updegrove. *Indomitable Will*. 269.

6. Ibid., 270.

7. The author replaced this Washington reporter in the position.

8. Perlstein, Rick. *Nixonland: The Rise of a President and the Fracturing of America*. New York: Scribner, 2008. 346. Print.

9. This commercial can be viewed at the website of the Museum of the Moving Image: http://www.livingroomcandidate.org/commercials/1968/vietnam.

10. The *Delta Democrat Times*, September 27, 1968, carried a UPI story datelined Washington by Ed Rogers on page 5: Rogers, Ed. "Uh Well, That Was Different." *Delta Democrat-Times* [Greenville, Mississippi] 27 Sept. 1972: 5. *Delta Democrat-Times Archive*. Delta Democrat-Times. Web. <http://newspaperarchive.com/delta-democrat-times/1972-09-27/page-5>.

11. Nossiter, Bernard. "Nixon: He Attacks HHH For Loosest Tongue." *Washington Post*. 5 Nov. 1968, A-1.

12. For Mitchell's prisoner number, see Hitchens, Christopher. *The Trial of Henry Kissinger*. London: Verso, 2001. 10. Print.

13. Abrams' comments are recalled by LBJ's national security advisor Walt Rostow in *Nixon: The Arrogance of Power*, a 2000 TV documentary made for the History Channel.

14. Gardner, Lloyd C., and Ted Gittinger. *The Search for Peace in Vietnam, 1964-1968*. College Station: Texas A & M University Press, 2004. 336. Print.

15. Taped conversation between President Johnson and Sen. Everett Dirksen on November 2, 1968. The transcript of this call can be accessed at the Miller Center, http://prde.upress.virginia.edu/conversations/4006123.

16. This tape can be heard at the LBJ Library website: http://www.lbjlib.utexas.edu/johnson/archives.hom/dictabelt.hom/highlights/may68jan69.shtm.

17. This tape can be heard at the LBJ Library website: http:// www.lbjlib.utexas.edu/johnson/archives.hom/dictabelt. hom/highlights/may68jan69.shtm.

18. Kettle, Martin. "Nixon 'wrecked Early Peace in Vietnam.'" *The Guardian.* Guardian News and Media. 08 Aug. 2000. Web. 15 Mar. 2014. <http://www.guardian.co.uk/world/2000/ aug/09/martinkettle1>.

19. Bundy, William P. *A Tangled Web: The Making of Foreign Policy in the Nixon Presidency.* London: I.B. Tauris, 1998. 37. Print.

20. Document 29-1 of the X Envelope. From FBI Director to White House Situation Room, attn: Bromley Smith. 2 Nov. 1968. Courtesy LBJ Presidential Library.

21. This tape can be heard at the LBJ Library website: http:// www.lbjlib.utexas.edu/johnson/archives.hom/dictabelt. hom/highlights/may68jan69.shtm.

22. This tape can be heard at the LBJ Library website: http:// www.lbjlib.utexas.edu/johnson/archives.hom/dictabelt. hom/highlights/may68jan69.shtm.

23. U.S. Constitution at the National Archives and Records Administration website: http://www.archives.gov/ exhibits/charters/constitution.html/.

24. Edelson, Chris. Personal correspondence with the author. 2011.

25. Congressional Research Service report on the Logan Act: http://www.fas.org/sgp/crs/misc/RL33265.pdf.

26. Kettle. "Nixon 'wrecked Early Peace in Vietnam.'"

27. Califano, Joseph. *The Triumph and Tragedy of Lyndon Johnson.* Touchstone Books, 1992, 328.

28. Updegrove. *Indomitable Will.* 308.

29. Ibid.

30. Rowan, Ford. Personal e-mail correspondence with the author. 2013.

31. Hitchens. *The Trial of Henry Kissinger.* 10.

32. Spivak, Al. Personal correspondence with the author. 10 Aug. 2010.

33. Hitchens. *The Trial of Henry Kissinger.* 136.

Chapter 2

1. Kurtz, Kenneth Franklin. *Nixon's Enemies.* Los Angeles: Lowell House, 1998. 273. Print.
2. Limpert, Jack. "Remembering Joe McGinnis and The Selling of the President 1968." *About Editing and Writing.* 12 Mar. 2014. Web. http://jacklimpert.com/2014/03/remembering-joe-mcginniss-selling-president-1968/.
3. Humphrey, Hubert H. *The Education of a Public Man: My Life and Politics.* Minneapolis, MN: Univ. of MN Press, 1991. 4. Print.
4. Solberg, Carl. *Hubert Humphrey: A Biography.* New York: W. W. Norton & Co., 1984. 35-36. Print.
5. Humphrey. *The Education of a Public Man.* 4.
6. Ibid.
7. Solberg. *Hubert Humphrey.* 35.
8. Ibid., 37.
9. Ibid.
10. Humphrey. *The Education of a Public Man.* 3.
11. Ibid., 6.
12. Ibid., 8.
13. Ibid.
14. Solberg. *Hubert Humphrey.* 42.
15. Humphrey. *The Education of a Public Man.* 8.
16. Ibid., 9.
17. Ibid., 10.
18. Ibid., 15-16.
19. Ibid., 20.
20. Solberg. *Hubert Humphrey.* 47.
21. Ibid.
22. Ibid., 50-52.
23. Ibid., 51.
24. Ibid., 53.
25. Summers, Anthony, with Robbyn Swan. *The Arrogance of Power: The Secret World of Richard Nixon.* New York: Penguin, 2000. 4. Print.
26. Aitken, Jonathan. *Nixon: A Life.* Washington, DC: Renergy, 1994. 11. Print.
27. Spalding, Henry D. *The Nixon Nobody Knows.* Middle Village, NY: Jonathan David, 1972. 36-39. Print.

28. Gannon, Frank. Interview with Richard Nixon. Day 1, Tape 1. 3:36. Oral History. University of Georgia, Walter J. Brown Media Archives and Peabody Awards Collection. http://www.libs.uga.edu/media/collections/nixon/ohms/.

29. Spalding. *The Nixon Nobody Knows.* 39.

30. Gannon, Frank. Interview with Richard Nixon. Day 1, Tape 1. 3:46. Oral History. University of Georgia, Walter J. Brown Media Archives and Peabody Awards Collection. http://www.libs.uga.edu/media/collections/nixon/ohms/.

31. Nixon, Richard. *RN: The Memoirs of Richard Nixon.* New York: Grosset & Dunlap, 1978. 6. Print.

32. Summers. *The Arrogance of Power.* 7.

33. Ibid., 9.

34. Nixon. *RN.* 13-14.

35. Summers. *The Arrogance of Power.* 8.

36. Gannon, Frank. Interview with Richard Nixon. Day 1, Tape 1. Oral History. University of Georgia, Walter J. Brown Media Archives and Peabody Awards Collection. http://www.libs.uga.edu/media/collections/nixon/ohms/.

37. Ibid.

38. Summers. *The Arrogance of Power.* 9-10.

39. Ibid., 14-18.

40. Hersh, Seymour. *The Dark Side of Camelot.* New York: Little, Brown, and Company, 1997. 158. Print.

41. Brodie, Fawn M. *Richard Nixon: The Shaping of his Character.* New York: W. W. Norton, 1981. 425. Print.

42. Greenberg, David. *Nixon's Shadow: The History of an Image.* New York: W. W. Norton, 2003. 235. Print.

Chapter 3

1. Updegrove, Mark K. *Indomitable Will: LBJ in the Presidency.* New York: Crown, 2012. 242. Print.

2. Johnson, Tom. Personal correspondence with the author. April 2014.

3. National Archives and Records Administration. "Statistical Information about Fatal Casualties of the Vietnam War. National Archives and Records Administration. Last updated Aug. 2013. Web. http://www.archives.gov/research/military/vietnam-war/casualty-statistics.html.

4. Chambers, John Whiteclay, II, ed. *The Oxford Companion to*

American Military History, 1999. http://www.oxfordreference. com/view/10.1093/acref/9780195071986.001.0001/ acref-9780195071986.

5. Johnson, Tom. Personal correspondence with the author. April 2014.
6. Ibid.
7. Gregory, Joseph. "Gen. Vo Nguyen Giap, Who Ousted U.S. From Vietnam, Is Dead." *New York Times*. N.p., 4 Oct. 2013. Web. 17 Apr. 2014. http://www.nytimes.com/2013/10/05/ world/asia/gen-vo-nguyen-giap-dies.html?_r=0.
8. Johnson, Tom. Personal correspondence with the author. April 2014.
9. Brigham, Robert K. "Battlefield Vietnam: A Brief History." PBS. http://www.pbs.org/battlefieldvietnam/history/.
10. "Who, What, When, Where, Why: Report from Vietnam by Walter Cronkite." CBS Evening News. February 27, 1968.
11. Dallek, Robert. "Three New Revelations About LBJ." *Atlantic*. Apr. 1998: 42-44. Web.
12. Ibid.
13. Logevall, Fredrik. *Choosing War: The Lost Chance for Peace and the Escalation of War in Vietnam*. Berkeley: University of California Press, 2001. 77. Print.
14. Updegrove. *Indomitable Will*. 264.
15. Pugmire, Tim. "Eugene McCarthy, who galvanized a generation of war opponents, dies." Minnesota Public Radio. 10 Dec. 2005. Web. http://news.minnesota.publicradio.org/ features/2005/06/15_olsond_genemccarthy/.
16. Updegrove. *Indomitable Will*. 61.
17. Ibid.
18. Ibid., 265.
19. John F. Kennedy Presidential Library and Museum website. http://www.jfklibrary.org/.
20. Updegrove. *Indomitable Will*. 272.
21. Reedy, George E. *The Twilight of the Presidency: From Johnson to Reagan*. New York: New American Library, 1988. 73. Print.
22. Pugmire. "Eugene McCarthy, who galvanized a generation of war opponents, dies."
23. Johnson, Tom. Personal correspondence with the author. April 2014.
24. From a 1995 interview with BBC Washington correspondent

Charles Wheeler, courtesy of the BBC's current Washington correspondent David Taylor.

25. Ibid.

26. *The Fog of War: Eleven Lessons from the Life of Robert S. McNamara.* Sony Pictures. 2003.

27. Ibid.

28. Ibid.

29. Summers, Anthony, with Robbyn Swan. *The Arrogance of Power: The Secret World of Richard Nixon.* New York: Penguin, 2000. 293. Print.

Chapter 4

1. Gibbs, Nancy and Michael Duffy. *The Presidents Club: Inside the World's Most Exclusive Fraternity.* New York: Simon & Schuster, 2012. 230. Print.

2. Bernstein, Irving. *Guns or Butter: The Presidency of Lyndon Johnson.* New York: Oxford University Press, 1996. Print.

3. Forslund, Catherine. *Anna Chennault: Informal Diplomacy and Asian Relations.* Lanham, MD: Rowman & Littlefield, 2002. 53. Print.

4. Summers, Anthony, with Robbyn Swan. *The Arrogance of Power: The Secret World of Richard Nixon.* New York: Penguin, 2000. 299. Print.

5. Witcover, Jules. *The Year the Dream Died: Revisiting 1968 in America.* New York: Grand Central Publishing, 1998. 441. Print.

6. Summers. *The Arrogance of Power.* 299.

7. Ibid., 300.

8. Document 105 of the X Envelope. Memo from Office of DIRNSA Marshall Carter to the White House attn: Arthur McCafferty. Date partially redacted, 1968. "Delays Improve South Vietnam's Position." Courtesy LBJ Presidential Library.

9. "Nguyen Van Thieu." *The Telegraph.* Telegraph Media Group, 1 Oct. 2001. Web. 22 Mar. 2014. Web. http://www.telegraph. co.uk/news/obituaries/1358069/Nguyen-Van-Thieu.html.

10. Document 102 of the X Envelope. Memo from Office of DIRNSA Marshall Carter to White House attn: Arthur McCafferty. 29 Oc. 1968. "Vice President Ky Expresses Opinions on Conduct of Bomb Halt." Courtesy LBJ Presidential Library.

11. Document 109a of the X Envelope. Memo from Office of

DIRNSA Marshall Carter to White House attn: Arthur Mc-Cafferty. 19 Oct. 1968. "Thieu's Views on NLF Participation in Vietnamese Government." Courtesy LBJ Presidential Library.

12. Summers. *The Arrogance of Power.* 297.
13. Knott, Stephen F., Russell L. Riley, and James Sterling Young. Interview with Richard V. Allen. University of Virginia, Miller Center Presidential Recordings Program. 28 May 2002. http://web1.millercenter.org/poh/transcripts/ohp_2002_0528_allen.pdf.
14. Jarecki, Eugene. *The Trials of Henry Kissinger.* BBC, 2002.
15. Ibid.
16. Kimball, Jeffery. *Nixon's Vietnam War.* Lawrence: University Press of Kansas, 1998. 60.
17. Chafe, William H. *The Unfinished Journey: America Since World War II.* New York: Oxford University Press, 2010. 379. Print.
18. Perlstein, Rick. *Nixonland: The Rise of a President and the Fracturing of America.* New York: Scribner, 2008. 350. Print.
19. Ibid., 149.
20. Gibbs and Duffy. *The Presidents Club.* 226.
21. Ibid.
22. Ibid., 239.
23. Document 39 of the X Envelope. Memo from Walt Rostow for the Record. 14 May 1972. Courtesy LBJ Presidential Library.
24. Document 105 of the X Envelope. Memo from Office of DIRNSA Marshall Carter to the White House attn: Arthur McCafferty. Date partially redacted, 1968. "Delays Improve South Vietnam's Position." Courtesy LBJ Presidential Library.
25. Document 97b of the X Envelope. Memo from Office of DIRNSA to redacted recipient. 28 Oct. 1968. "Thieu's Views on Peace Talks and Bombing Halt." Courtesy LBJ Presidential Library.
26. Ibid.
27. Document 44 of the X Envelope. Walt Rostow to President Lyndon Johnson. 29 Oct. 1968, 6:00 a.m.; Document 44a of the X Envelope. Note signed by Eugene Rostow. 29 Oct. 1968; Document 45 of the X Envelope. Walt Rostow to President Lyndon Johnson. 29 Oct. 1968, 12:50 p.m.; Document 45a of the X Envelope. Eugene Rostow to Walt Rostow. 29 Oct. 1968. Courtesy LBJ Presidential Library.

28. Document 44a of the X Envelope. Courtesy LBJ Presidential Library.
29. Ibid.
30. Document 39 of the X Envelope. Courtesy LBJ Presidential Library.
31. Summers. *The Arrogance of Power*. 301.

Chapter 5

1. Summers, Anthony, with Robbyn Swan. *The Arrogance of Power: The Secret World of Richard Nixon*. New York: Penguin, 2000. 300-301. Print.
2. Ibid., 302.
3. Ibid., 298.
4. This tape can be heard at the LBJ Library website: http://www.lbjlib.utexas.edu/johnson/archives.hom/dictabelt.hom/highlights/may68jan69.shtm.
5. This tape can be heard at the LBJ Library website: http://www.lbjlib.utexas.edu/johnson/archives.hom/dictabelt.hom/highlights/may68jan69.shtm.
6. Document 29-1 of the X Envelope. FBI Director to White House Situation Room attn: Bromley Smith. 2 Nov. 1968. Courtesy LBJ Presidential Library.
7. Robb, David L. *The Gumshoe and the Shrink: Guenther Reinhardt, Dr. Arnold Hutschnecker, and the Secret History of the 1960 Kennedy-Nixon Election*. Solana Beach, CA: Santa Monica Press, 2012. 253. Print.
8. Document 30 of the X Envelope. Walt Rostow to President Johnson. 2 Nov. 1968. "The New Mexico Reference May Indicate Agnew is Acting." Courtesy LBJ Presidential Library.
9. Summers. *The Arrogance of Power*. 303.
10. Robb. *The Gumshoe and the Shrink*. 254.
11. This tape can be heard at the LBJ Library website: http://www.lbjlib.utexas.edu/johnson/archives.hom/dictabelt.hom/highlights/may68jan69.shtm.
12. "Tonight" likely refers to Sunday, when the news program aired.
13. Document 93 of the X Envelope. White House memorandum signed Jim J. 3 Nov. 1968, 11:25 a.m. Courtesy LBJ Presidential Library.
14. This tape can be heard at the LBJ Library website: http://

www.lbjlib.utexas.edu/johnson/archives.hom/dictabelt.
hom/highlights/may68jan69.shtm.

15. Summers. *The Arrogance of Power*. 305.

16. Campaign speech by Hubert Humphrey. Salt Lake City,
Utah. September 30, 1968.

17. Updegrove, Mark K. *Indomitable Will: LBJ in the Presidency*.
New York: Crown, 2012. 303.

18. Updegrove. *Indomitable Will*. 303.

19. Summers. *The Arrogance of Power*. 305.

20. Ibid.

21. Sherman, Norman. Personal correspondence with the author.
2012.

22. Ibid.

23. Document 91 of the X Envelope. Walt Rostow to President
Johnson. 4 Nov. 1968. "Herewith Full Account Saville Davis –
Bui Diem Conversation." Courtesy LBJ Presidential Library.

24. Document 91b of the X Envelope. Continued from Document
91. Walt Rostow to President Johnson. 4 Nov. 1968. "Herewith
Full Account Saville Davis – Bui Diem Conversation."
Courtesy LBJ Presidential Library.

25. Summers. *The Arrogance of Power*. 305.

26. Document 27 of the X Envelope. Walt Rostow to President
Johnson. 4 Nov. 1968. "Report on meeting with Secretary
Rusk and Secretary Clifford." Courtesy LBJ Presidential
Library.

27. Ibid.

28. Ibid.

29. Summers. *The Arrogance of Power*. 306.

Chapter 6

1. Knott, Stephen F., Russell L. Riley, and James Sterling
Young. Interview with Richard V. Allen. University of
Virginia, Miller Center Presidential Recordings Program. 28
May 2002. http://web1.millercenter.org/poh/transcripts/
ohp_2002_0528_allen.pdf.

2. Isaacson, Walter. *Kissinger: A Biography*. New York: Simon &
Schuster, 1992. 135. Print.

3. Smith, Terrance. "Kissinger Role in '68 Race Stirs Conflicting
Views." *New York Times*. 13 Jun. 1983. Print.

4. Ibid.

5. Nixon, Richard. "Address Accepting the Presidential Nomina-
    tion at the Republican National Convention in Miami Beach,
    Florida." 8 Aug. 1968. University of California–Santa Barbara.
    Web. http://www.presidency.ucsb.edu/ws/?pid=25968.
6. Reedy, George. *The Twilight of the Presidency.* New York:
    Signet, 1971. 74. Print.
7. Kutler, Stanley I. *The Wars of Watergate: The Last Crisis of
    Richard Nixon.* New York: W. W. Norton, 1992. 205-206. Print.
8. Ibid.
9. Agnew, Spiro T. *Go Quietly . . . Or Else.* New York: William
    Morrow, 1980. 212. Print.
10. Cohen, Richard M. and Jules Witcover. *A Heartbeat Away: The
    Investigation and Resignation of Vice President Spiro T. Agnew.*
    New York: Viking, 1974. 272. Print.
11. This tape can be heard at the LBJ Library website: http://
    www.lbjlib.utexas.edu/johnson/archives.hom/dictabelt.
    hom/highlights/may68jan69.shtm.
12. Kutler. *The Wars of Watergate.* 72.
13. "Those Who Have Had a Chance . . ." University of
    Washington Library, Special Collections Division, Vietnam
    War Era Ephemera Collection. Web. http://digitalcollections.
    lib.washington.edu/cdm/ref/collection/protests/id/402.
14. This and the preceding Ehrlichman quotes can be found in
    his book, *Witness to Power: The Nixon Years.* New York: Simon
    & Schuster, 1982. 38-39. Print.
15. Lukas, J. Anthony. *Nightmare: The Underside of the Nixon Years.*
    Athens, OH: Ohio University Press, 1999. 363. Print.
16. Kutler. *The Wars of Watergate.* 66.
17. Ibid., 72.
18. McManus, Jim. Personal e-mail correspondence with the
    author. 2014.

Chapter 7
1. Dallek, Robert. "Three New Revelations about LBJ." *Atlantic.*
    April 1998.
2. Ibid.
3. Jones, Jim. 2011 interview with Larry Sabato in *The Kennedy
    Half-Century: The Presidency, Assassination, and Lasting Legacy*

of John F. Kennedy. New York: Bloomsbury, 2013. 301. Print.

4. Baker, Bobby. *Wheeling and Dealing: Confessions of a Capitol Hill Operator.* New York: W. W. Norton, 1980. 274. Print.

5. Dallek. "Three New Revelations about LBJ."

6. This juicy historical morsel comes to us courtesy of the LBJ Library in audiotapes released in 2008.

7. Sherman, Norman. Personal e-mail correspondence with the author. 6 March 2015.

8. Updegrove, Mark K. *Indomitable Will: LBJ in the Presidency.* New York: Crown, 2012. 303. Print.

9. Connell, Bill. Personal e-mail correspondence with the author. 2013.

10. Nafalti, Timothy. Interview with Tom Huston. 27 Jun. 2008. Accessed 5 Aug. 2014. Web. http://www.nixonlibrary.gov/virtuallibrary/documents/histories/huston-2008-06-27.pdf.

11. Ibid.

12. Ibid.

13. Drosnin, Michael. *Citizen Hughes: The Power, the Money, and the Madness.* New York: Holt, Rinehart, and Winston, 1985. 275. Print.

14. Sherman, Norman. Personal e-mail correspondence with the author. 2013.

15. Ibid.

16. All preceding quotations from Bill Conell were obtained from his personal e-mail correspondence with the author in 2013.

17. Dallek, Robert. *Nixon and Kissinger: Partners in Power.* New York: HarperCollins, 2007. 356.

18. BBC quotes courtesy of BBC's Washington Correspondent David Taylor.

19. Updegrove. *Indomitable Will.* 308.

20. Summers, Anthony, with Robbyn Swan. *The Arrogance of Power: The Secret World of Richard Nixon.* New York: Penguin, 2000. 307. Print.

21. Updegrove. *Indomitable Will.* 308.

22. Stewart, John. Personal correspondence with the author. 2013.

23. Sherman, Norman and John Stewart. "Hubert Humphrey and the lost art of unity." *StarTribune* (Minneapolis, MN).

12 May 2012. Web. http://www.startribune.com/opinion/commentaries/151197105.html.

24. Stewart, John and Norman Sherman. "Humphrey's lesson in bipartisanship for today's politicians." knoxnews.com. June 16, 2012.

Chapter 8

1. Document 86a of the X Envelope. From FBI Director to White House Situation Room attn: Bromley Smith. 7 Nov. 1968, 3:51 p.m. Courtesy LBJ Presidential Library.

2. Summers, Anthony, with Robbyn Swan. *The Arrogance of Power: The Secret World of Richard Nixon.* New York: Penguin, 2000. 305. Print.

3. Document 21a of the X Envelope. FBI Director to White House Situation Room, attn: Bromley Smith. 8 Nov. 1968. Courtesy LBJ Presidential Library.

4. Document 21 of the X Envelope. Walt Rostow to President Johnson. 8 Nov. 1968, 7:35 a.m. Courtesy LBJ Presidential Library.

5. Parry, Robert. "LBJ's 'X' File on Nixon's 'Treason'." *Consortium News.* N.p., 3 Mar. 2012. Web. 22 Mar. 2014. http://consortiumnews.com/2012/03/03/lbjs-x-file-on-nixons-treason/.

6. Summers. *The Arrogance of Power.* 307.

7. Ibid., 306.

8. Ibid.

9. Document 71 of the X Envelope. Walt Rostow to President Johnson. 20 Nov. 1968, 3:10 p.m. Courtesy LBJ Presidential Library.

10. Document 71a of the X Envelope. Central Intelligence Agency Intelligence Information Cable. 18 Nov. 1968. "President Thieu's Comments on Peace Talks Impasse at Private Dinner Parties on 11 and 12 November 1968." Courtesy LBJ Presidential Library.

11. Ibid.

12. Document 74 of the X Envelope. Pearson, Drew, and Jack Anderson. "Washington-Saigon Feud: Details Leak Out of Backstage Fight Between U.S. and South Vietnam." *The*

Washington Post. B7. 17 Nov. 1968. Courtesy LBJ Presidential Library.

13. Document 75 of the X Envelope. Geyer, Georgie Anne. "Saigon Boast: We Helped Elect Nixon." *Chicago Daily News*. 15 Nov. 1968. Courtesy LBJ Presidential Library.

14. Document 15 of the X Envelope. Walt Rostow to President Johnson. 10 Dec. 1968, 10:00 a.m. Courtesy LBJ Presidential Library.

15. Document 15a of the X Envelope. From FBI Director to White House Situation Room, attn: Bromley Smith. 9 Dec. 1968. Courtesy LBJ Presidential Library.

16. Document 13a of the X Envelope. Transcript of telephone conversation between Tom Ottenad of the *St. Louis Post-Dispatch* and Walt Rostow. 3 Jan. 1969, 11:40 a.m. Courtesy LBJ Presidential Library.

17. Document 13 of the X Envelope. Walt Rostow to President Johnson. 3 Jan. 1969, 2:25 p.m. Courtesy LBJ Presidential Library.

18. Document 11 of the X Envelope; Ottenad, Tom. "Was Saigon's Peace Talk Delay Due to Republican Promises?" Courtesy LBJ Presidential Library.

19. Document 11 of the X Envelope. Courtesy LBJ Presidential Library.

20. Document 55 of the X Envelope. "Did HHH's 'Fair Play' Cost Election?" *The Austin Statesman*. 9 Jul. 1969. Page 1; Document 59 of the X Envelope. Kelly, Harry. "White Reports Nixon Backer Tried to Block Peace Talks." *The Evening Star*. Washington, D.C. 9 Jul. 1969. Courtesy LBJ Presidential Library.

21. Document 63 of the X Envelope. "Humphrey Agrees with 'Sabotage' Charge." *The Austin American*. 11 Jul. 1969. Courtesy LBJ Presidential Library.

22. Document 62 of the X Envelope. "Mrs. Chennault Denies Seeking Peace Talk Delay." *The New York Times*. 23 Jul. 1969. Page C5. Courtesy LBJ Presidential Library.

23. Nixon, Richard. "Inaugural Address." 20 Jan. 1969. Accessed through the American Presidency Project, University of California at Santa Barbara. 3 Mar. 2015. http://www.presidency.ucsb.edu/ws/?pid=1941.

Chapter 9

1. Forslund, Catherine. *Anna Chennault: Informal Diplomacy and Asian Relations*. Lanham, MD: Rowman & Littlefield, 2002. 83. Print.
2. Miller Center Presidential Recordings Program. Richard Allen, interview with the Miller Center. http://millercenter. org/president/bush/oralhistory/richard-allen.
3. From an LBJ Library film dealing with the month of November, 1968.
4. Summers, Anthony, with Robbyn Swan. *The Arrogance of Power: The Secret World of Richard Nixon*. New York: Penguin, 2000. 306. Print.
5. "Anna Chennault Works to Stop Vietnam War," *Shanghai Star*, 19 Sept. 2002.
6. Woodward, Bob and Carl Bernstein. *The Final Days*. New York: Simon & Schuster Paperbacks, 1976. *The Final Days*. 168, 424. Print.
7. Hersh, Seymour. *The Price of Power: Kissinger in the Nixon White House*. New York: Summit, 1983. 448. Print.
8. Jarecki, Eugene. *The Trials of Henry Kissinger*. BBC, 2002.
9. Forslund. *Anna Chennault*. 83.
10. Haldeman, H. R. *The Haldeman Diaries: Inside the Nixon White House*. New York: Berkley Books, 1995. 271. Print.
11. Reeves, Richard. *President Nixon: Alone in the White House*. New York: Simon & Schuster, 2002. 447. Print.
12. Haldeman. *The Haldeman Diaries*. 40-41.
13. Shawcross, William. *Sideshow: Kissinger, Nixon and the Destruction of Cambodia*. New York: Cooper Square Press. 395. Print.
14. Morroco, John. *Rain of Fire: Air War 1969-1973*. New York: Time Life Education, 1985. 13. Print.
15. Nixon, Richard. Address to the Nation on the Situation in Southeast Asia. 30 Apr. 1970.
16. Duiker, William J. *Sacred War: Nationalism and Revolution in a Divided Vietnam*. New York: McGraw-Hill, 1995. 229-30. Print.
17. Reeves. *President Nixon*. 209.
18. Ibid.
19. Ibid., 199.
20. Summers, Anthony and Robbyn Swan. *The Arrogance of Power:*

The Secret World of Richard Nixon. New York: Viking, 2000. 372. Print.

21. Ibid.

22. This conversation comes from a tape that can be heard at the Nixon Library. The conversation took place on April 25, 1972. The Library has yet to make the recording available online.

23. Ibid.

24. Summers. *The Arrogance of Power.* 463. This comes from JCS member Adm. Elmo Zumwalt.

25. Ibid., 480.

26. Hitchens, Christopher. "Let Me Say This About That." Review of *The Arrogance of Power* by Anthony Summers. *New York Times.* 8 Oct. 2000.

27. "Military Coup Fears Denied." *Washington Post.* 27 Aug. 1974.

28. Summers. *The Arrogance of Power.* 481.

Chapter 10

1. Brinkley, Douglas and Luke Nichter. *The Nixon Tapes.* New York: Houghton Mifflin Harcourt, 2014. 602. Print. Most of the tapes in this volume are newly transcribed using state-of-the-art audio equipment.

2. Ibid., 606.

3. Reeves, Richard. *President Nixon: Alone in the White House.* New York: Simon & Schuster, 2002. 107. Print.

4. Nixon, Richard. Interview by Frank Gannon. *American Presidents.* C-SPAN. C-SPAN, United States: 19 Nov. 1983.

5. Reeves. *President Nixon.* 529.

6. Recorded White House call between Nixon and Kissinger. 20 Jan. 1973, 9:32 a.m. Accessed via the Nixon Presidential Library and Museum. http://www.nixonlibrary.gov/forresearchers/find/tapes/tape036/036-021.mp3.

7. Recorded Oval Office conversation. 6 Oct. 1972, 9:06 a.m. Accessed via the Nixon Presidential Library and Museum. http://www.nixonlibrary.gov/forresearchers/find/tapes/tape036/036-021.mp3.

8. Ibid.

9. Haldeman, H. R. *The Haldeman Diaries: Inside the Nixon White House.* New York: Berkley Books, 1995. 515. Print.

10. Ibid., 517.
11. Reeves. *President Nixon.* 533.
12. Haldeman. *The Haldeman Diaries.* 517.
13. Berman, Larry. *No Peace, No Honor: Nixon, Kissinger, and Betrayal in Vietnam.* New York: Touchstone, 2002. 162. Print.
14. Ibid., 163.
15. Reeves. *President Nixon.* 535.
16. Berman. *No Peace, No Honor.* 163.
17. Haldeman. *The Haldeman Diaries.* 517.
18. Reeves. *President Nixon.* 536.
19. Ibid., 537.
20. Ibid.
21. Haldeman. *The Haldeman Diaries.* 524.
22. Ibid.
23. Ibid., 525.
24. Author's personal notes from Kissinger's October 26 press conference.
25. Recorded conversation between Nixon and Haldeman. 26 Oct. 1972, 2:05 pm. Accessed via the Nixon Presidential Library and Museum. http://www.nixonlibrary.gov/forresearchers/find/tapes/tape375/375-014.mp3.
26. Haldeman. *The Haldeman Diaries.* 521.
27. Reeves. *President Nixon.* 521.
28. Haldeman. *The Haldeman Diaries.* 524.
29. Reeves. *President Nixon.* 540.
30. Ibid., 531.
31. Berman. *No Peace, No Honor.* 180.
32. Brinkley and Nichter. *The Nixon Tapes.* 643.
33. Recorded Oval Office conversation between Nixon and Kissinger. 14 Dec. 1972, 9:59 a.m. Accessed via the Nixon Presidential Library and Museum. http://www.nixonlibrary.gov/forresearchers/find/tapes/tape823/823-001a.mp3.
34. Dallek, Robert. "The Kissinger Presidency." *Vanity Fair.* N.p., n.d. Web. 22 Mar. 2014. http://www.vanityfair.com/politics/features/2007/05/kissinger200705.
35. "Return with Honor." *The American Experience.* PBS. 14 Nov. 2000. Television. http://www.pbs.org/wgbh/amex/honor/.
36. Sloyan, Pat. *The Politics of Deception.* New York: St. Martin's, 2015. 235. Print.

37. *Vietnam War Secrets*. Directed by Chris Noonan and John Duigan. 2007.

38. Butterfield, Fox. New York Times Obituary of Nguyen Van Thieu. 01 Oct. 2001. http://www.nytimes.com/2001/10/01/obituaries/01THIE.html.

39. Berman. *No Peace, No Honor*. 204.

40. National Archives and Records Administration. "Statistical Information about Fatal Casualties of the Vietnam War. National Archives and Records Administration. Last updated Aug. 2013. Web. http://www.archives.gov/research/military/vietnam-war/casualty-statistics.html.

41. United States Department of Defense. "American Forces Press Service, Operation Iraqi Freedom U.S. Casualty Status." http://www.defense.gov/news/casualty.pdf.

Chapter 11

1. Kutler, Stanley I. *The Wars of Watergate: The Last Crisis of Richard Nixon*. New York: W. W. Norton, 1992. 3. Print.

2. Nixon, Richard. Interview by David Frost, Part 3. 19 May 1977. Original CBS broadcast.

3. Kutler. *The Wars of Watergate*. 6.

4. Mitchell, Paul and Mick Gold. *Watergate*. Discovery Channel, 1994. DVD.

5. Nixon, Richard. Interview by David Frost, Part 3. 19 May 1977. Original CBS broadcast.

6. Mitchell and Gold. *Watergate*.

7. Summers, Anthony, with Robbyn Swan. *The Arrogance of Power: The Secret World of Richard Nixon*. New York: Penguin, 2000. 387. Print.

8. Corell, John T. "The Pentagon Papers." *Air Force Magazine* 90, no. 2 (2007). http://www.airforcemag.com/MagazineArchive/Pages/TableOfContents.aspx?Date=02/2007.

9. Ellsberg, Daniel. *Secrets: A Memoir of Vietnam and the Pentagon Papers*. New York: Penguin, 2003. 289.

10. Cooper, Michael, and Sam Roberts. "After 40 Years, the Complete Pentagon Papers." *New York Times*. 7 Jun. 2011. http://www.nytimes.com/2011/06/08/us/08pentagon.html?pagewanted=all&_r=0.

11. Corell. "The Pentagon Papers."

12. Ibid.
13. Ibid.
14. Editorial. "Vietnam: The Public's Need to Know." *Washington Post.* 17 Jun. 1971. http://www.washingtonpost.com/wp-srv/inatl/longterm/flash/july/edit71.htm.
15. Gravel, Mike, ed. *The Pentagon Papers, Gravel Edition.* Vol. 2. Boston: Beacon, 1972. 738.
16. Ibid., Vol. 3, 695.
17. Above quotes from the Pentagon Papers can be viewed online at the National Archives and Records Administration website: http://www.archives.gov/research/pentagon-papers/.
18. Tape 525-001. 17 Jun. 1971, 5:15 pm–6:10 pm. University of Virginia, Miller Center Presidential Recordings Program. http://millercenter.org/presidentialrecordings/rmn-525-001.
19. Hersh, Seymour. "Kissinger and Nixon in the White House." *Atlantic Monthly* 249, no. 5. 35-58. Web. http://www.theatlantic.com/past/docs/issues/82may/hershwh3.htm.
20. Matthews, Chris. "Nixon Personally Ordered Break-in." *San Francisco Chronicle.* 21 Nov. 1996.
21. Document 39 of the X Envelope. Memo from Walt Rostow for the Record. 14 May 1972.
22. University of Southern California. "Timeline." Annenberg Center for Communication. 2012. http://topsecretplay.org/timeline/. Courtesy LBJ Presidential Library.

Chapter 12

1. Nafalti, Timothy. Interview with Tom Huston. Part 1, 30 Apr. 2008. Accessed 5 Aug. 2014. http://www.nixonlibrary.gov/virtuallibrary/documents/histories/huston-2008-04-30.pdf.
2. Lukas, J. Anthony. *Nightmare: The Underside of the Nixon Years.* Athens, OH: Ohio University Press, 1999. 31. Print.
3. Ibid.
4. Reeves, Richard. *President Nixon: Alone in the White House.* New York: Simon & Schuster, 2002. 229. Print.
5. Ibid., 237.
6. Gentry, Curt. *J. Edgar Hoover: The Man and the Secrets.* New York: W. W. Norton, 2001. 658. Print.
7. Greenberg, David. *Nixon's Shadow: The History of an Image.* New York: W. W. Norton, 2003. 105. Print.

8. Huston's interviews with then-Nixon library director Tim Naftali can be found at the library's website, http://www.nixonlibrary.gov/.

9. Transcript from Presidential Recordings Program provided by the Miller Center of the University of Virginia. WH68 10-04-13547-13548. Original tape courtesy of the LBJ Library.

10. Ibid.

11. Nafalti, Timothy. Interview with Tom Huston. Part 1, 30 Apr. 2008. Part 2, 27 Jun. 2008. Accessed 5 Aug. 2014. http://www.nixonlibrary.gov/virtuallibrary/documents/histories/huston-2008-04-30.pdf; http://www.nixonlibrary.gov/virtuallibrary/documents/histories/huston-2008-06-27.pdf.

12. In 2008, the LBJ Library released riveting audiotapes dealing with Nixon's 1968 attempts to torpedo U.S. peace efforts. Included is the president's description of Nixon's actions as "treason." Johnson opined that the GOP candidate had "blood on his hands." And in 2010, declassified documents from the Nixon White House revealed just how eager the president was to obtain the CIA's intelligence data on candidate Nixon's 1968 anti-peace machinations.

13. Tape 525-001. 17 Jun. 1971, 5:15 p.m.–6:10 p.m. University of Virginia, Miller Center Presidential Recordings Program. http://millercenter.org/presidentialrecordings/rmn-525-001.

14. Ibid.

15. Matthews, Chris. "Nixon Personally Ordered Break-in." *San Francisco Chronicle*. 21 Nov. 1996.

Chapter 13

1. Updegrove, Mark K. *Indomitable Will: LBJ in the Presidency*. New York: Crown, 2012. 308. Print.

2. Ibid.

3. Conversation with Senator George Smathers, 23 Nov. 1968. LBJ Library Archives. http://transition.lbjlibrary.org/items/show/67315.

4. Updegrove. *Indomitable Will*. 308.

5. *Nixon: Arrogance of Power*. History Channel, 2000.

6. Haldeman, H. R. *The Haldeman Diaries: Inside the Nixon White House*. New York: Berkley Books, 1995. 567. Print.

7. Ibid.

8. Documented in author's personal press conference notes.
9. Liddy, G. Gordon. *Will: The Autobiography of G. Gordon Liddy*. New York: St. Martin's Paperbacks, 1991. 237. Print.
10. Anderson, Jack and Daryl Gibson. *Peace, War, and Politics: An Eyewitness Account*. New York: Forge, 2000. 222. Print.
11. Kutler, Stanley I. *Abuse of Power*. New York: Simon & Schuster, 1998. 44. Print.
12. "Senate History: Select Committee on Presidential Campaign Activities (The Watergate Committee"). United States Senate. http://www.senate.gov/artandhistory/history/common/investigations/Watergate.htm.
13. Robenalt, James and John W. Dean. "The Legacy of Watergate." *Litigation Journal* 38.3 (Spring 2012): The American Bar Association. Web. 29 Jul. 2014.
14. Recorded Oval Office conversation between Nixon and Kissinger. 12 Jul. 1973, 4:48 p.m. Accessed via the Nixon Presidential Library and Museum website. http://www.nixonlibrary.gov/forresearchers/find/tapes/tape949/949-011.mp3.
15. United States v. Nixon 418 U.S. 683 (1974).
16. Haldeman. *The Haldeman Diaries*. 473.
17. Recorded White House conversation. 1 Aug. 1972. Accessed via the Nixon Presidential Library and Museum. http://www.nixonlibrary.gov/forresearchers/find/tapes/tape758/758-011.mp3.
18. Recorded Oval Office conversation. 12 Jul. 1973, 4:48 p.m. Accessed via the Nixon Presidential Library and Museum. http://www.nixonlibrary.gov/forresearchers/find/tapes/tape949/949-011.mp3.
19. Kutler, Stanley I. *The Wars of Watergate: The Last Crisis of Richard Nixon*. New York: W. W. Norton, 1992. 548. Print.

Chapter 14

1. McCloskey, Bill. Personal e-mail correspondence with the author. April 2014.
2. Lukas, J. Anthony. *Nightmare: The Underside of the Nixon Years*. Athens, OH: Ohio University Press, 1999. 166. Print.
3. *Washington Post*. 28 Apr. 1973.

4. Angers, Trent. "Nixon and the My Lai Massacre Coverup." *New York Post* 15 Mar. 2014. Web. 8 Apr. 2014. *Post* quotations in the preceding two paragraphs were taken from this article as well.
5. Greenfield, Meg. "Memorial Frenzy." *Newsweek*. 30 Jun. 1997.
6. Recorded Oval Office conversation. 19 Sept. 1972, 3:42 p.m.–5:41 p.m. Tape 783, conversation 26. Accessed via the Nixon Presidential Library and Museum. http://www.nixonlibrary.gov/forresearchers/find/tapes/tape783/783-026a.mp3.
7. Lukas. *Nightmare*. 167
8. Summers, Anthony, with Robbyn Swan. *The Arrogance of Power: The Secret World of Richard Nixon*. New York: Penguin, 2000. 277. Print.
9. Ibid.
10. Recorded Oval Office conversation between Nixon and Haldeman. 5 May 1971, 9:58 a.m.–10:15 a.m. University of Virginia, Miller Center Presidential Recordings Program. http://millercenter.org/presidentialclassroom/exhibits/guy-wholl-get-out-and-tear-things.
11. Emery, Fred. *Watergate: The Corruption of American Politics and the Fall of Richard Nixon*. New York: Touchstone, 1994. 125. Print.
12. Transcript, Lawrence F. O'Brien Oral History Interview XXVI, 8/26/87, by Michael L. Gillette, Internet Copy, LBJ Library; Updegrove, Mark K. *Indomitable Will: LBJ in the Presidency*. New York: Crown, 2012. 308. Print.
13. Summers. *The Arrogance of Power*. 379; recorded conversation between Nixon and aides, accessed via the National Archives and Records Administration.
14. McCullough, Frank. Phone conversation with author. 2011.
15. Anderson, Jack. "Rebozo Helped in Double Cross." *Palm Beach Post*. 1 Nov. 1973.
16. Kutler, Stanley I. *Abuse of Power*. New York: Simon & Schuster, 1998. 438. Print.
17. Yost, Peter and Lara Jakes Jordan. "FBI Searched Long, Hard for Jack Anderson Sources." *USA Today*. 11 Oct. 2008; Garner, Dwight. "The Supersnooper Pursuing the Paranoid

Politician." Review of *Poisoning the Press,* by Mark Feldstein. *New York Times.* 28 Sept. 2010. http://www.nytimes.com/2010/09/29/books/29book.html.

18. Drosnin, Michael. *Citizen Hughes: The Power, the Money, and the Madness.* New York: Holt, Rinehart, and Winston, 1985. 91. Print.

19. Feldstein, Mark. *Poisoning the Press.* New York: Farrar, Straus, and Giroux, 2010.

20. Ellsberg, Daniel. "Edward Snowden Is a Hero and We Need More Whistleblowers." *The Daily Beast.* Newsweek/ Daily Beast, 10 June 2013. Web. 9 Apr. 2014. http://www.thedailybeast.com/articles/2013/06/10/daniel-ellsberg-edward-snowden-is-a-hero-and-we-need-more-whistleblowers.html.

Chapter 15

1. Document 06 of the X Envelope. Walter Rostow. 26 Jun. 1973. Courtesy LBJ Presidential Library.

2. Document 0 of the X Envelope. Walter Rostow to Harry Middleton, Director, LBJ Library. 26 Jun. 1973. Courtesy LBJ Presidential Library.

3. Document 39 of the X Envelope. Memo from Walt Rostow for the Record. 14 May 1972. Courtesy LBJ Presidential Library.

4. Greenberg, David. *Nixon's Shadow: The History of an Image.* New York: W. W. Norton, 2003. 116. Print. 116.

5. Goodman, Amy. "Barack Obama: The Least Transparent President in History." Reader Supported News. N.p., 29 Mar. 2014. Web. http://readersupportednews.org/opinion2/277-75/22837-barack-obama-the-least-transparent-president-in-history.

6. At the time, the private's name was Bradley Manning, but the leaker has since come out as transgender, taken the name Chelsea, and expressed the desire to undergo sex reassignment surgery to become physically female. Her decision will be reviewed by proper authorities, given her current incarceration in military prison.

7. Goodman. "Barack Obama."

Chapter 16

1. United States Constitution, Article 3, Section 3.
2. "18 U.S. Code Â§ 2381 - Treason." Legal Information Institute. Cornell University Law School, n.d. Web. http://www.law.cornell.edu/uscode/text/18/2381.
3. "18 U.S. Code Â§ 953 - Private correspondence with foreign governments." Legal Information Institute. Cornell University Law School, n.d. Web. 12 Apr. 2014. http://www.law.cornell.edu/uscode/text/18/953.
4. Unger, Irwin and Debi Unger. *LBJ: A Life.* New York: John Wiley & Sons, 1999. 492. Print.
5. Walt Rostow to Lyndon B. Johnson. 28 Oct. 1968. X Envelope. Courtesy LBJ Presidential Library.
6. Berman, Larry. *No Peace, No Honor: Nixon, Kissinger, and Betrayal in Vietnam.* New York: Touchstone, 2002. 33. Print.
7. *Nixon: Arrogance of Power.* History Channel, 2000.
8. Summers, Anthony, with Robbyn Swan. *The Arrogance of Power: The Secret World of Richard Nixon.* New York: Penguin, 2000. 298. Print.
9. Updegrove, Mark K. *Indomitable Will: LBJ in the Presidency.* New York: Crown, 2012. 307. Print.
10. Recorded Oval Office conversation between Johnson and Nixon. 8 Nov. 1968, 9:23 p.m. Accessed via the U.S. Department of State Office of the Historian. http://history.state.gov/historicaldocuments/frus1964-68v07/d207.
11. Ibid.
12. Summers. *The Arrogance of Power.* 307.
13. The full transcript of this press conference can be found on the University of California at Santa Barbara's website, http://www.presidency.ucsb.edu/ws/?pid=3548.
14. Rosen, James. *The Strong Man: John Mitchell and the Secrets of Watergate.* New York: Doubleday, 2008. 495. Print.
15. Ibid., 15-16.
16. Davis, Sid. Personal e-mail correspondence with the author. 2014.
17. Ibid.
18. Hitchens, Christopher. *The Trial of Henry Kissinger.* London: Verso, 2001. 135. Print.

Chapter 17

1. Haldeman, H. R. *The Ends of Power*. New York: Dell, 1978. 122. Print.
2. Summers, Anthony and Robbyn Swan. *The Arrogance of Power: The Secret World of Richard Nixon*. New York: Viking, 2000. 8-9. Print.
3. Hutschnecker, Arnold. "The Stigma of Seeing a Psychiatrist." *New York Times*, November 20, 1973, 39.
4. John Dean, *Lost Honor: The Rest of the Story*. New York: Stratford Press, 1982. 126.
5. Shannon, William. "Warning in Scary Days of August." *New York Times,* September 1, 1974.
6. Greenberg, David. *Nixon's Shadow: The History of an Image*. New York: W. W. Norton, 2003. 120. Print.
7. Kutler, Stanley I. *The Wars of Watergate: The Last Crisis of Richard Nixon*. New York: W. W. Norton, 1992. 548. Print.
8. These remarks are on a videotape of the pre-speech remarks obtained by the author from the National Archives and Records Administration.
9. Greenberg. *Nixon's Shadow*. 235.
10. Kessler, Ronald. *Inside the White House: The Hidden Lives of the Modern Presidents and the Secrets of the World's Most Powerful Institution*. New York: Simon & Schuster, 1995. 41. Print.
11. Editors of the American Heritage Dictionary. "Psychopath." *Webster's II New College Dictionary*. 914.
12. *Nixon: Arrogance of Power*. History Channel, 2000.
13. Personal correspondence with the author. 2002.
14. *Nixon: Arrogance of Power*. History Channel, 2000.
15. Summers. *The Arrogance of Power*. 235.
16. Haldeman. *The Ends of Power*. 75.
17. This incident is confirmed in a newly released 1968 memo from Rose Woods to Bob Haldeman. Drew Pearson and Jack Anderson referred to the incident in their October 4, 1968, column in the *Washington Post* titled "Dirty Fighter."
18. Aitken, Jonathan. *Nixon: A Life*. Washington, DC: Renergy, 1994. 265. Print.
19. Von Hoffman, Nicholas. "El Flippo Rides Again." *Washington Post*. 24 Aug. 1973.

20. Butterfield, Alexander. Oral History released in 2014 by the Nixon Presidential Library and Museum.

21. December 1970, on a tape made by Kissinger and released in 2004.

22. To Nixon's suggestion, Kissinger replied: "That, I think, would just be too much."

23. Shribman, David. "Nixon Suffered from Alcohol Abuse." *New York Times*, May 20, 2006.

24. Haldeman. *The Ends of Power*. xxi.

Chapter 18

1. Mankiewicz, Frank. *Perfectly Clear: From Whittier to Watergate.* Quandrangle, 1973. 32.

2. Kutler, Stanley I. *Abuse of Power: The New Nixon Tapes.* New York: Simon & Schuster, 1998. 69. Print.

3. Mello, Michael. "Nixon Library Exhibit Gives New Perspective on Watergate." *Orange County Register.* 31 March 2011. Accessed 27 Aug. 2014.

4. Haldeman, H. R. *The Ends of Power.* New York: Dell, 1978. Print.

5. Recorded conversation between Nixon and Chuck Colson. 5 Jan. 1973. Accessed via the National Archives and Records Administration.

6. Ibid.

7. Rush, George. *Confessions of an Ex-Secret Service Agent.* New York: Dutton, 1988. Print.

8. Krogh, Egil. *The Day Elvis Met Nixon.* Pejam, 1994. Print.

9. Nixon, Richard. Interview by David Frost. 19 May 1977. Original CBS broadcast.

10. Summers, Anthony and Robbyn Swan. *The Arrogance of Power: The Secret World of Richard Nixon.* New York: Viking, 2000. 18. Print.

11. Ibid., 121.

12. Kutler, Stanley I. *The Wars of Watergate: The Last Crisis of Richard Nixon.* New York: W. W. Norton, 1992. 34. Print.

13. Nixon, Richard. *In the Arena: A Memoir of Victory, Defeat, and Renewal.* New York: Simon & Schuster, 1990.

14. *Nixon: Arrogance of Power.* History Channel, 2000.

15. Haldeman, H. R. *The Haldeman Diaries: Inside the Nixon White House.* New York: Berkley Books, 1995. 205. Print.

16. Documented in the author's personal notes from Nixon's Phoenix campaign stop.

17. Haldeman. *The Haldeman Diaries.* 206.

18. Modzelewski, Joe. "Loser's Corner." *Miami News.* 21 Oct. 1986.

19. C-Span. "George Shuktz Oral History Interview." 10 May 2007.   http://www.c-span.org/video/?298581-1/george-shultz-oral-history-interview.

20. Documented in a Nixon Presidential Library and Museum display.

21. O'Neill, Thomas P. *Man of the House: The Life and Political Memoirs of Speaker Tip O'Neill.* New York: Random House, 1987. 86.

22. Nash, Bruce and Allan Zullo. *Football Hall of Shame.* New York: Pocket Books, 1986. 67.

23. Cook, Kevin. *The Last Headbangers: NFL Football in the Rowdy, Reckless '70s, the Era That Created Modern Sports.* New York: Simon & Schuster, 2012.

24. Woodward, Bob and Carl Bernstein. *The Final Days.* New York: Simon & Schuster Paperbacks, 1976. 238. Print.

25. Summers. *The Arrogance of Power.* 202.

26. Jung, C. G. "On the Psychology of the Trickster Figure." Accessed via the16types.info. http://www.the16types. info/vbulletin/content.php/211-On-the-Psychology-of-the-Trickster-Figure-Jung.

27. Fulsom, Don. "Nixon's Greatest Tricks." *Regardie's.* January 1991.

Appendix
1. Multiple documents were labeled "4."
2. Multiple documents were labeled "7."

Index